ENCOUNTER WITH HISTORY

Edmund Richard Pitman Shurly.
From: *Officers of the Army and Navy (Regular) Who Served in the Civil War*, ed.
Major William H. Powell, U.S. Army and Medical-Director Edward Shippen, U.S. Navy,
Philadelphia: L. R. Hammersly & Co., 1892.

ENCOUNTER WITH HISTORY

The Memoirs, Reminiscences, and Amazing Life of
Captain Edmund Richard Pitman Shurly, 1829–1909

Robert Vanderzee

iUniverse, Inc.
New York Lincoln Shanghai

Encounter with History
The Memoirs, Reminiscences, and Amazing Life of
Captain Edmund Richard Pitman Shurly, 1829–1909

iUniverse books may be ordered through booksellers or by contacting:

iUniverse
2021 Pine Lake Road, Suite 100
Lincoln, NE 68512
www.iuniverse.com
1-800-Authors (1-800-288-4677)

Because of the dynamic nature of the Internet, any Web addresses
or links contained in this book may have changed
since publication and may no longer be valid.

The views expressed in this work are solely those of the author and do not necessarily reflect the views of the publisher, and the publisher hereby disclaims any responsibility for them.

ISBN: 978-0-595-46963-5 (pbk)
ISBN: 978-0-595-70670-9 (cloth)
ISBN: 978-0-595-91248-3 (ebk)

Printed in the United States of America

Jan, forever the love of my life.

And to Fredricka Shurly Wormer, my mother's closest sister. This story would not have been written without her recollections of Shurly family life, her documentation of little-known facts concerning the Shurly family, her suggestions as to where much of this information could be found, and especially her constant encouragement.

CONTENTS

PREFACE

I HAVE ALWAYS CONSIDERED LIFE AN ADVENTURE, for some, more of an adventure, for others, sadly less, depending on one's inclination and determination. My own experience has been something of an adventure, but when I began research into this work I was not prepared for the scope and breadth of the adventures that had befallen my great-grandfather. Almost none of the story had been passed down to me from my family.

This is the story of the Shurly family after they arrived in America; in particular, of Captain Edmund R. P. Shurly and his adventures in the Civil War and the subsequent Indian War on the western frontier. I will release a second volume about the Shurly family, to be published soon after this one reaches the book shelves that will tell of Edmund's brother Ernest, and his son, Burt Russell Shurly, both of whom became preeminent doctors in the city of Detroit.

I decided to research this story after receiving a short history of these exploits from my aunt, the late Mrs. Clark Wormer, Edmund Shurly's youngest granddaughter. It was this obscure document that set me to looking for more information about my family. As more stories surfaced I realized the Shurly descendants would want to know of the accomplishments and incredible events that shaped and enriched the lives of their forefathers. As these stories and facts grew even further in length and convolutions, it finally dawned on me that this was a story for a wide-ranging audience. It was evident this story was one that should be published, not just copied and distributed to relatives and friends.

To portray more fully the Shurly family's experience in the second half of the nineteenth century, I melded graphic descriptions of some of the monumental world events in which Edmund Shurly participated, with the facts and data describing his life. The Civil War and the Indian War, as well as the Great Chicago Fire that destroyed his home and business, had a major impact on the life of Edmund Shurly. These events are described as the Shurlys would have seen and experienced them—from *their* point of view.

The reader will also see, soon after delving into these chronicles, that I have generously included passages from letters and newspaper articles written by the Shurlys as well as other writings about these events, produced by authors far better equipped than I to describe them, wherever I felt it would more clearly illuminate the Shurly story.

One serious word of caution! This is not a "politically correct" depiction of history. The stories you will read of Indian atrocities are documented eyewitness accounts and often extremely graphic. I made no effort to weed out descriptions that might offend. Instead, I wanted the reader to see the world as it was presented to the Shurlys.

I hope serious students of the Shurly family story will find this work useful. Those of you who are inspired to look further by the information collected here are encouraged to visit the Burton Historical Library in Detroit, the Walter Reuther Library at Wayne State University, also in Detroit, and the Sheridan County Fulmer Public Library, Sheridan, Wyoming, where much more information is available about members of the Shurly family and about the Francis Palms family into which Colonel Shurly's son married.

I believe you will find this work an enjoyable read and something of an education in history. For the Shurly family, I write this volume so succeeding generations will know of and appreciate their heritage. This work is a challenge to each of them to excel in his or her life's endeavors and strive to leave a legacy at least as rich as that of their ancestors whose stories begin here. Those readers who trace their lineage to this Shurly family will find it difficult, but hopefully an obligation, to live up to the standard their forebears established.

As revealed in the following pages, this challenge imposes a heavy burden on the Shurly descendants.

Au clair de la lune,
Mon ami Pierrot,
Prete-moi ta plume
Pour ecrire un mot.

—Anonymous
Au Clair de la Lune[1]

---

[1] By the light of the moon,/My friend Pierrot,/Lend me your pen,/To write a word.

Chapter One

RED BLANKETS AND
BILLOWING SAILS

*The discovery of America offered a thousand new paths to fortune,
and placed riches and power within the reach of the adventurous and obscure.*

—Alexis de Tocqueville,
Democracy in America

As Lieutenant Edmund Richard Pitman Shurly and seven of his men struggled to lower the last three of the Wells-Fargo wagons down the snow-covered slope, the Sioux attacked. The Indians had been watching the wagon train for days and now, after fourteen of the wagons had eased down the ridge, they saw an opening. Swarms of arrows filled the sky, and return fire from the wagons below the slope crackled as seven hundred Sioux in their war paint, egged on by none other than Sioux Chieftain Red Cloud, screamed their war whoops and rose into sight on the ridges surrounding the wagon train.

"Save the gun at all hazards!"[1] bellowed the young lieutenant. He meant, of course, the twelve-pound mountain howitzer limbered and pulled by two mules. It always followed behind the last wagon and now would mean the difference for his men between life or death by torture and mutilation. The Sioux desperately

1

wanted the howitzer and especially the three wagons stranded on the hill loaded with bright red blankets heaped up in plain sight.

Corporal Peter Donnelly's howitzer responded again and again with canister shot and seemed to slow the Indian advance but did not stop it. One Sioux appeared behind Shurly and put an arrow into his foot before Shurly realized he was there. Instantly, Shurly pulled out his trusty horse pistol, wheeled around, and fired. A jagged fifty-caliber hole opened in the middle of the red warrior's chest as the bullet tore through his stomach and severed his spine. The jolt punched him backward, dead before he hit the ground. Two other Indians attempted to scalp Shurly but were killed by bullets from U.S. Army muskets.[2]

William Freeland, a civilian driving the limbered howitzer, and "as brave a man as ever mounted a mule,"[3] sagged forward in agony from a ball in his thigh, but was able to start his rig down the slope, toward the wagons already there and beginning their defensive corral. Due to his heroism, the Sioux would not get the gun.

Corporal Donnelly had been the first to sight the Indian attack and, reacting as ordered, shot off the gun both to sound the alarm and delay the attack. This accomplished both objectives, but it also frightened the six-mule team harnessed to the lead wagon at the bottom of the slope. Its driver, D. V. Bowers, a civilian teamster, had been ordered to remain at his driver's post on the lead wagon, but instead had disobeyed his orders and climbed up the hill to help get the last of the wagons down. With no driver, the startled mules jumped forward, pulling their wagon and its valuable cargo straight toward the Indians massed on the trail ahead.

As Freeland started the gun down the slope, Shurly and his men, all now wounded but one, abandoned the three wagons on the hill and stumbled down the slope and into the defensive circle of wagons. Private Harold Partenheimer was dead from arrows in both lungs and was left on the hill. Donnelly and Private James McGeever were mortally wounded, Corporal Gordon Fitzgerald would lose a hand, and, while painful, the wounds to Private Michael Kerr and Freeland would heal. D. V. Bowers, who had left his post on the lead wagon, was not wounded and would later face a disciplinary hearing when he returned to the fort.

Shurly's wound was serious, with the arrow protruding from both sides of his boot. Gingerly, he cut the tail feathers from the shaft and pulled it from his foot.

Then, removing his blood-filled boot, he tightly bound the wound with his kerchief. This stopped most of the bleeding, but it did not stop the pain, and he had lost a lot of blood.

The bluffs were now "black with Indians"[4] and they had infiltrated a thicket of brush near one side of the corral and were firing from it indiscriminately. Shurly ordered a skirmish line forward to drive them back. Twelve men answered the call and cleared the area with the help of several well-placed canister shots from the howitzer. At the same time they were able to pull two wagons stranded at the base of the hill into the corral.[5]

Next, Shurly ordered more ammunition to be brought forward from the lead wagon and was stunned when told the Indians had run off the wagon. Pausing to collect his thoughts, Shurly asked for an ammunition count and was dismayed to find there were no more than forty rounds per soldier, and just six cannon balls for the howitzer. The seventeen Wells-Fargo teamsters had an assortment of pistols, but few bullets. All the rest of the ammunition was in the missing lead wagon, carefully tucked under a mail pouch and the knapsacks containing warm clothing and food for his men. Shurly immediately ordered that no one was to fire a shot without his approval on penalty of death.

By now the men had emptied the cargo of hundred-pound bags of corn from the corralled wagons and shoved them under and around the wagon for added protection from arrows and bullets. This corn was intended to feed the men of an isolated Montana outpost, Fort C. F. Smith, over the winter of 1867–68. Fort Smith, a key part of the U.S. Army strategy to maintain a route from the Oregon Trail to the Montana gold fields, was so far north that, within weeks, winter would completely isolate it from the outside world.

Now this corn would serve a more immediate need. If the men kept their heads down behind these bags of corn, they would be relatively safe. But without the ammunition in the lead wagon, Shurly knew they would not last more than a day without help. And help was twenty miles to the south in Fort Phil Kearny, where he knew no one had the slightest inkling his train was in jeopardy.

To make matters worse, Shurly was getting weaker from loss of blood and no longer able to stand. Finally realizing that he was getting weak, he ordered Wagonmaster William Harwood, a civilian, but nevertheless a well-experienced civilian, to assume command of the train in the event Shurly could not maintain his control.

The Sioux hated the cannon and had learned a new respect for these soldiers with their breech-loading rifles after bloody defeats in the Wagon Box Fight and the Hayfield Fight three months earlier. Shurly had been in on the Hayfield Fight. So, after the initial onslaught, the Sioux backed off to carry away their wounded and their precious red blankets and to mutilate the dead body of Private Partenheimer. In mid-afternoon, the Indians renewed their attack, but well-aimed shots from the howitzer discouraged more massed attacks from the surrounding ridges.

Two days before, Colonel John Eugene Smith, noting how lightly defended Shurly's wagon train was as it departed their rendezvous north of Fort Phil Kearny, had transferred the howitzer to Shurly's command. Now the howitzer was vital to their survival. Once the ammunition for this gun was gone, the Sioux would know it and come in for the kill. Someone would have to get past the surrounding Indians and bring word to the fort. Just after dark, two men slipped quietly out of camp with the last two live horses and headed south. The Sioux were waiting for them.

The young lieutenant was very tired now and perhaps dreaming of other days. It was getting difficult for him to focus on his immediate situation. With his serious loss of blood, the relative quiet of the battlefield, and temperatures dropping to the low twenties, it is easy to believe his thoughts might have drifted to the huge billowing sails he remembered from his childhood—sails that pushed the great ship that brought his family to the New World and to the inconceivable adventures that followed. Indeed, the vision of those huge sails had remained with him since his youth and reassured him again and again that man could conquer nature. He had resolved early on he would be one of those men who persevered over nature. Always.

*   *   *

BORN IN CAMBRIDGE, ENGLAND, on January 27, 1829, to John Martin Shurly and his wife, the former Elizabeth Catharine Chumly, the child was christened Edmund Richard Pitman Shurly. Prior to his birth, a sister, Marian Winifred, had, on March 20, 1827, already joined the family.[6]

Elizabeth Chumly Shurly, mother of Edmund Shurly, as she appeared in about 1845. Courtesy of the Reuther Library, Detroit.

The boy was eight years old when his father sat his children down and explained to them the family was moving across the ocean to America. John and Elizabeth Shurly did not, of course, go into much detail about their decision to their young children, but they were only too aware that even with the defeat of Napoleon some twenty years earlier, the threat of war in Europe still lingered. In 1830, France again was confronted by revolution as Louis Philippe ascended the throne and fear arose that the Duke of Wellington would have to occupy the Low Countries to prevent a world power from facing England across the channel.

Then King George IV died and was succeeded by the good-natured but rather simple-minded William IV. No one had respect for their new king, and everyone knew "Sailor William," as he was called, was not the leader England needed to ease poverty and relieve the stresses the Industrial Revolution was imposing. Like his friends, John Shurly was caught up in the radical idea of representative government that was taking hold in France and America. But in England the king still ruled and seats in the House of Commons were bought and sold like real estate. The Tories were in power and vigorously opposed control of Commons by the propertied class. When the middle classes finally joined with a bitter, poverty-stricken underclass to demand wider representation in the House of Commons, the resulting "reform," as it was cynically called, put the Tories out of power but added few voters to the electorate. Only one in six male adults could vote, and poverty was unchanged. For John Shurly, "reform" had accomplished nothing more than to convince him, and many like him, to renounce the stratified society of the Old World and immigrate to the new, where class was a thing of the past.

Every story John heard or read about America filled him with a yearning for a better life—for adventure. As he prepared to leave his mother country, John realized he had a spark, an inner thirst for adventure. It was a thirst that would emerge often in succeeding generations of American immigrants and shape their stories.

In 1837 the Shurly family made their way to the ship that would take them to America.[7] For a lad of eight, climbing aboard that great ship, with his father firmly gripping his hand, was the biggest thrill of his young life. Before the voyage was over, the boy would discover every nook and cranny in the vessel and marvel at the huge billowing sails reaching up to the sky. Any concern John and Elizabeth may have had about their son's reluctance to travel was gone. Edmund, they could see, even at this early age, had all his father's thirst for adventure.

Chapter Two

THE ADVENTURES BEGIN

There's a long, long trail a-winding
Into the land of my dreams,
Where the nightingales are singing
And a white moon beams.

—Stoddard King,
The Long, Long Trail

KING WILLIAM IV DIED IN 1837 with the reputation and honor of the monarchy
at a low point, and was succeeded to the throne by an eighteen-year-old princess. John Shurly could well have believed, as did most other Englishmen of the
day, that this naive maiden, Victoria by name, would send the reputation of the
monarchy even lower. However, one Englishman, Lord Palmerston, later to be
prime minister, wrote, "Few people have had opportunities of forming a correct
judgment of the Princess; but I incline to think that she will turn out to be a
remarkable person, and gifted with a great deal of strength of character."[8] He was,
of course, correct. On the evening before her coronation this young lady wrote in
her diary: "Since it has pleased Providence to place me in this station, I shall do
my utmost to fulfill my duty towards my country; I am very young, and perhaps
in many, though not in all things, inexperienced, but I am sure that very few have
more real good will and more real desire to do what is fit and right than I have."[9]

If Shurly had appreciated Princess Victoria's spirit and resolve, he might not have ventured to America.

The family disembarked in New York and settled first in Brooklyn. There young Edmund could, when he was not occupied with family chores, visit the waterfront and watch the sailing ships arrive and depart under their huge sails.

Andrew Jackson, ending his tenure as president when the family arrived in their new country, had attacked the Second Bank of the United States, a private corporation holding most of the public funds of the country. That, and a wild land and stock speculation bubble that was soon to burst, produced the Panic of 1837. Martin Van Buren, who followed Jackson into the White House, was unable to come to grips with these economic problems and actually aggravated them with his ineffectual handling of what came to be known as the Swartwout Affair in which a politically appointed tax collector for the Port of New York absconded to Europe with over a million dollars.

John Shurly and his family stayed in Brooklyn for a time—perhaps a year—to become acclimated with their new surroundings and to decide where in this vast new country they would settle. Everyone he talked to had ideas. Reports were circulating of a new canal that had just opened the Ohio interior to settlement and growth, and settlers were pouring into the area. There, commercial wheat farming, manufacturing, and even boat building were booming. Because of this new canal, Ohio would soon be the third most populous state in the Union. John Shurly was finally convinced that a move to Ohio would be best for his family. And he knew from reports the trip to Ohio's interior would be long and arduous.

When the Shurlys completed their preparations, they began their odyssey up the Hudson River to their first stop in Albany. They were there only a short time to regroup, and perhaps to become acquainted with the Godwin family, who would cross their paths again in the years to come. Then they boarded a small vessel that took them across the length of the famous Erie Barge Canal to Buffalo. From there, they crossed Lake Erie by steamer to the thriving village of Cleveland and to the starting point of the new canal everyone had been talking about. Their steamer eased up to its pier on the Cuyahoga River near the boarding area for the canal barge that would take them on the new Ohio and Erie Canal to the top of Portage Summit where the small village of Akron was starting to take hold, and then to their final destination, New Philadelphia.

What a spectacular adventure this portion of the trip must have been for the eight-year-old boy, one he would never forget. With gigantic virgin timber extending to the edge of the towpath on one side of the narrow waterway and nearly to the water's edge on the other—in places the trees entirely covered the sky over their heads—it would appear to Edmund that he was passing through a tunnel of trees, sometimes for hours on end. As the travelers were towed south through the beautiful Cuyahoga Valley they were presented with a spectacular abundance of wild animal life—bear, elk, deer—that inhabited the Ohio forest. Aside from the billowing sails that had mesmerized him crossing the ocean, passage of the tiny vessel through this forest may well have been the most fascinating part of the trip for Edmund.

Occasionally, the family would spy Indians emerging from the underbrush, peering at them with guarded suspicion. At least once during their passage to New Philadelphia, John Shurly must have pondered the thoughts of these native peoples who had hand-carried their canoes and goods over the Portage Summit for uncounted millennia, until, without warning, some three thousand white people invaded their land and, with hand shovels and pick axes, dug, in just two years, a ditch, which, when filled with water, transported entire ships uphill and over the summit, seemingly without effort.

Opened in 1832, the Ohio and Erie Canal elevated travelers four hundred feet through more than thirty locks, past the prosperous and thriving little villages of Independence, Brecksville, and Peninsula, to Akron and Massillon. Then it lowered them gently into the open plains of central Ohio. From there the canal wended its way south to Dover and its twin village, New Philadelphia, before continuing on through 130 more locks to the Ohio River at Portsmouth.[10]

When Shurly's family arrived in New Philadelphia, the town had become a thriving wheat market for the farmers who had settled central Ohio. Even before disembarking from the boat, John Shurly could see warehouses and stores everywhere, and across the river the first water-powered flourmill was operating in Dover. Beside the canal, spewing thick black smoke, was a newly constructed blast furnace that used the "kidney" ore found nearby along with limestone and coal.[11]

By all accounts, New Philadelphia and Dover were rough towns in the 1830s, and perhaps not what John Shurly had in mind for his family. The canal, he found, had brought disease along with wealth. In 1832 Dover had been hit hard with smallpox and cholera, devastating and feared diseases in those days. Then too, the waterfront was inhabited by all manner of scurrilous characters attracted by the steel furnaces and the bars and taverns along both sides of the river.

Perhaps young Edmund actually met or heard stories about some of these characters who lived in New Philadelphia at the time. One such character who would have fascinated the young lad was Captain Titus Gehenna, who navigated the Sandy and Beaver and the Ohio and Erie Canals in his barge, *City of Dungannon*, named after a nearby Irish shanty town. This was a canal barge typical of the time and place, probably sixty feet long and powered by tow horses. Gehenna's barge, as with most barges of similar construction, had room for both the traveler and his horse.

Captain Gehenna, however, was a thrifty man who often operated his boat without a crew or tow horses. He would offer a traveler free passage for himself and his horse and then, once aboard, would order the hapless passenger to help pull the boat with his horse on the tow path, explaining that refusal was mutiny under maritime law. It was not long before Gehenna no longer had prospective passengers showing up at his pier, so he modified his boat with a horse-powered treadmill that turned a paddle wheel at the stern. The boat now was used to haul cargoes of horses and mules, and Gehenna could temporarily "borrow" them to run his treadmill. Sharp spikes to the rear of the horse enclosure encouraged the animal forward when its pace slackened. For many years anyone planning to buy horses along the Ohio and Erie looked at the rump as well as the teeth of the animals before buying.

Captain Gehenna was a good friend and customer of the German brewers of Dover and the nearby town of Zoar, as well as of the Irish distillers of Columbiana County. His boat brought Irish whiskey into Tuscarawas County and took German beer out. His drinking exploits were legendary, and he is thought to have originated and named his favorite shot of whiskey followed by a drink of beer the "boilermaker." In Dover, after the steel and tin mills came, it was called a "puddler and a helper." But by one name or the other, the concoction became widely known across the country.[12]

Once settled in New Philadelphia, young Edmund could stretch his legs in the open countryside and play along the banks of the Tuscarawas River, flowing south beside the newly opened canal. Long afterward Edmund remembered the "rope ferry" that crossed the river at New Philadelphia. He would watch with fascination as the ferryboat harnessed the current to propel it across the river tethered to a rope strung across the river and angled downstream. To return the boat, one end of the rope was relocated to a tree upstream and the boat obediently drifted home. This was amazing stuff to a nine-year-old boy in 1838, and it became fixed in his memory, as many unusual spectacles do in the minds of children.

After a year in New Philadelphia, John Shurly decided that what he had seen of Buffalo on their way west would better fit with the future he had in mind for his family. They picked up their belongings and headed back north to Cleveland where they boarded a ship to return to Buffalo. There the family settled for good.

By 1840 John Martin Shurly sensed the country was coming out of the "Jackson-Van Buren" depression, but bitterness toward the existing political parties was so strong that a third party, the Whigs, emerged from disparate political elements in the country and elected fragile old Army General William Henry Harrison president. Having come from the rigid political climate of England, John Shurly had to have marveled at how, in his newly adopted country, a new political party, the Whigs, could form, then, rather than discuss important issues, win the election by resorting to showmanship—by smothering the country in songs such as:

> Let Van from his coolers of silver drink wine,
> And lounge on his cushioned settee;
> Our man on his buckeye bench can recline,
> Content with hard cider is he.

When the opposition tried to mention the "issues," the Whigs yelled out their mind-numbing chant:

> Tippecanoe—Tippecanoe,
> Tippecanoe and Tyler too.

Thirty days after assuming office, Harrison succumbed to flu contracted while he delivered an overly long inauguration speech and Vice President John Tyler would serve out Harrison's term. The economy, left to fend for itself, steadily improved. The next ten years would see inventions of the telegraph, ether anesthesia, rubber-soled shoes, and the Eccaleobion, an automatic egg-hatching machine! Railroads pushed into the South and West to nearly the Mississippi River, and the voters showed little concern for what went on in Washington. Even the war with Mexico in 1846 seemed to have little effect on the mood of the country. By the end of the decade, the Polk administration had shaped the country, and California, which had been acquired in the Mexican War, was applying for statehood after gold was discovered there in 1848.

AT LAST, AFTER A SHAKY START, John Shurly could see his decision to immigrate to America was vindicated. Two more sons joined the family in Buffalo: Cosmus[13] J. Shurly, birth date unknown, and Ernest Lorenzo Shurly, born June 11, 1846.[14]

After 1846, John and Elizabeth Shurly fade from the family chronicles. One must assume they lived out their lives in Buffalo, but this cannot be corroborated. In 1848 an obituary appeared in a Rochester, New York, newspaper stating that "Mrs. Elizabeth Catharine Shurly, aged thirty-seven and six months, wife of John Shurly and mother of Mrs. G. S. Jenning[s] of this city," died on February 1 in Milwaukee. A "John Shurly" is listed in the records of Saint Matthias Church in Waukesha, Wisconsin, in 1857. This, most likely, was John Martin Shurly. If so, why or how the family drifted to Wisconsin is a mystery. Their sons, however, remained in New York to begin their adventures, already recorded in history books and national archives, and now in the pages that follow.

Edmund attended school for a few years and then, at the age of fourteen, entered the employ of H. O. Hood, a jeweler in Buffalo, with whom he stayed one year. After a brief visit to Saint Catharines, Ontario, Canada, he returned to Buffalo and found work with a Mister C. H. Goodrich, another jeweler in Buffalo, as an apprentice in the jewelry business. He remained with him until Goodrich died, seven years later. Thus, in 1851, at the early age of twenty-two, Edmund Shurly got an offer to purchase the business. Seizing the opportunity, with P. C. Stambaugh as his partner, he bought the store of his late employer and started in the jewelry business. Within two years he bought out Mister Stambaugh's equity in the firm and continued the business with the help of his younger brother C. J.[15]

Edmund was now a fine-looking young man, six feet tall, with fair skin, brown hair and blue eyes, solidly built, and able to handle himself well. Later, after joining the army, he would grow a full beard, similar in appearance to those of Generals

Stonewall Jackson and James Longstreet of the Confederate Army. Edmund had an active mind and he was fascinated by much that was happening around him. A lad of only seventeen when the Mexican War broke out, he followed newspaper reports of the combat with keen interest and, as soon as he was old enough to enlist, joined the New York State Militia.[16] In 1850 he was attending regular drills at Camp Woll, near Niagara Falls, and by 1856 he had been promoted to the rank of lieutenant.[17]

Around this time sister Marian found herself a beau, Gilbert Silas Jennings, and married him. Gilbert was twelve years Edmund's senior, but the two of them and Gilbert's younger brother John became close friends. Little is known of the Jennings' lives after they were married other than Gilbert's army service. It is known that Gilbert and Winifred had at least three children.

Ominously, the issue of slavery would not go away. It was the subject of discussion everywhere, and even with the Compromise of 1850 few were reassured the question had been put to rest; it had been only postponed. The Compromise of 1850 did nothing to still the fury in the hearts of Southern slaveholders or Northern abolitionists.

We hear nothing more about the jewelry business until after Edmund's military career ends, but in 1856 we know Edmund was appointed mail agent for the railroad that passed through Buffalo, and he helped man the mail cars that shuttled between Buffalo and Syracuse.[18] This travel broadened his horizons and very likely provided him with an opportunity to meet a beautiful young lady from Albany, Charlotte Augusta Godwin,[19] born in Canada in 1836. On November 25, 1856, they were married by the Reverend George N. Cheney, rector at the Trinity Church in Rochester, New York. In 1859 their first child, a lovely daughter, Edna, was born.

One year later, a lawyer favoring the abolition of slavery, Abraham Lincoln, was elected president. This was too much for the Southern states. They had had enough of the North's incessant condemnation of their slave economy and declared that they were leaving the Union. At precisely 4:30 a.m. on April 12, 1861, the Civil War began in earnest when Confederates began firing cannon balls at Fort Sumter on an island in Charleston Harbor, forcing its surrender.

At the first call for troops, just three days after the attack, the three comrades, Edmund, Gilbert, and Charles, Gilbert's younger brother, eagerly enlisted in the

Union Army. They were sure when they enlisted, as were most of their compatriots, that this would be a short, exciting ninety days as officers in the 26th New York Infantry Volunteers. Edmund left his jewelry business in the capable hands of his brother C. J. Too young to join in the coming struggle, his fifteen-year-old brother Ernest remained at home, in complete awe of his older brother marching off to war in his fine uniform.

Why did Edmund give up his promising business career and his family to join the fighting? Many writers and historians, such as George Bradley, writing in the *Harrisburg Dispatch,* a Pennsylvania Civil War bulletin, in 1995, believed the Union boys simply loved their country. After all, their country had been attacked by traitors, the "damned secesh" as the Confederates were soon called. But Edmund had a family and a successful business established in Buffalo. Why would he leave all this and, in effect, abandon his wife and child?

In 1885 Shurly answered the question when he wrote his comrades at the first reunion of the 26th New York Volunteers Infantry Regiment: "[T]he men who enlisted at the first call were patriots. No bounty lured them, in fact many did not expect any pay. We enlisted at the sound of Sumter's guns to sustain the Union and the flag. If any body of men deserves honor it is the survivors of those who responded to the first call."[20]

And there may have been something more driving him toward the military life. A thirst for adventure threads its way through generations of these American immigrants, from John Martin Shurly, and his search for a new life in America, to the present day. As these chronicles will show, this quest for a full and rewarding life is never far from the surface in John Shurly and his generation and those that followed.

Chapter Three

THE CIVIL WAR AND THE 26TH NEW YORK VOLUNTEERS INFANTRY REGIMENT

Said I: "Joe, I suppose you are rejoiced you will so soon see your master."
In reply he said: "If it was not for de old woman and the children, I would rather die."

—E. R. P. Shurly, in a conversation with one of
"Old Mason's" escaped slaves, 1862[21]

BEFORE MOST MEN REALIZED THAT WAR WAS IMMINENT, Colonel William Henry Christian, a revered native of Utica, New York, and a veteran of the Mexican War, championed the establishment of the 26th New York Volunteers (NYV) Regiment. Foreseeing the conflict ahead for the nation, Christian resolved to raise a regiment of volunteers from northwestern New York, principally from the towns of Utica, Rochester, and Oriskany, and surrounding counties.

When the call went out for volunteers, Christian, a Democrat politically, immediately organized the regiment and was the first man in Utica to offer his services to President Lincoln. The three lads, Edmund, Gilbert, and Charles, some of the first to join the regiment, were placed in Company G, which would be commanded by Gilbert. By April 24, 1861, Christian had enrolled over three hundred men in the regiment, and by early May there were nearly a thousand, and all marched to Elmira for training and discipline. On May 21 the regiment was mustered into the service of the United States for a period of ninety days.[22]

Christian drilled the men mercilessly in Elmira and formed them into the fighting unit they remembered proudly for the rest of their lives. Captain George Arrowsmith, of the 26th NYV, would later write that "he [had] no confidence in any general or colonel near here but Colonel Christian." Colonel Kerrigan of the famed New York Zouaves said "the 26th was one of the best drilled volunteer regiments he had yet seen."[23] As soon as it was judged ready for service, the 26th New York Volunteer Infantry Regiment exchanged the muskets they had trained with for Austrian rifles and, on June 19 they were loaded into freight cars and moved south. In just over two months, and with only the training he had received in the New York State Militia and the month spent training in Elmira, Edmund Shurly would be introduced to the ugly world of military conflict.

PRIVATE CORNELIUS RIGHTMIRE,[24] of Company K, 26th New York, later described in his memoirs the rousing welcome the troops received when they arrived in Williamsport, Pennsylvania, where they were treated to a "good dinner."[25] Afterward, they returned to their train and continued a slow, tedious journey past Harrisburg and Havre de Grace, Maryland, to the outskirts of Baltimore.

> Then, [Rightmire continued], we were ordered off the train, [and] drawn up in line. A command [was] given to load [our weapons] and the bayonets of the 26th New York glistened in the morning sun. We obeyed; we loaded our Springfield rifles; we were in the borderland of Dixie; we were prepared for our enemies.
>
> About [two o'clock in the afternoon], we marched through the streets of Baltimore in the order of street firing, a pretty movement and well executed. A Massachusetts regiment that preceded us had been mobbed. I think [that] had [the Baltimore street gangs] attempted to mob us the score would have been different. After marching through the city, we boarded the [railroad] cars and journeyed to Washington

without further incident, and on Mary's Heights we were bivouacked for the night.[26]

The next morning the troops awoke to see a vast training camp spread out over fields dotted with tents that stretched for miles. "Regiments, brigades [and] whole divisions were being drilled for the oncoming struggle."[27] At first, the Quartermaster Corps could not keep up with the demand for uniforms and other supplies, and the troops were "ragged, dirty and absolutely penniless."[28] Slowly, however, the situation improved and new uniforms and eight dollars in silver were issued. With the new supplies came orders to move south. Cornelius Rightmire recalls:

> We crossed the Potomac River to Alexandria. The day was dark with a drizzling rain and, marching through King Street, I beheld a sight that chilled my blood. At the top of a long building or stockade was lettered "Slave Pen." My ire was raised to the highest pitch. I told my comrades if I ever got the chance, I would shoot to kill at so diabolical an institution. Alas! I learned my southern brothers could shoot as well as I.
>
> Our move to the higher ground near Alexandria occurred near the middle of July, and quite soon after, we smelt the smoke of battle. We were sent by rail (in the early hours of the night) to the battleground of First Bull Run but were not engaged, for upon our arrival the Union forces were routed.[29]

THE 26TH NEW YORK VOLUNTEERS had arrived by rail on the field of the First Battle of Bull Run on July 21, 1861, just in time to witness the humiliating retreat of the Army of the Potomac from its debacle at Bull Run, a brilliantly planned but badly executed invasion of the South. Army Generals Winfield Scott and Irvin McDowell, who led the Union forces into this battle, had begged the recently elected and militarily unseasoned President Lincoln not to commit completely untrained soldiers to a complicated offensive aimed at an important supply center such as Manassas. But politicians in Congress, and in the president's

Cabinet, as well as the newspapers of the day, had demanded action and cried out, "On to Richmond!"[30]

Calls for troops had already produced 35,000 men under arms near Washington, D.C., and ten artillery batteries for the Federals, far more than the cadre of army officers had ever seen, much less trained and exercised in mass. The regiments had been organized into brigades only a week before; inexperience was everywhere and discipline was nowhere to be seen. Movement and maneuver of such a large army required precise attention to order and punctuality. This army had none of that, and most soldiers had not even been trained in the use of muskets. Many had not even fired a rifle. Moreover, freight wagons were in short supply and wagon masters were untrained and insubordinate.

His top army leaders, Scott and McDowell, presented this to Lincoln, but to no avail. A politician with no military experience, Lincoln would make mistakes throughout the Civil War, mistakes no different from those made by the inexperienced wartime presidents who preceded and would follow him to the office. Once again, and not for the last time, events would teach the Republic and the president of the United States the importance of military preparation and respect for the lessons of history.

On July 16, 1861, a spectacular sight greeted the assembled dignitaries. Thirty thousand soldiers paraded before President Lincoln, and, accompanied by hundreds of civilians, scores of congressmen, senators and their wives in carriages, and newspaper reporters, marched south to put an end to this Southern foolishness. Their spirits were buoyed by their new uniforms and rifles, and by the martial music coming from the marching bands that accompanied them. How, at this point, could they possibly have known of the importance of training and discipline in war? G. F. R. Henderson, in his book, *Stonewall Jackson and the American Civil War*, writes:

> The return of a victorious army could hardly have been hailed with more enthusiasm than the departure of these untrained and unblooded volunteers. Yet, pitiful masquerade as the march must have appeared to a soldier's eye, the majority of those who broke camp that summer morning were brave men and good Americans. To restore the Union, to avenge the insult to their country's flag, they had come forward with

no other compulsion than the love of their motherland. If their self-confidence was supreme and even arrogant, it was the self-confidence of a strong and a fearless people, and their patriotism was of the loftiest kind. It would have been easy for the North, with her enormous wealth, to have organized a vast army of mercenaries wherewith to crush the South. But no! Her sons were not willing that their country's honor should be committed to meaner hands.[31]

It was not long before the officers would learn the full extent of the problems presented to them by undisciplined troops. Virginia roads were hot and dusty, and knapsacks, rifles, blankets, and ammunition became too burdensome for many of the raw recruits. Their compact formations began to stretch out and stragglers fell farther and farther back from their units. Men became separated from their regiments. By the end of the first day the army had marched no more than six miles, and it was not until late the next day that all the men had returned to their units.

Finally, on July 18 the forward elements of the army made their first contact with the Confederates, with chilling results. Eighty-three Union officers and men were lost, and nearby Union soldiers tried not to look at the first bloody victims carried past them to the surgeon's tent. Some officers did not avert their gaze soon enough and vomited in front of their men. One regiment turned and ran to the rear; and, despite appeals from the secretary of war, another regiment and one battery of three-month enlistees demanded their discharge. This was not a good beginning.

The Battle of Bull Run started in earnest on the morning of July 21 after a march to the battle line that began at midnight. Samuel P. Heintzelman's 3rd Division, along with David Hunter's 2nd Division, was ordered to cross Bull Run at Sudley Ford and make a sweeping movement around the left flank of the Confederates. Initial contact was made with Colonel Nathan G. "Shanks" Evans' Confederate troops shortly after daybreak. One can only imagine the Union soldiers' exhilaration after two hours of battle as untrained Union regiments decimated the brigades of Brigadier General Barnard E. Bee and Colonels F. S. Bartow and Evans, forcing them back toward Henry House Hill, toward General Thomas Jonathan Jackson's 1st Brigade, hidden in the tree line at the far side of the hill. The Union right flank continued its advance into the early afternoon as Jackson resolutely assured Bee he would hold the hill. Bee then rallied his troops with his famous words: *"There stands Jackson like a stone wall. Rally behind the Virginians!"*[32] Jackson's troops fired a volley from their hidden positions, then charged the disoriented Union soldiers with fixed bayonets.

"Yell like furies when you charge!" Jackson had ordered, and for the first time in the war the Union soldiers heard the famous, earsplitting Rebel yell. Jackson's tactics effectively stopped the Union soldiers on Henry House Hill, and the tide of battle turned in favor of the Confederates. The Union soldiers' exhilaration turned to panic and despair, and they bolted back across Bull Run. Retreat turned to rout all the way back to Washington.

The sight of the Union Army fleeing in panic was the first exposure Edmund Shurly and the 26th New York had to the skills of Stonewall Jackson, but it was not to be their last. It would in fact be their misfortune to engage units of Stonewall Jackson's army in nearly every battle they fought during Edmund Shurly's tenure with the 26th. And, in every engagement with Jackson, they took a licking. They had picked a foe who was one of the finest generals ever to wear an American military uniform, albeit a Rebel uniform.

After this disaster it was obvious to Lincoln that his soldiers needed new leadership and more training. But Lincoln himself lacked any formal military training and, what was worse, he had only second-rate generals to pick from for direction of the Union forces. The best soldiers in the army had chosen to represent their home states rather than their country. Lincoln was left with an assortment of army politicians rather than fighting military officers imbued with that extra spark needed to produce victory. For the next three years he would be enticed by the likes of Generals George McClellan, John Pope, and Ambrose Burnside into believing that they, in turn, could win the war against Robert E. Lee. Of the three, McClellan was probably the "least worst," having exceptional charisma and the trust of his army, but who, when Lincoln could coerce him into fighting, allowed his caution and self-doubts to turn what could have been victories into defeats and his defeats into catastrophes. To his eternal credit, Lincoln was quick to recognize and dismiss his failed generals and continue his search for success until at last he found it late in the war in General Ulysses Simpson Grant. By then Edmund Shurly had departed the active army.

IT ALSO WAS APPARENT that the ninety days the volunteers had originally enlisted for was not going to be sufficient to bring the South to its knees. Accordingly, on August 7 Colonel Christian announced to his troops that he wanted only those officers prepared to stay for two years to remain in the regiment. Lieutenant Shurly, along with almost the entire 26th New York, chose to extend their enlistments to two years. Shurly had performed well and was promoted from ensign to lieutenant on May 21, and then to captain on August 7, and given command of Company C,[33] replacing John H. Fairbanks, who may have been one of fourteen soldiers who had decided that ninety days was enough.

Shortly after receiving his promotion Edmund was assigned to recruiting duty in Rochester and Buffalo, allowing him to return home to Augusta and baby Edna. By now the hometown folks knew he was embarking on serious business and in gratitude presented him with a fine sword and a telescope engraved with his name followed by "C-26-NYV." The following April he returned to duty with his regiment, again leaving behind his wife and daughter.[34]

Meanwhile, the 26th New York spent the months following Bull Run constructing and garrisoning Forts Lyon, Worth, Ward, and Ellsworth, forts surrounding Washington, D.C., to guard it against a Confederate attack. In September the regiment was assigned to a brigade under General Henry Slocum and camped on the plain above Fort Lyon, building rifle pits and other defenses. In October the brigade moved to Camp Franklin near Fairfax Seminary, Virginia. By November 1861 the unit was detached from Slocum's brigade and garrisoned Fort Lyon for the winter.

Many years later Shurly would write of some of the incidents that befell him after his return to the 26th in April. Shurly tells one such tale with a flair that illustrates his ability to relate a story and his sympathy for the Negro slave:

> During the World's Fair, I met a few members of my old regiment, the 26th New York. I was walking along, looking at the sights, when someone said, "Hello, Captain," and an old gentleman caught my hand and said, "How do you do! It is many a year since we met. Now you don't know me; I was in your company."
>
> My eyes closed for an instant, and in my mind I saw [Company] C in line as they answered to their names. My eyes opened and I looked upon

that old but pleasant face. Like a flash, memory came to the rescue. "Brown, 2nd!" I said and grasped his hand. No one but the old soldier comrades who have stood together when the bullets were flying can appreciate the tie of friendship that links comrade to comrade—very much stronger than any society! The present generation cannot realize the feeling.

After talking of old times—you know how it is; telling of this one and that one who had crossed the "dark river"—my friend said, "Say, Captain, do you remember when we lost the niggers belonging to old Mason of Virginia?"

"Well, I declare," said I, "it is many a day since I thought of that."

In the winter and spring of 1861 and 1862, our regiment was stationed at Fort Lyon, Alexandria, Va. (By the way, we built that Fort.) I think it was about this time of the year, April, when I received an order from Colonel Christian to report with my company to the Post Quartermaster at Alexandria for duty. I have mislaid the order. The substance came from Washington to our Colonel, and it was about as follows:

"Special order, No.—: Capt. E. R. P. Shurly in command of Company C, 26th New York, will report with his company to the Depot Quartermaster for escort duty, and take charge of private property, and turn the same over to Ex-Senator Mason, of Virginia, or his agent, taking his receipt for the same."

As soon as possible, with my company, I reported to the Quartermaster, and received the following property: 6 horses, 2 cows, 2 mules, 1 wagon and harness, 5 Negro slaves—consisting of father, mother, and three children. Somehow after receipting for this property, I did not like the slave part and told the Quartermaster that I did not come to the war to take back Negroes to their masters. He said, "You are green in the business, and will have to do many things that are distasteful while in Uncle Sam's service." But, as he said, "Orders must be obeyed." I saw the Negro family placed in the wagon, detailed a guard to prevent escape, and gave the order to march.

It was early spring—one of those delightful days peculiar to Virginia. The trees were leafing out, the birds making the woods musical. The weather was warm, and as I was not limited for time, we marched along at an easy gait, stopping often to rest at some of the inviting little creeks and streams.

During the march, I talked with the Negro and his wife. They were quite intelligent and had been born and raised on the Mason place. The woman was almost white and had been reared as a house servant. It seemed that they had escaped, hoping to reach the North, but were arrested in Alexandria. This was early in the war, at a time when politicians hoped to compromise with the South.

I enjoyed the play of the children, especially a three-year-old girl [who] reminded me of one I had left home, perhaps never to see again. The nearer we came to the end of our journey, the more reluctant I was to turn these slaves over.

Before God I said to myself, "What a mistake our government is making—returning human beings to slavery." Did I sacrifice business, leave family and friends, to become an instrument of enforcing the Fugitive Slave Law? I saw that my company had the same feeling in regard to these chattels, and I did a heap of thinking. We had arrived within four miles of our destination. The road was narrow through the woods—bridle paths crossed in every direction. A rippling stream of water near the road afforded a charming place for a halt and rest. I ordered a halt.

I spoke to the Negro. I noticed that the nearer we came to the place of his birth the sadder he became. Occasionally a tear coursed down his dark cheek, and his wife was also in tears. The children had ceased to play. Said I, "Joe, I suppose you are glad that you will soon see your master."

In reply, he said, "If it were not for the old woman and de children, I would rather die."

Said I, "Do you know this country well?"

"I was born here, Massa. I know every path," he answered.

"How far is it to the next water?" I asked.

"About a mile," he answered.

"Well now," I said, "when we arrive at that creek we will halt. I will march the company to the left, in the shade of the trees, and will take the guard from the wagon, leave you in the wagon on the right side in the woods, and stop about ten minutes. Do you think you can get away with your family?"

"Just give me the chance, Captain. I know every part in these woods. If it were not for my wife and children, I would kill myself before being sent back to Massa Mason."

Fall in, forward march. We soon arrived at the next halting place. My plan was carried out. The Negro and his family escaped. Found the horses hitched to a tree. I made a great racket, formed the company in a skirmish line and scoured the woods on the left side of the road. Negroes gone. Forward, company! Proceed on the march. As we started the men began to cheer. We soon reached the end of our journey.

The most angry man I had met for some time was old Mason when I told him that the slaves had escaped. [He] said his son commanded a company of [Confederate] cavalry and he knew where to reach him and would give me a lively time marching back. I finally told him that if he did not sign my receipt and stop his talk I would take him back with me. "I will have you dismissed from the army," he said. "It was a damned Yankee trick."

I returned to the regiment and made a written report and enclosed the receipt to the colonel, who forwarded the papers to Washington. The next day, there came an order to place me in arrest, and sent me to General McClellan's HQ at Washington. I reported there the next day. The general was away. His adjutant told me to come back at 2:00 p.m.

Before the war I had met Secretary [William H.] Seward a few times. I made up my mind to call on him. I sent in my card and was admitted. I told him my story. He said, "As you have to cross the [Potomac] river back to your regiment, I will see the president at once, as I have some other business with him." He returned in about half an hour with an order to go back to my regiment, and he would see that I was released from arrest. Mister Seward said Mister Lincoln said that somehow a U.S. officer was not worth his salt to return Negroes to their owners.

After the battle of the 2nd Bull Run, I was walking up Pennsylvania Ave., when I heard a voice say, "Stop, Captain! Stop!" I looked back and there was my escaped darkey, full of thanks. He said his wife prayed for me every night. I think perhaps I needed the prayers. He was doing well, at work at Brown's Hotel—happy and free.[35]

IN EARLY 1862, exasperated over lack of army movement, Lincoln issued a direct order to McClellan to march on Richmond. Ever the cautionary, and with what some conclude was cowardice, McClellan devised a plan to attack the Confederate capital, by way of a circuitous route through the peninsula formed between the James and York Rivers rather than risk attacking what he believed was an easily defended Manassas railroad junction, scene of the First Battle of Bull Run. He did not seem to appreciate that the Rebels had abandoned it.

As his army landed and proceeded up the peninsula, the outnumbered Confederates became very concerned, and Robert E. Lee and Stonewall Jackson, the latter now in command of a division in the Shenandoah Valley, endeavored to fool Lincoln into believing Jackson was preparing to attack Washington through Harper's Ferry from the west and thus draw Union troops away from the Peninsula Campaign.

By May 24 McClellen's troops could see the spires of Richmond in the distance. Citizens, along with the Confederate Congress, were fleeing the city. Nevertheless, the always-fearful McClellan begged Secretary of War Edwin Stanton for forty thousand more troops before invading the town. By now, his generals, disgusted with the progress of the campaign, were calling him "The Virginia Creeper."

Rather than give McClellan the troops he asked for, Stanton instead called for the formation of the 3rd Corps of the Department of the Rappahannock under the command of the luckless General Irvin McDowell and, with the troops McClellan wanted for himself, ordered it to move west of the Potomac from Washington and south toward Fredericksburg and Richmond. McClellan was furious that these troops were not under his own direct command.

FOR EDMUND SHURLY this was good news. At last the 26th was to move out. On May 4, the 26th, assigned to the 3rd Corps, broke camp and proceeded south along the Potomac River to positions above Aquia Creek that had been occupied by Confederate forces the previous winter. From Aquia Creek the 26th marched farther south to the vicinity of Fredericksburg and, on May 11, was attached to General John C. Ricketts' 1st Brigade, General Edward O. C. Ord's 2nd Division, 3rd Corps.

Transfer to McDowell's 3rd Corps was in fact a mixed blessing for Shurly. He had wanted to see action, and now his regiment was marching toward it. But McDowell, in addition to being perhaps the unluckiest of the Union generals, was also said to be hated by his men and rumored by some to be secretly favoring victory by the Confederates. It was a spurious rumor, of course, but it always seemed to reappear after each successive Union defeat. For Edmund's commander, Colonel Christian, sadly, McDowell's reputation only aggravated his growing misgivings over Union battlefield leadership.

Abruptly on May 25 the 3rd Corps halted its advance to the south just as it was placing pontoon bridges across the Rappahannock at Fredericksburg. Stonewall Jackson's strategy had surprised Lincoln. For no reason apparent to Shurly and the other troops, the 26th abruptly pulled back north to Manassas Junction, and by late the next day were camped at Thoroughfare Gap, west of Manassas and not far from the Shenandoah Valley. Rumors flying through the regiment said they were headed for a small town in Virginia called Front Royal. The men knew something big had happened and that constant marching back and forth through the Virginia countryside meant confusion and indecision in the top ranks, but not much else. At this point Edmund Shurly could not have known that Jackson, in a classic military maneuver studied ever since in military classrooms, had successfully hoodwinked Lincoln into believing he was going to attack Washington, D.C. (Some historians say with some justification that Lincoln was in fact attempting to trap Jackson in the valley and destroy his army.)

Years later, Shurly's foreboding would be forgotten, but the humorous incidents that occurred during these incessant marches across Virginia would not.

> We had marched about three days over a rough country [he later wrote], the sticky clay of old Virginia not adding to our pleasure. We thought from the appearance of our little general, Ord, commanding, that it looked like a fight. Certainly something was up. Hence this forced march—no rations, the orders being strict, no foraging, not a rail

fence to be touched, or rebel hog, sheep, or ox killed, on pain of severe punishment.

About 2:00 p.m. we bivouacked upon the plantation of the late Chief Justice Marshall, a most pleasing rural landscape. The fields ornamented with many hogs and sheep; but alas, they were not for the hungry soldier. We were in camp. It was rumored that the commissary train would soon be up, but as the time passed on proved to be an illusion. It was not long before some of the home Rebs (all Union men to me) came into our company lines. I was looking attentively from a point in the front of my company for the missing train, when a man handed me an order from my colonel to detail two men as guards for the house. In conversing with the man I ascertained that he was the overseer and had charge of the place.

Said I, "Who owns those hogs and sheep?"

"They belong to the estate," he replied.

A thought flashed in my head. If I could buy only one and have my men catch it, the meat problem was solved. "Do you have any gold in circulation here?" I asked.

"Not seen such a thing since you'uns came to war with we'uns."

I had in my pocket a gold dollar, the last of the Mohicans. I showed it to my man. "See this dollar? It is genuine. I will give it to you for one of your hogs."

He closed the bargain at once.

"Stop," I said, "I will give you this dollar with the understanding that I send five of my men to catch it."

"Only one hog," he said.

"That is all the five men will take."

"That is all right," he answered.

"Sergeant Church—detail four men and with them catch one hog from that herd."

They started for that herd on a run. They had scarcely reached the herd when the whole brigade gave a cheer and were on the run for the hogs. In less time than I can tell it, there was not a living hog or sheep on the plantation. The men were supplied with meat, but a few minutes afterwards a staff officer was at the colonel's tent.

I was sent for, and the colonel appeared very much out of temper. But if I was not mistaken, I scented meat cooking in the rear of his tent. I told him the story, but General Ord had directed that the officer who had command of the men who "led the charge" should be ordered to report in arrest to him. Upon appearing before him, he said, "Who are you?"

"I have the honor, sir, to command Company C, 26th N. Y. Volunteers."

"What is your name?"

"E. R. P. Shurly."

"You are a disgrace to the service," said he. "I shall have your shoulder straps torn off in the presence of the troops."

My dollar man was there, the picture of woe.

"General," said I, "what is the offense?"

"Not a word, sir."

"But you must listen to me." I turned to the man and said, "Did I not buy a hog from you for a gold dollar? Was it not in the bargain that five of my men should catch it?"

"Yes," said the man.

"General Ord, am I to blame if the whole of your brigade turned into a mob? Am I responsible for their discipline? You see how it was."

I saw his staff officers in a broad grin. The general said, "Go to your quarters, sir. I will attend to this later!"

About three years afterwards, I was ordered to report to General Ord at Detroit for mustering duty. After I had been [t]here two or three days, the general said to me, "Have you been in the hog and sheep trade since you left Virginia?"

"General, how was that Southern mutton?"

"Well, it was fine. But there was a little trouble over it at Washington."

This took place early in the war.

[Signed]
E R P Shurly, USA, April 7, 1904.[36]

Military life for Edmund until now had been filled with humorous incidents such as this, but that would change. Stonewall Jackson had just struck savagely at Front Royal.

Chapter Four

THE BATTLE OF
FRONT ROYAL

*"There is a ferry at Front Royal, Va., in which we have passed
a regiment of infantry, a section of artillery,
60 baggage wagons, and a squadron of cavalry."*

—Telegram from General McDowell to
Secretary of War, Edwin M. Stanton, June 15, 1862
concerning a rope ferry Shurly built over the Shenandoah River[37]

SHORTLY AFTER THE WAR BEGAN, Lincoln put Major General Nathaniel P. Banks
in command of the troops defending the western approaches to Washington.
Before the war, Banks had a very successful political career, rising to the position
of speaker of the U.S. House of Representatives in only his second term and later
becoming governor of Massachusetts. However, as a general he was incompetent
and would never have become one had it not been for his political connections and
his strong abolitionist feelings.[38] It has been said that Secretary of War Stanton felt
that Banks had a fine career before him until Lincoln undertook to make of him
what the good Lord had not: a general.

Banks had forty thousand men arrayed against Jackson's fifteen thousand[39] but
had divided them into smaller groups including a 4,500-man force defending

Strasburg; one thousand men defending Front Royal; two thousand troops defending Rectortown; and fifteen hundred men defending Winchester, to the north of Front Royal, each unit too far distant to help the others in an attack.

On May 8, 1862, Jackson's troops mauled a Union force at McDowell, Virginia, a village just west of Staunton on the Bullpasture River, and Banks mistakenly assumed he would remain in this area. Instead, Lee, a student of Napoleonic strategy, ordered Jackson to threaten an attack on Washington to draw Union forces away from McClellan's Peninsula Campaign against Richmond. As ordered, Jackson's forces secretly marched north toward the Strasburg-Front Royal line.

Colonel John Kenly commanded the thousand-man garrison that guarded Front Royal. On the night of May 22, he and some of his officers were invited to a party given at the home of an attractive young woman by the name of Belle Boyd. In the course of the evening festivities she was able to draw from him and his officers details of the deployment of his men in and around Front Royal. When the party broke up, she saddled her horse and rode to Jackson's headquarters, three miles southwest of the town,[40] to provide him with the final pieces of information he needed to make an attack on the Union garrison the next day.[41] These secrets confirmed other information he had received earlier and there is little doubt that it was this intelligence that caused him to choose that town for the opening battle of his Valley Campaign.

Meanwhile, plans were afoot to send a squadron of New York cavalry into the Front Royal area on May 23. The squadron, probably no more than fifty to seventy men, commanded by a Major Vought, was assembled from various army units and ordered to proceed to Front Royal.[42]

So it was on the evening of Thursday, May 22, 1862, not more than eighty miles from Washington, D.C., that Stonewall Jackson encamped with fifteen thousand troops in the Luray Valley, just to the south of Front Royal, while a few miles to the north, Major Vought, with perhaps seventy men, was preparing to bed down for the night. Between these disparate forces were a thousand men of the 1st Maryland Regiment guarding Front Royal under the nearly universal Union misapprehension that the war was near an end. After all, Kentucky, Missouri, and western Virginia had been taken by Federal forces; the Mississippi River, from Memphis north, was controlled by the Union, and New Orleans had been occupied.[43] McClellan's Peninsula Campaign was going well at this point, and few in Washington could see how the Sessionists could last out the summer. In fact Washington was so sure of imminent Confederate collapse that army enlistment offices had been closed.[44]

The Front Royal campsite was one of immense natural beauty and at the same time militarily difficult to defend. To its southeast stood the majestic Massanutten mountain range, which flanks the Shenandoah Valley to its east; and to the east of the campsite, in the distance, were the Blue Ridge Mountains. Kenly was camped east of the Shenandoah just south of where its two forks join to form the Shenandoah River, wending its way north to Harper's Ferry. From this junction, one fork extends west to Strasburg and then bends south through the heart of the Shenandoah Valley. In 1862 two wooden bridges crossed the river from the east at Front Royal. One was a railroad bridge for the Manassas Gap Railroad, the other for wagon traffic passing along the Winchester Turnpike. From these bridges the road travels west toward Strasburg then turns north, crossing a third wooden bridge toward Cedarville and Winchester. With a thousand men and only two small howitzers, Kenly had little chance of defending this town against a determined enemy.

Henderson's words begin the story:

> On the morning of May 23 there was no token of the approaching storm. The day was intensely hot, and the blue masses of the mountains shimmered in the summer haze. In the Luray Valley to the south there was no sign of life, save the buzzards sailing lazily above the slumberous woods.[45]

Confederate bugles announced the surprise attack. A skirmish line of Confederate soldiers emerged from the trees south of town and fired on the thin line of Union pickets. At first Union cannons effectively slowed the Confederates, and from the woods to their north came a squadron of New York cavalry unexpectedly galloping in to join the battle. When Kenly saw another column of Rebels approaching his right flank, however, he quickly ordered the camp and its supplies burned and retreated across the bridges to defensive positions on Guards Hill. Then he ordered the bridges burned to prevent the Rebels from crossing to his defensive lines. By quick action the Southerners were able to save the road bridge, and, although heavily damaged, the bridge to Guards Hill allowed some Confederates to get across. The 6th Virginia, accompanied by Jackson himself, found fords to cross the river despite turbulent water from heavy rains, and he immediately ordered the regiment forward.

By the time Jackson could assemble four squadrons of cavalry to continue his attack, the Union forces were fast disappearing down the Winchester Turnpike, toward the little village of Cedarville, three miles to the north. The New York cavalry was doing what it could to slow the 6th Virginia but was far outnumbered.

When his men reached Cedarville, Kenly ordered them to dig in for a last-ditch holding action. The land near Cedarville on either side of the turnpike was farmed and fenced in and appeared suitable for a defense. Then, just as his men began tearing down fences and digging in, they heard the sound of furious hoof beats and pistol shots, and a dense cloud of dust appeared to their front.

Jackson had ordered his 6th Virginia to attack vigorously without waiting for reinforcements, and they were rapidly overwhelming the relatively feeble resistance of the New York squadron of cavalry. Finally, the New Yorkers broke and ran for the Winchester Turnpike with the southerners arrayed across the fields behind them. Through the cloud of dust and into the defenses of Kenly's troopers rode the New Yorkers. The lead Confederate squadron of cavalry had held to the confines of the Winchester Turnpike and, when it burst through the cloud of dust, it received a full volley of rifle fire. The flanking units of the Confederate cavalry, however, swept on around the Union troops and quickly surrounded them, killing many and wounding Colonel Kenly. In total for the day, Jackson captured over seven hundred of the Union soldiers that had garrisoned the town. Confederate losses were eleven killed and fifteen wounded. It was an unmitigated disaster for the Federals.

TEN DAYS LATER, on June 1, engulfed in a torrential downpour, General Ord's 2nd Division, including John C. Ricketts' 1st Brigade, marched into Front Royal from Manassas Gap. They were to bring order to the town and defend it against any new attack from Stonewall Jackson.[46] The division halted at the east bank of the Shenandoah River, but the 26th NYV, a section of Captain Hall's battery attached to the 2nd Maine, sixty baggage wagons, and a squadron of cavalry crossed the only remaining bridge over the river and occupied Federal Hill to the south of town. There they directly faced Jackson's forces camped six miles farther south, with Confederate pickets not more than a mile from their position. One Union company was detailed to form a defensive line facing Jackson.

Stonewall Jackson had by now earned deep respect in the hearts of the Union command for his fighting prowess, and any Federal force this close to him was understandably nervous. Moreover, their concern was only deepened when they saw that the bridge, severely weakened in the recent fighting, was their only avenue for reinforcement if Jackson attacked, and the only avenue of escape if Jackson attacked in overwhelming numbers as he had done the week before.

After the war, 1862 was long remembered by both the North and South as the wettest in memory, and the rain seemed endless as the 26th Infantry crossed the river and established its bridgehead. The river, swollen with turbulent water, had become impassable except by this bridge. But it apparently had not occurred to anyone that the bridge might collapse from the rising water.

That evening, after the 26th made camp, Lieutenant Shurly borrowed a horse from his commander, Major Jennings, and, in the driving rain, rode to the main encampment across the bridge. In 1894, and again in 1904, he would write about what happened when he tried to return to his unit.

It was known that General Jackson and his division were encamped about six miles from the river, his pickets extending within about two miles of the ford. There was a bridge across the Shenandoah when General McDowell advanced General Ricketts' division to the river. Our regiment, 26th N. Y., and the 2nd Maine Battery were ordered to cross the bridge. I remember the water was very high. It was raining, and there had been more or less rain for some days past. After camping on the other side, ... Major [Jennings] said, "How are you off for tobacco?"

"Out," said I.

"Well," he said, "take my horse and go to Front Royal." The rain was coming down only as it could in Virginia at that time. I rode to Front Royal and purchased tobacco for the major and myself, and returned, speedily as possible. When within about fifty feet of the bridge crossing the Shenandoah the center arch dropped in the river. The river had raised many feet in a short time. I rode as quickly as possible to General Ricketts' tent, found the general and told him of the trouble. He said, "This is bad. If the Confederates ascertain that the bridge is destroyed, your regiment and the battery will be captured." He ordered an aide to tell the Chief of Artillery to place some guns on the bank of the river to cover the troops on the opposite bank. The river kept rising. I was sorry to be cut off from the regiment and feared that the Rebs would find out the situation. General Ricketts said, "I hope they will not. The rain will stop and the water will lower. We will repair the bridge and probably pass over reinforcements."

I remember when a boy living in New Philadelphia, Ohio, there was a rope ferry across the Tuscarawas River. The current ran the boat. "General," I said, "if it is possible to procure a rope long enough to reach across the river ... I will have a ferry across—providing I can procure a boat."

The general said, "There is a chance that you may succeed." He wrote the following order: "To the commanding officer of any regiment under my command: You will detail as many men as the bearer, Captain Shurly, may require for the purpose to insure transportation across the Shenandoah River."

The first regiment I visited was the 1st Maine, if I remember right. Their colonel detailed two hundred men under a major to repair the bridge. The colonel (I have forgotten his name), said, "We will not only do our military duty, but will do everything possible to rescue your regiment."

Now the trouble was to find a boat. We had the rope from the engineer department. We interviewed quite a number of residents of Front Royal, but they all said General Jackson had destroyed all the boats. While on the march to the river we met a Negro, and asked him if he knew what had become of all the boats that were on the river. He said, "Before the Lord, I does not, but I suspects the miller does."

"Where is the miller?" I asked.

"Massa, you turn to the left and go down dat road you will come to the mill."

We proceeded on our march and soon arrived at the mill. It was of the old fashioned Virginia style. I entered the mill with one of the Maine officers and two men, found the miller and his family. I forgot to say that before parting from the darkey, he told me that two days before, when Jackson's army passed through, the flat boats were taken up the river and that the miller knew where they were. The miller denied all knowledge of the flat boats; said that two or three had been destroyed. Finding that I could get no satisfaction from the miller by fair means, I spoke to the lieutenant of the Maine Regiment who was with me and told him that we must take serious means as the night was passing away. One of the men with us was a sergeant. I told him to bring a rope that was hanging near by, and said to the miller that unless he informed me at once where to find the boats I would hang him.

He said, "I do not know." His wife had come in, was in tears, begging for his life. I had told the sergeant, aside, that I did not propose to take the life of the miller, only to go as far as we could without that result. I was sure the darkey was right, hence these drastic means.

The soldier passed the rope round the miller's neck, ran it over a beam in the mill. Two more men came in. I said to the miller, "This is your last chance."

He answered, "I do not know."

"Up with him," said I, and they drew him up so that his toes just touched.

"Lower him down," said I, "Now then will you talk?"

"No!" he said.

"Up you go!"

At that moment his wife rushed in, having passed the sentinel. She said, "Stop! My God, for the sake of me and the children," she said to her husband, "tell them, or I will."

The miller said, "There are two boats in the bushes about three miles up the river—I will show you."

We started with the miller between a file of men. My orders were to kill him if there was any treachery. We proceeded about two miles up the river and there found the flat boats. They were about twenty-five feet in length. We secured both boats and had a terrible ride until we came near the dam. We procured the necessary tackle and ropes, and by six o'clock in the morning the boat, propelled by the current, began to pass over the 26th regiment, and by 2:00 p.m., we had passed [all of the regiment] over.

On the second day after the ferry was erected, General [Samuel W.] Crawford with his staff and escort of cavalry, his brigade in the distance, came to the ferry. I had orders from General Ricketts not to pass anybody until the quartermaster and his supplies were transported across the river. General Crawford, before I had completed my order, insisted on passing his cavalry. He took possession of the boat and ordered me to run it. I refused to do so. So he put some of his men at the rope. Just before [the boat] reache[d] the east shore of the river, much to my delight, [the] bow of the boat went under, wetting the general and his staff. He ordered me to report to General Ricketts in arrest.

I waited until we were through with the ferry and then called on General Ricketts. I told him what General Crawford said.

"Well," he said, "You do not want any of his medicine. You return to your company. You will hear from me later." Some little time after, I received a letter from General Ricketts which was very complimentary for the work performed.

[Signed] E. R. P. Shurly[47]

After a stay of three weeks in Front Royal the 26th, along with the rest of Ord's division, moved out of the Shenandoah and back to Manassas.

Chapter Five

THE SECOND BATTLE
OF BULL RUN

It seemed as if every arm and all the projectiles known in modern warfare
had been let loose upon us at once.

—Private Charles McClenthen, 26th New York Volunteers

ON JUNE 26, 1862, SECRETARY OF WAR EDWIN M. STANTON created a new army, the Army of Virginia, and placed Major General John Pope in command. This army combined the units of Generals John C. Fremont, Nathaniel P. Banks, and Irvin McDowell and was to press against Confederate forces along the Rappahannock near Gordonsville and Charlottesville in order to relieve Rebel pressure on the beleaguered Union forces on the peninsula. Its mission was also to protect the capital and to clear Confederates from the Shenandoah (which they did not know had already been accomplished by the departure of Jackson).

In John Pope, Lincoln had found a general not only more detested by his immediate subordinates and his men in the field than McDowell, but also, incredibly, personally hated by Robert E. Lee as well. Lincoln, who had known Pope before his appointment, was taken in by his stories and flattery.[48] But for those who knew him well, Pope was known as a blow-hard and a "blatherskite." He was egotistical, tactless, and pandered to anyone whom he thought could improve his position.

Postmaster General Montgomery Blair once told Lincoln that Pope and his entire family were cheats and liars.

Lincoln may have understood all this but had little better to choose from. None of this boded well for the future of the Union. Within weeks of his appointment, instead of inspiring his army, Pope, in a speech highly critical of his troops, managed to lose the last vestige of respect by his soldiers, by McClellan and his Army of the Potomac, and by the rebel Army of Northern Virginia.

FOR SHURLY'S REGIMENT, the change in leadership meant that on June 26 its 1st Brigade leader, General James B. Ricketts, would move up to replace General Ord as commander of the 2nd Division, and the 26th would transfer to Brigadier General Zealous B. Tower's 2nd Brigade.

On July 4, 1862, the 26th New York found itself in Gainsville, Virginia. From there it advanced south to Warrenton, to Waterloo Bridge over the Rappahannock, and finally to Culpeper, south of the Rappahannock. But morale was slipping to new lows with each new scathing criticism by the hated General Pope, and the march to the Rappahannock became slow and halting. No one took the criticism harder or had less confidence in his army's leadership than Colonel Christian.

On August 9 the 26th New York Volunteers brushed against Stonewall Jackson's men at Cedar Mountain where they were positioned opposite Jackson's left. A little before dark, Shurly and the 26th found themselves on the right flank of the battlefield, very close to a Rebel battery furiously shelling Union positions to their rear and to their left. The display of fire in the sky as the Confederate shells passed overhead was spectacular, and Private Charles McClenthen, of Company G, later wrote, "Our division, [was] near enough to see the flash and smoke of almost every gun fired from the enemy's batteries planted on the side of the mountain, and distinctly hear the rattle of the musketry."[49]

McClenthen went on to write:

> [The Rebels] were not suffered to continue this amusing pastime very long, however, for moving us still further to the right, the 2nd (Hall's) and 5th (Lapier's) Maine, [along] with Thompson's and Matthew's Pennsylvania batteries, took up their positions on the same ground we had just occupied, and opened up on them with such perfect shower

of shot and shell that an ordinary sized thunderstorm would be but a "tempest in a teapot" compared to it. I don't believe anyone could tell when the Rebel battery ceased firing, but it was soon silenced, and most of the men manning it, forever. The next day some of the pieces were found dismounted and the ground strewn with dead men and horses. This was a splendid sight, and as we seemed to be perfectly safe we enjoyed it hugely.

This battle has been set down as a Union victory [and] perhaps it was, but the loss on each side was nearly equal. The Rebels gained ground on us and held possession of the battlefield, carrying off arms, ammunition, etc. before our eyes, while we were allowed to touch nothing except our dead and wounded.[50]

Pope shamelessly proclaimed victory, but everyone knew Stonewall Jackson had whipped them.

BRANDY STATION

MEANWHILE, LINCOLN HAD FINALLY LOST PATIENCE with McClellan's timid approach to the Peninsula Campaign and ordered him to withdraw his troops from the peninsula. McClellan was transferred to a desk in Washington where he would supervise the defense of the capital. Pope assumed command of McClellan's troops, which were separated by a considerable distance from his newly formed Army of Virginia, and Lee was quick to recognize an opportunity. As Pope moved his Army of Virginia south toward the Rappahannock River, Lee ordered a rapid strike by Jeb Stuart's cavalry around Pope's right flank against his relatively undefended headquarters. There, on August 23, Stuart seized $350,000 in cash,[51] Pope's dress coat, and his personal papers, which divulged the disposition of his forces. Pope was stunned.

With this information Lee now had what he needed to attack the superior Union forces. Three days later, on August 26, he sent Stonewall Jackson on a sixty-five-mile march around Pope's right flank through Thoroughfare Gap, then east on the Warrenton Pike to capture Pope's supply depot at Manassas Junction and cut

Pope's supply line from Washington. That evening his hungry, tattered, shoeless soldiers dined joyously on General Pope's fine food and wine. Not only was John Pope's humiliation complete, but he could not have been more confused.

AFTER JEB STUART'S RAID, the shaken Pope ordered his troops back behind the Rappahannock River to Brandy Station, just north of Culpeper where the Orange and Alexandria Railroad crosses the Rappahannock River. For the men of the 26th New York, Stuart's raid would mean double-time marches on empty stomachs and a hellish return to the Bull Run battlefield.

Ricketts' division quietly, under cover of darkness, moved north toward Culpeper, but soon found itself snarled in the traffic of other units with their supply trains and artillery blocking the road and stopped for the night. The next day they slowly threaded their way through Culpeper, along the Orange and Alexandria Railroad tracks, reaching the Rappahannock at Brandy Station around midnight, "tired, hungry, and completely worn out."[52]

The next day the Rebel cavalry made itself known and Hartsuff's brigade had to recross the river to support a Union battery under fire. The Rebels were driven back with heavy losses, and the skirmish simmered down to not much more than an artillery duel. McClenthen commented:

> During these four days [of] cannonading, the infantry, although most constantly under fire, took no really active part in the fighting, and sustained but very little loss from the fact that our artillery and sharpshooters prevented their batteries from occupying the positions where they could have done us the most injury. During this time General Ricketts was everywhere present, personally superintending the planting of batteries and posting infantry, his gallant bearing and earnest zeal diffusing confidence and challenging the admiration of every beholder.
>
> Captain Hall's (2nd Maine) battery particularly distinguished itself during this time for the rapidity and accuracy of its fire and the boldness of the positions occupied.[53]

By the fourth day at Brandy Station Jackson's raid on the Union supply center at Manassas was beginning to have its effect. Food rations were in very short supply, and Rebels were threatening the Union right flank; Pope ordered a retreat toward Warrenton. Shurly's company and Jennings' Company G were ordered to fire the Rappahannock bridge, Brandy Station, and, to prevent the repair of the bridge, its surrounding buildings. General Tower himself was there to supervise the operation, and it was proceeding smoothly when, as Private McClenthen remembers:

> A heavy storm of wind and rain set in, displacing and thoroughly drenching the kindlings we had prepared, making the task of burning them a very difficult one to perform. The buildings nearest the river which we apportioned [to] Company C, were already in full blaze, and we were busy trying to kindle ours, when a Rebel battery on the other side of the river, which had moved up immediately upon the withdrawal of ours, opened upon us with shot and shell which came crashing through the buildings we were burning, causing us to perform this portion of our duty with more alacrity than Company G has ever been noted for. We made one attempt to form the company, but Major [Jennings] rode up and told us to make the best of our legs until we got out of range of the battery, taking especial care to assure himself by his own personal observation that General Tower's orders had been thoroughly executed. There were crowds of stragglers from the Pennsylvania Reserves (who were on their march from Fredericksburg) coming along at this time, but fortunately for us the Rebel's shells did not explode! We could dodge their solid shot, and although they fell thick and fast all around us for more than a mile, I did not see a man hurt.[54]

By the evening of August 24 Companies C and G had rejoined their regiment at Warrenton amid swirling rumors that Confederate forces were about to capture their supplies at Manassas Junction—rumors that by August 26 proved to be true.

THOROUGHFARE GAP

POPE LEARNED ON AUGUST 27 that Jackson had made an end run around his army with an entire corps, not just a cavalry unit, and was plundering his supply depot.

Other reports told him that, even more menacingly, Longstreet was marching with five divisions to reinforce Jackson, who was now settled into a heavily wooded area just to the west of the Bull Run battlefield of 1861. To reinforce Jackson, Longstreet would have to pass through a narrow gorge in the Bull Run range of the Appalachian Mountains between Salem Village and Haymarket, known as Thoroughfare Gap, the only location where there was even a remote chance of stopping him. Pope ordered Ricketts' 2nd Division there to block Longstreet's army.

At six in the evening of August 27, Ricketts and his division set out for Thoroughfare Gap. As was usual, Shurly's Company C and Jennings' Company G brought up the rear of the column, acting as rearguard. Private McClenthen had much to say about this action:

> The men were completely tired and worn out, disheartened and suf-
> fering from hunger. Many could not, and others would not, try to keep
> up but would lie down and try to obtain a little rest in every corner of
> the fence and under every tree along the road. Threats and persuasion
> were unavailing and General Tower who remained with us, and who
> was more active and persevering than any one else, was kept in a tower-
> ing passion all night.[55]

Hartsuff's brigade arrived at the Gap just in time to see the Confederate forces emerging from the gorge and deploying into lines of battle, and he attacked them immediately, driving them back into the mountains. Amazingly, Captain Hall managed to position his rifled guns on the crest of a hill overlooking the gorge and, protected by a regiment of sharpshooters, kept up a brisk and accurate volley of exploding shells along the passage through the gap until well after dark.

> Having thus far accomplished our mission and obeyed orders, which
> were to hold Longstreet in check for six hours, [McClenthen reported
> that] we again turned our faces towards Gainsville, which we reached
> after midnight, and [where we] halted until daylight on the 29th.[56]

Ricketts received considerable criticism for having left the field of battle and not having held Longstreet's army at the Gap for a longer time, but it was general knowledge in the 26th that their orders were to hold for only six hours, then back off to Gainsville. Furthermore, after six hours of bombardment of the Gap by Hall's battery, Ricketts saw that Rebels were bypassing him in large numbers through other mountain gaps on either side and were forming into units to his rear. His division was in serious danger of being surrounded and captured. He had to retreat. McClenthen later wrote, "Nothing but General Ricketts' skillful and hasty retreat prevented the certain capture or annihilation of his whole command."[57]

Ricketts moved his men east, then angled southeast, and headed for Bristow Station. As the Rebels, now fully through the Gap, marched directly east toward Jackson's positions, the clatter of supply wagons and clouds of dust stirred up by Longstreet's five divisions were clearly evident to Ricketts' rearguard made up of Shurly's Company C and Gilbert Jennings' Company G. Several times they stopped and formed a defensive line, expecting an attack that never came. "But Longstreet seemed in too great hurry to join the rest of the Southern army to pay any attention to us after we were … out of his way."[58]

Long afterward, Shurly would discuss the actions of the 26th at Thoroughfare Gap with Longstreet himself at a reunion of Northern and Southern Civil War veterans at the Palmer House in Chicago. Longstreet told him, "Your division gave me some trouble at Thoroughfare Gap, so that we had to give up forcing our way on the road through the Gap, and go over the mountains, by which I lost some valuable hours."[59] Shurly replied that it was his understanding that Ricketts' orders were to hold the Gap only until dark and then pull back toward Manassas, which of course he did.

SECOND BULL RUN

RICKETTS' DIVISION FELL BACK TO GAINSVILLE, then to Bristow Station, "supperless as usual."[60] As they approached Bristow Station, "after twelve days and nights of almost constant marching and fighting, a portion of the time without rations, many of us barefoot, without tents, overcoats or blankets; dropping rather than lying down to sleep whenever we were halted, waking again upon the command to fall in, wet, stiff, and chilled through with the cold heavy dews that prevail in this region; and moving on again like so many automatons, without life or spirit except such as might be produced by some momentary excitement, and which subsided with the cause; officers and men alike, ragged, dirty, and worn almost to skeletons from hunger and fatigue,"[61] Shurly knew, from the cannon fire and musketry he could hear in the distance, that his men were in for a ferocious fight.

The Second Battle of Bull Run began the afternoon of August 28 when Gibbon's "Iron Brigade" came under fire from Confederate cannon as they marched east on the Warrenton Turnpike toward Groveton, a small settlement near the site of the first Manassas battle. The next morning, Pope ordered a massive attack on a badly outnumbered but safely dug in Confederate Army commanded by—whom other than—Stonewall Jackson. The result was predictable: Union losses for the afternoon exceeded six thousand men. What was not predictable, however, was Pope's inexplicable conclusion the following morning that Jackson was retreating. So, against all advice to the contrary, Pope ordered his army to advance toward woods he was sure were held only by a limited Confederate rearguard. Ricketts' division moved up along Sudley Road, between the Stone House and Sudley Church, and attacked the left flank of the Confederate Army. McClenthen describes the action as Edmund Shurly and the men of the 26th experienced it:

> After dispatching a hasty breakfast we were marched around the left of our line, across a portion of what had been the battlefield of the day before, to the position assigned us near the center, with the Pennsylvania Reserves on our right, and Porter's corps, or a portion of it, on our left.
>
> Duryea's brigade was in front, advancing as skirmishers towards the long range of woods which lay extended before us, and which were supposed to be in the occupation of the Rebels. We lay here until one or two o'clock in the [afternoon], during which time, our skirmishers having failed to draw more than an occasional volley from the enemy, the troops on our right were advanced into the woods. We also received the much needed rations at this time, and I recollect seeing Generals Hooker, Heintzelman, Siegel and McDowell conversing together just behind us, which to me was a sufficient contradiction of the absurd report we had

heard the night before of a difficulty having occurred between Generals
Siegel and McDowell during the battle on the day previous.[62]

As the Union Army pressed against Jackson, Pope's second in command,
McDowell, for a reason that has never been explained, moved reserves away from
his left toward the center of the line, leaving his left flank open to attack from
Longstreet whom Pope believed had left the field. McDowell's supreme blunder
quickly became obvious and Longstreet's army promptly advanced against Pope's
weakened left flank. To counter Longstreet's move, McDowell, dividing Ricketts'
division, desperately rushed Brigadier General Zealous B. Tower's brigade, which
the 26th NYV had now rejoined, to Bald Hill. There General Tower and his outnumbered men fought furiously against repeated attacks by Longstreet's overwhelming force before backing off to Henry House Hill, eventually crossing over
The Stone Bridge, "the road ... filled with trains of wagons, ambulances and artillery, going steadily but without hurry or confusion toward Centreville."[63]

McClenthen described the furious action Edmund Shurly and the men of the
26th went through:

> About two o'clock we ... started up the road leading by the left of
> the woods to Gainsville ... [then] halted opposite the woods where we
> remained standing some half or three [quarters] of an hour. Then we
> were recalled at double quick and reached the left of our line just in
> time to find [the left] and the center [of our line] giving way under the
> terribly impetuous and well-sustained attack of an overwhelming force
> which the enemy had, with marvelous skill and rapidity, succeeded
> in massing at this point. Regiments, brigades and divisions had here
> broken and fallen back, and as we moved up the ascent [to Bald Hill]
> which partially hid the rage of battle from us, the shot and shell which
> went flying over or on either side of us and the crowds of wounded men
> hurrying to the rear told us [all] too plainly what we might expect when
> we arrived at the summit.
>
> We were marched onto the field [of battle] by a left flank at double
> quick (the other regiments of the brigade arriving and taking their posi-
> tion first). As the left, now the head of the column, filed off to the left

for the purpose of forming a line, the caissons of the 5th Maine Battery and part of a regiment of retreating infantry came plunging through our columns creating considerable confusion. But we formed as well as we could and commenced firing. We were now under as heavy and as galling [a] fire as ever has been poured upon any body of troops during this war: shot, shell, grape, and canister with a heavy enfilading fire of musketry. It seemed as if every arm and all the projectiles known in modern warfare had been let loose upon us at once.

No troops in the world could stand it and we commenced falling back, slowly at first—the officers trying to rally and re-form their men—but as the confusion increased we [got] orders to leave the field and retire to the woods [on Henry House Hill] in our rear. Once during this time there was an order, from what source I know not, to cease firing—that we were firing upon our own men. Some of the men obeyed it; others did not. As for myself I paused for a few moments—undecided how to act—[until] I could distinctly see the colors of the enemy advancing upon us, and I again commenced firing. Upon looking around soon after, I found that the colors of my own regiment were gone, and I saw no one of the regiment near me. I can assure you I did not stay long to hunt them up, but made the best of my way towards the rear. I had not gone far, however, before I found [our] colors which were [being] borne from the field by Corporal Paul McCusky of Company F, the color sergeant having been badly wounded. Upon these [colors] Captain Carrol, of Company K, had rallied a portion of the regiment and was now awaiting the Rebels who were fast advancing.

We had not long to wait. When they approached, we fired two or three volleys and again retired. Instead of following the colors, I came across a portion of the 9th N. Y. M., of Hartsuff's brigade, where they had formed a line in the edge of a piece of woods unseen by the advancing Rebels, and delivered one of the most deadly volleys almost in their faces. This seemed to stagger them for a moment, but they soon recovered, advancing and returning the fire with interest. As the 9th fell back, I again found our own colors and remained with them afterwards.

... Almost directly in the rear of us at this point, [we joined] a major of the 21st N. Y. V. [who] had collected quite a body of men composed of various regiments, forming on our colors. When the major ... was wounded in three places, [he] proceeded to the rear [for medical help] leaving his command with Lieutenant Colonel Richardson. It was now as near as I can judge between 6:00 and 7:00 p.m.[64]

At day's end Ricketts' men had escaped the worst of the casualties. Still, the 26th lost 169 killed and wounded out of an original strength of around four hundred men.[65] General Tower was badly wounded and Captains Cassleman, Company A, and Davis, Company H, and Lieutenant Leonard, Company D, were killed. Shurly was devastated to find that Gilbert Jennings' brother, Captain Charles Jennings, serving under him in Company G, was mortally wounded.[66] William K. Bacon, Adjutant, and Lieutenant Enoch Jones, Company A, were wounded while leading their men on Chinn Ridge. Later, as the men of the 26th encamped in the rain and drizzle that began as the fighting ended, many would remember that evening as the worst, most miserable night of the war.

Colonel Christian was felled temporarily by sunstroke during the melee, but, more seriously, his morale and loss of respect for army leadership was drifting into clinical depression, and his men were beginning to notice. Perhaps he had heard of the out-generaled Pope's disingenuous report he telegraphed to Washington: "The enemy is badly whipped, and we shall do well enough."[67] Christian could see only that the fine regiment of New York boys he had assembled and trained for the Union cause would inevitably be shredded by Rebel bullets. His New York boys might fight bravely and heroically, but they would never overcome the incompetence, blunders, and deceit of his army superiors.

CHANTILLY

THE NEXT DAY, Lee, realizing that although he had inflicted a humiliating defeat on the Union he had not destroyed its army, feigned a strike on Washington. Seeing this, Pope followed and, on September 1, near Chantilly, a fine old mansion built by an uncle of Robert E. Lee, attacked the Confederates.[68] McClenthen describes the action of the 26th NYV that day:

> We marched in the direction of Fairfax [for] some two or three miles. [Then], turning to the left from the main road, we passed, [at] some distance, through a piece of woods. Along the edge of these [woods] we formed a line of battle. [Before us was a hollow] with a small creek running through [it] which was crossed on the road by a stone bridge similar to the old [stone bridge] at Bull Run.
>
> [Here] General Ricketts and staff rode along the line, addressing us with a few spirited words of encouragement. Skirmishers were thrown across the creek ascending the hill beyond, and we awaited the expected attack of the enemy. Certainly, no position could have been better chosen to repel an attack, and the men, somewhat recovered from their fatigue and with unlimited confidence in the veteran, General Hooker—to whose corps we were now assigned—longed for an opportunity to avenge their defeat of the Saturday before.
>
> It was not long before the sharp and continued rattle of musketry and the heavy roar of artillery convinced us that a battle was in progress but a short distance to the left and a little in advance of us.[69]

That day the Federals fought Stonewall Jackson to a standstill in torrential rain, with the battle ending only after losing about a thousand men and two of their best fighting generals—colorful, one-armed Phil Kearny[70] and Issac Stevens—and when the gunpowder on both sides had become too wet to fire.

Pope and the Federal Army would repair to Washington where seething hatred and bitter jealousy awaited them. And Lee, with exalted confidence gained from repeated victories over every Union general who opposed him, began to plan for replenishment of his supplies and final victory. He would invade the North and march to Harrisburg.

Chapter Six

ANTIETAM

"Shoot if you must this old gray head,
But spare your country's flag," she said.
A shade of sadness, a blush of shame,
Over the face of the leader came;
The nobler nature within him stirred
To life at that woman's deed and word;
"Who touches a hair of yon gray head
dies like a dog! March on!" he said.

—John Greenleaf Whittier, *Barbara Frietchie*

SHURLY KNEW BIG CHANGES HAD TO BE MADE SOON. His men hated McDowell for what he had done to his army, and often when the general passed his troops Shurly would hear "Scoundrel" and "Traitor" shouted out at him. What was worse, Shurly could see Colonel Christian becoming increasingly morose and uncommunicative. Although the recent battle casualties had been fairly evenly divided between North and South, everyone knew Lee had hoodwinked their generals at almost every turn. And now their only really popular general, General Philip Kearny, had been killed in a blundering exchange of gunfire.[71]

ON THE MORNING OF SEPTEMBER 2, 1862, while Shurly was mulling these thoughts, and the army around him was assembling for its march to Washington, President Lincoln and General-in-Chief Henry W. Halleck, visited the home of George McClellan in Washington, interrupting his breakfast. They came, hats in hand, to ask him to return to command of the disheartened troops falling back on Washington. Both Lincoln and Halleck knew that they were appointing a man far too young for the job and far less aggressive than a general with superior forces should be, but their situation was desperate. McClellan had somehow inspired in the army a trust and confidence, and literally a bond that no other Union general could muster. In short, McClellan had charisma that some historians believe has never been equaled by an American army general before or since. How he could inspire this charisma mystified the leadership in Washington and, most of all, McClellan himself. Few suspected that the annoying egotism he displayed masked a distant voice that whispered to him whenever momentous decisions were to be made, asking if he really appreciated the strength of his opposition; was his army really ready for the fight; was he himself really up to the task ahead? He never seemed able to understand what in the world made everyone around him so sure he was the person to lead the vast Union armies to victory.

THAT AFTERNOON, as a long, sullen, straggling column of soldiers moved toward Washington, there in the distance ahead of them a small group of horsemen approached. A smart young general wearing a flashy yellow sash around his waist and riding a handsome, black stallion led them. Colonel Christian, Shurly, and the men of the 26th heard a distant roar of voices coming from the leading ranks of the forlorn army, and the cheering grew louder as the horsemen neared. Finally, the electrifying news of Pope's dismissal and McClellan's reappointment reached them too, and they were transformed by the exhilaration. In an instant they were a new army, ready to whip anything Johnny Reb could throw at them. The exhilaration the 26th New York felt now approached euphoria as General McClellan rode by. If Captain Edmund Shurly had had any inkling whatsoever of this army leader's self-doubts, he would have tempered his enthusiasm with a modicum of dread. Colonel Christian was not at all impressed.

Pope returned quietly to the Northwest Territories to fight Indians, and McDowell retreated to a desk job in Washington without the slightest objection.

The Army of Virginia was dissolved and its troops reassigned to the Army of the Potomac under McClellan. On September 12, Ricketts' division, along with his 26th Infantry Regiment, was transferred to "Fighting Joe" Hooker's 1st Army Corps, and it quickly readied for a march north to search for Lee, rumored to be moving into Maryland. With Zealous Tower now seriously wounded, Colonel Christian, disturbed as he was, assumed command of the 2nd Brigade, consisting of his beloved 26th New York, the 94th New York, and the 88th and 90th Pennsylvania Regiments.[72] Colonel Richard H. Richardson now commanded the 26th. The regiment returned to its camp at Hall's Hill where, as McClenthen writes, "We remained [for] several days and, more fortunate than the other regiments of the brigade, we received new shelter tents, clothing, blankets, etc., which had become absolutely necessary to our cleanliness and comfort."[73]

By now the news of Lee's march into Maryland was confirmed, and the Army of the Potomac would have to hurry to follow him. Elated by his devastating victory over the hapless Federals at Manassas, Lee resolved to strike north to Frederick, Maryland, west through South Mountain, then north again to Hagerstown, Carlisle, and Harrisburg, where he would find vital supplies for his soldiers. This would effect a final humiliation of the North that, he hoped, would bring France and England into the war.

The march north for the seventy-thousand-man Army of the Potomac began on the night of September 6 and was slow and cautious, as was McClellan's custom, even after his troops intercepted a Confederate dispatch revealing Lee's army was spread out between Harper's Ferry, Virginia (now West Virginia), and Hagerstown, Maryland. Their march would take them to Frederick, Maryland, to Turner's Gap through South Mountain, and beyond to the small village of Boonsboro, halfway between Hagerstown and Harper's Ferry, where McClellan would divide Lee's army and destroy it.

McClenthen describes the march of the 26th New York Volunteers Regiment to find Lee:

> Leaving our camp at Hall's Hill, [we] crossed the Potomac by the Aqueduct [Bridge] at Georgetown. Passing through Georgetown and Washington in the night, we left the last named city by the 7th Street turnpike. As we emerged into the open country beyond, on Sunday, the

highly cultivated fields, splendid dwellings and outhouses, open doors, and happy, cheerful faces within, together with the hearty welcome everywhere extended to us, afforded a pleasant and striking contrast to the waste and desolate fields, broken fences, and deserted dwellings we had been accustomed to in Virginia. For the first two or three days we made short marches and long halts, passing and being passed in turn by other corps of the army, until Thursday morning, September 11th, which found us in camp near Mechanicsville. [We pushed] rapidly forward, [passing] through Brookeville, striking the "Old National Road" at Cookesville, and on through Lisbon, "Poplar Springs" and Newmarket to Frederick, crossing the Monocacy, and encamping within a mile or so of the town on the night of Saturday the 13th.

On Sunday morning, the 14th, with drums beating and colors flying, we marched into the town of Frederick, from which the Rebels had been driven only the day before. Union flags were displayed from nearly all the houses and manifestations of pleasure at our presence greeted us in every direction. Occasionally, some vinegar-faced old man or closely veiled lady draped in mourning reminded us of the Secesh we had left behind, but these were hardly discernible amid the crowds of neatly dressed children waving their tiny banners and shouting their hurrahs for "McClellan." The porches were full of beautiful young maidens and staid matrons, all exhibiting unmistakable evidence of pleasure at their relief from the presence of their would-be benefactors.[74]

In Frederick the men of the 26th could hear the cannon fire ahead as Major General Jesse Lee Reno's men ran into elements of the Confederate forces dug in on the south side of the National Pike leading to Turner's Gap. General Gibbon and his men straddled the National Pike (now Route 40A) as they advanced while Hooker's regiments turned to the right off the pike at Mount Tabor Road, then, following steep Dahlgren Road, would move up the northern slope of the gap through South Mountain to the tiny village of Frosttown. It was there, on some of the most rugged terrain found on any Civil War battlefield, they would find and engage Confederate blocking forces. McClenthen vividly described the action of the 26th New York in this fight:

Upon arriving at the summit of [the Catoctin Mountains], a high range of hills to the east of Middletown, we could distinctly see the smoke of the cannonading on the side of the mountain beyond, and groups of citizens had been collecting with the expectation, no doubt, of seeing a battle in the valley beneath. Descending the hills, and passing through Middletown, some two or three miles beyond, we crossed a small creek, the bridge over which, as well as a house and a barn nearby, … [had been] burned by the retreating Rebels. Leaving the turnpike soon after this, we took a road leading off to the right, and, recrossing the creek, followed it, passing a small church, a mill and a little cluster of houses, to the foot of the mountain.

It was now late in the afternoon. We had heard no infantry firing, and, supposing the cannonading had been for the purpose of shelling the woods or ascertaining the position of the enemy, we thought, as we turned into a field to the left, we were to halt for the night. In this, however, we were disappointed, for hardly had we halted when the command "forward" was again given, and we commenced the ascent of the mountain. Rapid discharge of musketry now informed us that the infantry was already engaged. Halting part way up [the mountain], we formed in a line, and, led by our own gallant General Ricketts in person, we hurried forward into the woods which crowned the top, eager to share in the dangers and honor of the battle.

Obliquing to the left we came upon the first line of battle, occupied by Hatch's Brigade of King's Division, with the 14th Brooklyn directly in front of our regiment. [The 14th was] exhausted and out of ammunition [and] many of their men killed and wounded after having driven the enemy some distance, [and were about] to fall back … before the fresh [Confederate] troops [which] now opposed them. Upon seeing us, [the 14th] gave a cheer to which we responded with a yell that would have done credit to the demons of the infernal regions, and, rushing forward, took position along [a] line of fence at the farther edge of the woods and commenced firing.

We have ascertained by prisoners since taken that five fresh regiments of the enemy's infantry, commanded by Colonel [John Bowie]

Strange of [the 19th] Virginia, who was killed, … had just been led up to check our advance [and] were driven back by this fire, the murderous effects of which the ground before us, covered with dead and wounded, fully attested on the following morning. It was now dark, and the firing soon ceased; but long after we had lain down, and when we could no longer hear the report of their rifles, the bullets continued to whiz past us, cutting the leaves and branches over our heads. In this action Lieutenant Colonel Richardson, commanding our regiment, was struck by a spent ball in the forehead, which knocked him off his horse, leaving an ugly mark where it hit. We passed the night here on the ground where we had fought, amid the dead and dying.[75]

As Shurly's men stubbornly climbed the north slope of Turner's Gap they could not see Gibbon's soldiers taking cannon fire from Confederate batteries arranged along the road at the summit of the Gap, nor watch as one cannon ball took out a dozen men. Shurly's own work lay on the slopes above, and he could not dwell on the fate of those below.

When the evening's battles were over, the Federals, with their superior numbers, had finally pushed the Southerners back beyond Turner's Gap. Gratefully, the 26th ended the day with only two wounded enlisted men (not counting Richardson's dented head), and, what was unusual for Union forces, they commanded the battlefield. On the floor of the valley and on the south slope the army had not been so lucky. It had taken heavy casualties, including the death of popular General Reno, a name Edmund would become all too familiar with in the years to come.

The next morning, as the new day dawned, the men of the 26th finally saw the full extent of what had happened the night before. McClenthen recalled:

[We awoke] in the morning with a shudder at the close proximity of the distorted countenances and mangled forms of the fast stiffening corpses around us, to take a better survey of the battlefield and its surroundings than the darkness of the previous night had afforded us.

Directly in front of us was plowed ground with a cornfield a little to the right, across which the enemy's line must have extended. And here lay the bodies of their dead in almost every possible position, in some places three or four of them together in one pile, as if their ranks had been in confusion and huddled together where they had all fallen at once. Colonel Strange was one of those who fell nearest our lines, and upon his person were two canteens, one of whiskey, and the other of water. Their haversacks were generally well filled with biscuits, cold ham, etc., which they must have procured before they left Frederick; and some of our men, I believe, made a hearty breakfast off their contents, although the thought must seem revolting to any but hungry soldiers.

Our loss in this action was very small from the fact that nearly [the Rebel's] whole fire went over our heads, which must have been owing to the nature of the ground.[76]

South Mountain was a victory of sorts for the Federals, but the Confederate forces were able to delay them for another crucial day, giving Lee time to "dig in" near a little hamlet known as Sharpsburg just beyond the banks of rambling, serene Antietam Creek. Longstreet had been able, because of McClellan's caution, to depart Hagerstown and join Lee, and Stonewall Jackson was now arranged along Lee's left flank in front of a little white Dunker church just beyond a cornfield. By the evening of September 16 Lee had gathered all his troops except Confederate General Ambrose Powell Hill and his Light Division of five thousand men surrounding Harper's Ferry seventeen miles to the south. The next morning they too would be on the road to Sharpsburg, marching hard, marching so hard in fact that almost half of them would fall by the wayside from fatigue. The bloodiest day of the war lay just ahead.

Shurly could know none of this, of course, in the early morning of September 15 as his men arose and assembled for the march that would take them through Turner's Gap, to the village of Boonsboro, then south to the spires and house tops they could just make out in the distance as they passed over the summit. McClenthen described the move:

The command to fall in was soon given, and we moved off to the left, down the mountain and onto the turnpike again, along which we proceeded until within about two miles [of] Boonsboro. [There] we halted in a field with the rest of the division, and remained long enough to cook, and rest ourselves, while other portions of the army were passing. We were again moved forward, passing houses and tents on the way, which the enemy had used as hospitals, with their flags still flying. We soon reached Boonsboro, through which we passed, turning to the left at right angles with the main road, and took [the road] leading to Keedysville and Sharpsburg. Upon arriving at Keedysville, we halted, and, stacking arms by the roadside, remained [there] until 10 or 11 PM.

While we lay here, the road was almost constantly filled with troops passing towards Sharpsburg. During [this] time McClellan with his staff and a large cavalry escort came up. His approach was announced to us long before he appeared in sight by cheer after cheer given by the various regiments as he passed them. As he neared us, and our regiment took up the shout of welcome that preceded him, it seemed to me as if I never saw a man whose open smile and sparkling eyes more clearly denoted the inward satisfaction he must have felt at this heartfelt expression of unbounded confidence in, and admiration for, him entertained by the whole army.

Most of us were fast asleep when the order to fall in was given, but we soon roused ourselves, and marched through [Keedysville], across [Antietam Creek] which runs through it, and, turning to the right, soon recrossed it on the other road, and encamped in a large clover field where we remained until four o'clock the next day, Tuesday, the sixteenth.[77]

As the men rested and cleaned their weapons, their confidence in McClellan and his command and in the victory that they finally would achieve in the coming battle grew. "Little Mac," they were sure, had a grand scheme to bring Lee to battle. McClenthen and many of the men convinced themselves that McClellan's "plans [were] nothing less than the total annihilation of the whole Rebel army, to be immediately followed by the collapse of that magnificent humbug, the so-called Southern Confederacy, ending in our discharge and return to our homes, where, during the long evenings of the coming winter, we [will] astonish the natives by our tales of daring valor and hairbreadth escapes 'by flood and field.' The firm belief entertained by many [was] that [the Rebel] entrance into Maryland had been connived at for the purpose of entrapping them. The large force here under our favorite generals, and the absence of two or three corps under good leaders whom we hoped were in position to intercept their retreat, all combined to render us thus sanguine in our expectations."[78] All of this was idle speculation, of course, but, if nothing else, it helped to disperse the heavy anxiety they all felt.

For Shurly there were no idle thoughts of strategies or tactics that McClellan might or might not be concocting. His worry was building for a very real reason. He could see that his brigade commander, Colonel Christian, who knew far more about the situation than he, was as distressed as he had ever seen him, and this could not be good news for the regiment. The Union Army of seventy thousand soldiers gave them overwhelming superiority over their foe, but this meant very little. Shurly and Colonel Christian both knew in their guts that leadership, not numbers, had determined the outcome of all the past Union debacles.

Instead of immediately attacking the Confederates while they were still regrouping and achieving almost certain destruction of the Rebel Army, McClellan delayed. September 16 for Shurly consisted of positioning Company C with the rest of the 26th New York, along the left flank of the entrenched Confederates— Stonewall Jackson's men.

> About four o'clock, the order to fall in was obeyed with alacrity and, passing a mill and [again] crossing the Antietam, we moved with the rest of Hooker's corps towards the scene of the next day's conflict. After crossing the creek, we left the road and marched through the fields in a northwesterly direction, the Pennsylvania Reserves, King's division, and our own (Ricketts') proceeding by a flank and in nearly parallel lines for something over a mile, when we were halted (the Reserves and King's division passing on to the right). [Then], forming column by division, we advanced directly towards the front. About this time fire was opened by one of the enemy's batteries, some of the shot falling uncomfortably near us, but no one [was] hurt. It was now dark and after marching across plowed lots, through corn fields, over rail fences, stone walls, fallen trees, piles of wood, and ledges of rock, stumbling over all sorts of obstacles, and each other, we at last found ourselves in line along

the edge of a piece of woods, where, after posting a picket in advance, we remained until morning. Two or three times during the night we were awakened by musketry firing in the direction of the Pennsylvania Reserves, but upon ascertaining everything quiet along our line of pickets, we again lay down and slept soundly.[79]

Obliquely to Shurly's left front was a forty-acre cornfield that stretched between two copses of woods, later termed the East Woods on Shurly's left and the West Woods to his immediate front. Early in the morning of September 17, the twelve thousand five hundred men and forty guns of Hooker's 1st Army Corps assembled in double battle lines.[80] Hooker would order his corps to strike due south down the Hagerstown Pike and through that cornfield. McClenthen wrote:

> The heavier report of field pieces convinced us that the ball was about to open in earnest, and, as we were engaged for the first set, we hastily fell in and moved towards the right, in the direction of the firing. After marching some distance by a flank, we halted, and formed column by division, and with Duryea's brigade on the right, and Hartsuff's in line in front, we again moved forward. We were now under fire from the enemy's infantry and artillery, many falling (General Hartsuff among this number) from the discharges of infantry, while that of the [Rebel] artillery went mostly over us so uncomfortably close that some of the tallest did not have room to hold up their heads. Hartsuff's brigade soon halted at the edge of the woods through which we were advancing, and poured in their deadly discharges upon the Rebel lines in front of them as we deployed into line and took our position to the left. Before us was a plowed field, with a burning house and barn, and an orchard beyond, before which the Rebels were just forming a line as we moved up. Between them and ourselves was a slight rise of ground that prevented our seeing lower that the middle of their bodies, except to the right where their line ran in front of an enclosure we afterwards learned to be a graveyard, before which the ground was more level and their whole persons distinctly seen.

Immediately upon our arrival at the point indicated, we commenced firing and continued without intermission or change of position until we had exhausted the last round of ammunition, the Rebels returning our fire with promptness and spirit. We remained on the ground some few minutes after our ammunition was exhausted and they had commenced falling back on each side of us; but soon [we] had orders to retire, which was done without any more haste or confusion than would have attended the same movement upon battalion drill. As we retired, the Rebels advanced with a shout, but they paid dearly for their temerity as they were soon driven back with great loss by the fresh troops advancing to relieve us. After getting out of range of the enemy's guns, we received a fresh supply of ammunition and again started for the front when, upon our arrival, we found that ... the battle of Antietam, so far as Hooker's Corps on the right was concerned, was virtually ended.[81]

The cornfield had changed hands fifteen times that morning with dreadful loss of life. By 10:00 a.m. the fighting in the cornfield had claimed eight thousand killed or wounded, and Hooker's 1st Corps was shattered. Typical of many units that morning was the 12th Massachusetts, losing 224 men out of 338. General Ricketts had his horse shot out from under him and Hooker himself, wounded in the foot, was carried from the field. General Hartsuff, of the 2nd Brigade, was severely wounded while leading his troops, whose losses exceeded any of the other brigades of the division. McClenthen continues:

About this time, General McClellan and staff visited this portion of the field, and cheer after cheer rent the air as he made his appearance. He had just taken his departure when in reply to the enemy's batteries, who were now throwing shells at this [position], our batteries on [a nearby] knoll opened fire, first one, then another, and another, until it swelled to the most deafening cannonading to which I have yet listened. The reports from the pieces and the explosion of shells were so rapid and incessant that, with the exception of the difference in sound, it seemed like file firing by infantry. At first we could distinguish between the shots of the different batteries, but it soon became one long, continued and tremendous roar, causing the ground itself to quake and tremble as if with an earthquake. It was really terrific, and strong men, without once thinking of danger, bent their heads as if in awe.[82]

Around ten o'clock McClellan ordered the 1st Corps to withdraw. McClellan now struck at the center of the Rebel line, to Shurly's left, toward a sunken road, perfect cover for the defending Confederates. Again there was more slaughter before McClellan would order an attack across an Antietam Creek bridge against the Rebel right flank by General Ambrose E. Burnside, a general secure in the knowledge he was incapable of fulfilling his responsibilities. After repeated failed attempts, Burnside finally was able to get his men over the creek and they were approaching the outskirts of Sharpsburg only to be repulsed at the last minute when A. P. Hill arrived from the south to save the day for Lee. All of this Shurly could hear but not witness as he tended to the dead and wounded of his unit.

Shurly had survived the slaughter, and for him only the field glass presented to him by his friends in Buffalo was missing. By the end of the day eighteen generals from both sides were casualties. Luckier than many regiments, the 26th New York lost "only" sixty-six killed, wounded, or missing. "In many places the dead were so thick they had more the appearance of troops that had halted and lain down to rest than [of] dead left on the battlefield."[83] The holocaust, however, was more than Colonel Christian could accept. Christian's mind cracked that afternoon, and he resigned his commission and fled the battlefield. He returned home to Utica, New York, where he was received as a hero, but his mind was shattered and his sanity never completely returned. He had been as much a casualty of the cornfield disaster as if he had lost a limb. On May 8, 1887, he died in an insane asylum.[84]

Everyone in the 26th expected fighting to resume early the next day. The Rebels had lost over ten thousand men and now were outnumbered three to one. It was a unique chance to finally surround and destroy their army and put an end to the war. But McClellan dithered and waited and did not attack. Instead, on September 18 the Confederate Army slipped away and recrossed the Potomac to Virginia. A crestfallen McClenthen wrote:

On the morning of the nineteenth, our pickets were advanced as skirmishers to the banks of the [Potomac] River, which resulted in [the capture of] many stragglers, deserters, and others of the Rebel army, and the demonstration of the fact that their army itself had recrossed into Virginia. Why or how they were suffered to accomplish this without molestation on our part, it is not my province to explain.[85]

On the first of October, President Lincoln visited the troops at the Antietam battlefield, and Shurly and his men turned out to see him. They did not understand that Lincoln was there to vent his rage at McClellan for not having gone after Lee to finish him off. Finally, Lincoln secured McClellan's grudging promise to immediately move against Lee; but after the president returned to Washington, McClellan invented one excuse after another not to move. Lincoln sent blistering telegrams hoping to humiliate McClellan into action, but nothing could budge the "Virginia Creeper." The Army of the Potomac remained in camp at Sharpsburg and did not leave the field until October 30.

The men knew nothing of these exchanges and continued to adore McClellan. From their point of view they could not recognize his incompetence. So when on November 5, 1862, Lincoln relieved McClellan of his duties, they were thunderstruck.

Chapter Seven

FREDERICKSBURG

For once, war unmasked its terrible proportions
with a distinctness hitherto unknown in the
forest-clad landscapes of America,
and the plain of Fredericksburg presented
a panorama that was dreadful in its grandeur.

—Reverend R. L. Dabney (a Presbyterian clergyman whom
Stonewall Jackson had enlisted as his chief-of-staff)[86]

WHAT LITTLE CHANCE THE UNION HAD to defeat the Confederates at
Fredericksburg evaporated on November 5, 1862, when Lincoln, bending to criticism of McClellan by his political enemies in Washington, replaced him with the
even more incompetent Major General Ambrose Everett Burnside. Never a great
general, McClellan at least had been learning from his mistakes. Furthermore,
the army, for some reason, seemed to trust McClellan, and when he was replaced
by Burnside, morale faded precipitously. Burnside, the first to admit (to himself)
that he was unqualified to lead the Army of the Potomac, was widely questioned
as to whether he should even lead an army corps. Energetic, friendly, and modest,
his qualities made him liked by his associates, but they were not the qualities
required for the impending battles. His indecision and poor military judgment at
the bridge over the Antietam should have ended his army career.

In fairness to Burnside, however, it must be said that the strategy he developed upon assuming command from McClellan was sound, except that it depended upon a rigorous adherence to orders and schedules, something usually lacking in Union campaigns.

Burnside's idea was to bend the thrust of his southern troop movement toward the east to shorten supply lines during the oncoming winter. This meant an attack on the lightly defended town of Fredericksburg. The Rappahannock River that flowed beside the town could be forded in shallow water just to its north and crossed by pontoon bridges directly in front of the city. The town could be taken and the heights overlooking the town could be occupied if the Confederates did not bring forward additional forces to defend these heights. Success depended on an expeditious movement of the army and its equipment to the battle site and across the river. On November 14 Lincoln approved Burnside's plan to attack Fredericksburg, noting, however, that the strategy would succeed only if Burnside moved quickly; otherwise it would fail.

ON OCTOBER 27 the 26th New York Volunteers packed up and left the grim Antietam battlefield behind them, crossing South Mountain in beautiful weather near Crampton's Pass to Burkettsville and on to Brunswick where, the next day, they crossed the Potomac on a pontoon bridge. It was while camped near Philomont, Virginia, on November 4 that the men heard that General John Gibbon would replace their admired division commander General Ricketts. The march continued, this time in a severe snow storm, through the towns of Bloomfield, Upperville, Rectortown, and Salem to Warrenton where, on November 9, the troops got the news of McClellan's dismissal. McClenthen observed: "When it became known that [McClellan's] connection with the army was to cease altogether, the excitement for the time seriously menaced the discipline and morale of the army. Officers threatened resignation, men desertion, and all vented their indignation in curses both loud and deep, upon those whom they thought the cause of or in any way connected with his withdrawal. These feelings soon gave way to the despondency of hopelessness or utter indifference."[87]

The next day the Army of the Potomac broke camp at Warrenton and marched south to Bealeton, staying there a week to reorganize. Gilbert Jennings, Shurly's brother-in-law and erstwhile comrade-in-arms, was promoted to command the

26th NYV. Gibbon's 2nd Division was now attached to Major General John F. Reynolds' 1st Army Corps, a unit of Burnside's newly minted "Left Grand Division," commanded by General William B. Franklin. The 26th New York was still attached to the 2nd Brigade, which lost one regiment, dropping its strength to just four regiments. Its new commander was Colonel Peter Lyle.

On the morning of November 17 the army resumed its march south, passing Morrisville, Grove Church, and, the next day, past Hartwood Church to Falmouth where a left turn (on what is now U.S. Route 1) took them to their camp about a mile north of Falmouth, Burnside's staging area for the upcoming attack.

This march, sometimes through rain, snow, and half frozen mud in temperatures that neared zero at times, had been swift and caught Lee by surprise. Jeb Stuart's cavalry was far upstream, trying to determine if the Army of the Potomac had left Warrenton; Longstreet's Corps was in Culpeper; and Stonewall Jackson, recently appointed lieutenant general of a reorganized 2nd Confederate Army Corps, was positioned in the Shenandoah Valley. All that remained for a successful Union attack on Fredericksburg was the prompt arrival of several dozen rough wooden scows the army would need to construct its pontoon bridges over the Rappahannock.

But where were they? No one in the army command seemed to understand the urgency of their need, and many did not even know that the scows were with the weary 50th New York Engineers in Maryland, some fifty miles northwest of Washington. A week went by and still the scows for the bridges did not appear. Instead, scarce supplies for the Union troops were being used up, and more Confederate reinforcements were pouring into Fredericksburg to take up their defensive positions. And, perversely, a conviction that he must win this battle at any cost began to arise in Burnside. He decided he would wait as long as necessary for the vital bridge scows. Meanwhile, his troops, short of rations and supplies, suffered in the cold. The ground on which they camped became a quagmire, the surface freezing at night and thawing by day. The low morale of the veteran troops spread rapidly to the new recruits.

So this is what it had come to for Edmund Shurly in just over a year of fighting. In the few days preceding the battle he would have ample time to ponder how life could transform from the jubilation and confidence of that glorious march from Elmira to Washington at the time of the first Bull Run to this wretched condition at the edge of the Rappahannock River across from Fredericksburg. And he was well aware the worst was yet to come.

Orders finally reached the 50th Engineers to move the boats south but, because of bureaucratic bungling, they did not reach Stafford Heights, overlooking Fredericksburg, until December 10. By this time Lee had heavily reinforced the town with Longstreet's 1st Army Corps on Marye's Heights, directly behind the town, and with Jackson's 2nd Army Corps, straddling the right flank of the Confederate line extending some five miles southeast to Hamilton's Crossings.

The next morning at dawn the men of the 26th awakened to the thunder of 140 Federal cannons emplaced on Stafford Heights and moved to the bluffs overlooking the Rappahannock River. There they saw the 50th New York bridge builders beginning construction of their pontoon bridges. Under cover of an early-morning fog they had been able to extend the bridges about two-thirds the distance across the river before the fog lifted and Confederate sharpshooters opened fire with deadly effect. Their fire was returned by the Union artillery, and the town was soon reduced to rubble. McClenthen reported: "With the exception of these [sharpshooters], and two Shanghai roosters that were strutting up and down the opposite bank of the river, lustily crowing their defiance of the Yankees, not even the smoke of a single chimney gave evidence that the town was inhabited."[88]

The cannon fire did not dislodge the Confederate defenders, however, and the town was not cleared until that afternoon when Hooker ordered four regiments to cross the river in boats some distance upstream from the town. "How the Shanghais, before mentioned," wrote McClenthen, "escaped capture with the sharpshooters, I cannot well conjecture, as neither of them showed the white feather."[89] By four thirty in the afternoon three bridges had been secured across the river at Stafford Heights and an additional three bridges had been constructed farther downstream near the mouth of Hazel Run. These downstream bridges would be the ones that Shurly and the men of the 26th New York would cross to their fateful encounter with Stonewall Jackson.

As evening approached, Edmund Shurly could watch the awful scene before him. The town, which the day before had been a picture of tranquility, now was deformed and burning. Few of its buildings remained standing. Red sparks and jagged lightning occasionally spurted from cannon on Stafford Heights off to his right, soon to be followed by a gigantic crash of flame and smoke in the broken town across the river. Above it all the sky was serene as its colors changed from scarlet to purple and enveloped the black plume of smoke drifting aimlessly upward from Fredericksburg.

The next day was warm and sunny, much of the snow melting and forming deep quagmires wherever troops and equipment moved. Ponderously, eighty thousand men made their way across the six bridges to Fredericksburg and prepared for a frontal assault on the Confederates. For the 26th New York the day began at midnight when Gibbon's 2nd Division crossed a downstream bridge and was positioned near the Arthur Bernard residence. Four hundred yards beyond were Major General George Meade's Pennsylvania Reserves. Safely entrenched on ridges some two hundred yards beyond an embankment built for the unfinished Richmond and Potomac Railroad was Stonewall Jackson's army. Other than an occasional cannon duel and a brief Union cavalry reconnaissance, quickly routed by Jeb Stuart, there was no fighting that day.

Burnside had deluded himself into believing that the Confederates were at reduced strength and widely dispersed, perhaps as far down river as Port Royal, some eighteen miles from Fredericksburg. By crossing rapidly at Fredericksburg, he planned for Union forces to engage the Confederate left flank before the Southern troops in Port Royal could come to their assistance. Then, a gentle nudge from Franklin's men would crumple the Rebel right flank and leave the main body of the Confederate Army defending Marye's Heights open to defeat. But with the same lack of resolution that stained his reputation at Sharpsburg, Ambrose Burnside held off his attack for still another day, allowing Lee to bring in even more reinforcements. That night the assembled Union forces slept on their arms anticipating a terrible conflict. All were certain they would be wounded or killed.

A thick fog enveloped the Union forces the next morning, allowing them a peaceful breakfast and coffee as they assembled at the edge of the river for their assault. In the vicinity of the 26th New York, visibility was so poor they could barely see Meade's division to their immediate left.

By nine o'clock, the sun was burning the heavy fog from the plain below the Confederate lines, and Lee could see what the Union Army was preparing for him. On his right, opposite Stonewall Jackson's 2nd Corps, was Union General William B. Franklin's Left Grand Division, fifty-five thousand men and 116 cannons in all.

Extending toward Fredericksburg were the forty thousand troops of Union General Edwin V. Sumner's Right Grand Division, who were soon to begin their attack on Longstreet who was defending Marye's Heights.

Across the Rappahannock Lee also saw the masses of reserve Union troops and the artillery on Stafford Heights beginning their bombardment. Looking down on this scene, as they met just before the battle to coordinate their plans, Longstreet, welcoming the sight, turned to Jackson and said, "General, do not all those multitudes of Federals frighten you?" "We shall very soon see whether I shall not frighten *them*!"[90] With that, Jackson spurred his horse and returned to his corps. A witness to this conversation later noted that it was the only time Jackson had ever been known to smile before the start of a battle.

The cannon fire intensified, and Captain James Hall, whom Shurly had saved at Front Royal with his makeshift rope ferry across the Shenandoah River, was engaging the enemy with his 2nd Maine battery not far from the 26th New York. One story has it that as he sat on his horse conversing with Lieutenant Colonel Charles W. Tilden, commander of the 16th Maine Regiment, and Colonel Adrian Root, 1st Brigade commander, a Confederate cannon shell flew between them nearly killing all three. Hall, chagrined, dismounted and personally adjusted the aim of a nearby cannon. He then signaled the gun crew to fire the weapon. It landed a direct hit on an enemy gun emplacement, sending up a cloud of fire and earth. Satisfied, he remounted and resumed his conversation.

Burnside, still believing the Confederate 2nd Army Corps was at Port Royal, now ordered Franklin to attack Stonewall Jackson's entire corps with but two divisions: Meade's 4,500 Pennsylvanians and Gibbon's 2nd Division on Meade's right flank. The rest of the Left Grand Division would stand by idly.

Meade advanced in three-brigade strength and Gibbon advanced with his 2nd and 3rd Brigades; Root's 1st Brigade brought up the rear as reserve. Heavy fire erupted from the Rebel lines and the Federals were soon pinned down in an open field of thawing mud and water some four inches deep beyond the Richmond road paralleling the unfinished railroad. For the next several hours the men were in this freezing mud, taking fearful casualties, awaiting a slackening in the fire, rolling onto their backs to load their rifles, then rolling over onto their stomachs to fire at the enemy. If there were any lulls in this fierce exchange, Captain Shurly, flat on the ground with his men, would have heard the sound of cannon and rifle fire from Sumner's Right Grand Division as it vainly attacked Marye's Heights just beyond the center of town with catastrophic losses. The battle for Fredericksburg was now fully joined.

The battle on the Union left flank intensified, and Rebel cannons dueled with Federal cannons until finally the Federals exploded a Rebel caisson. Rebel fire slackened and at about one in the afternoon, the men regained their feet and charged the Rebel lines. Brigadier General Nelson Taylor's 3rd Brigade opened fire at fifty yards and Lyle's 2nd Brigade advanced to the left of the 3rd and opened fire. By this time Meade's division had made splendid progress across the road, past the railroad embankment, and into the woods beyond in hand-to-hand combat, taking prisoners belonging to North Carolina and Tennessee brigades of A. P. Hill's division. The Rebel first line of defense was broken and they were retreating when Meade's division began to run short of ammunition, and, seeing no sign of reinforcement, wavered, then fell back, leaving Gibbon's troops exposed and with several of his regiments out of ammunition.

The Rebels, now fully reinforced, pushed forward with rifle and bayonet and advanced to well beyond the railroad embankment to exposed positions that subjected them to strong return fire from the Union cannon.

Root's 1st Brigade then rushed forward, passing over the 26th and the 90th Pennsylvania to cover their withdrawal, taking over two hundred Rebel prisoners in the process. The 26th and 90th were ordered to pull back to a small ravine to collect ammunition from the dead and wounded, but then, before they could reload, they were ordered to fix bayonets without a round of ammunition in their rifles and charge. By the time they came up even with the lead regiments, all the Federal troops were falling back.

Seeing the need for more troops to exploit Meade's opening, Colonel Root raced back to Gibbon to plead for more help but got nowhere. Battle instructions from Burnside were so vague Franklin was unwilling to commit more men to the fight. Meade had made good progress through a swampy, densely wooded section of forest that Jackson had neglected to fortify and had developed a large salient between two Confederate brigades. Had he been effectively assisted, military analysts believe Meade might have broken through.

Franklin did call Birney's division from the 3rd Corps forward from across the river to cover the withdrawal of Meade and Gibbon, and in so doing Birney's men were able to inflict considerable losses on the counterattacking Rebels.

Forty-five minutes later the fighting for this section of the battlefield was over. The 26th had sustained over 50 percent casualties in this four-hour debacle, including Captain Shurly, brought down by a bullet through his upper thigh. Nearby lay Gilbert Jennings, lightly wounded, and regiment favorite Adjutant William K. Bacon, dead. In all, the 26th New York had lost 170 men out of a strength at the start of the fight of around three hundred.

It was not long before Captain Shurly was recrossing the Rappahannock on a horse-drawn ambulance, assisted by two privates who undoubtedly were very relieved to be able to help anyone out of the battle zone. Orders had been given that no one was to leave ranks to aid the wounded but, nevertheless, many of the injured officers were assisted across the river.

Burnside ordered Franklin to attack again, but he refused the order. Franklin had so little confidence in his superior that he could see no point in continuing. Meade and Gibbon together had lost four thousand officers and men in their fight against Stonewall Jackson, and the battle lines had not moved. Sadly, the Union commanders on the Marye's Heights front obeyed Burnside's orders for more assaults on the Confederate lines, and the result was more appalling slaughter.

For Edmund Shurly Civil War combat had now ended and, as he lay recovering from his painful wound, he would reflect upon his good luck. He was still alive and had not lost a limb, as did many of the other seriously wounded in that war. Most fortunately of all, he was now out from under the bumbling commanders of the Union forces: McClellan, Pope, and Burnside.

What he could not have realized this soon after the battle, though, was his extraordinary luck in again having evaded capture or death. At Fredericksburg the Federals were handed a humiliating and devastating defeat, losing over 12,000 men, including 877 officers, against a Confederate loss of 3,415 men. The Rappahannock River, however, prevented Lee from following up his victory with a strike that could have encircled and destroyed the Union Army. After the war, military analysts concluded that had Jefferson Davis granted the request of Lee and Jackson to withdraw from Fredericksburg before the battle and make their stand twenty-five miles farther south at the North Anna River, they could have annihilated General Burnside's army by blocking the Union line of retreat with blows against the flanks of the Union troops.[91] Fortunately for Edmund Shurly, neither Davis nor Lincoln recognized until later in the war that their prime objectives were to destroy their opposing armies rather than to take and hold territory.

The bullet that wounded Edmund Shurly just barely grazed the main artery in his leg. Here, Shurly's descendants have something profound to ponder as they continue on through the pages of this story. If the trajectory of the bullet that incapacitated Shurly had changed by as little as a fraction of an inch—whether because of wind direction, a nearby explosion, an unexpected jostling by a comrade, a better sighted Confederate rifle, or, most likely, the hand of God—our story would have ended as it did for thousands of poor souls that fateful day in December, and been recorded, if at all, by others. Today, of course, there would be no descendants to contemplate this turn of events or write this story.

Soon after the battle ended, Shurly was transported to a hospital in Washington, D.C., curiously named the Patent Office Hospital. He remained there for two months and then furloughed to his home in Buffalo to further recuperate. Recovery was slow, however, and doctors recommended either a lengthy stay at home or a discharge from the army. Edmund Shurly opted for the discharge.

THE 26TH NEW YORK continued on after Fredericksburg and followed Jackson to Chancellorsville to participate in arguably the most humiliating defeat ever inflicted on the United States Army—again by Stonewall Jackson who would die of wounds inflicted by his own men who had, in the dusk that followed the battle, confused him for the enemy. Ironically, Captain Shurly was honorably discharged from the army on April 25, 1863, just fifteen days before Stonewall Jackson passed away.

On April 28 the 26th New York was disbanded, having served the Union forces for the agreed upon two years. The officers and men whose enlistments were not yet completed were absorbed into the 97th New York Regiment. Shurly and the men of the 26th could be proud of their efforts. The regiment had seen hard duty in nearly every important battle since the first Bull Run and had served the cause proudly, losing 407 men killed or wounded. The 26th New York had courageously withstood for two years the best the Confederacy could throw at them.

Some years later, a priest dedicating a monument to Stonewall Jackson in New Orleans may have correctly noted the true turning point of the war when he said:

> "When in Thine inscrutable decree it was ordained that the Confederacy should fail, it became necessary for Thee to remove Thy servant Stonewall Jackson."[92]

Chapter Eight

CAMP DOUGLAS

"even rats were hard to obtain"

—From an article in a Chicago newspaper
reporting the "yarns" told at a reunion
of John Morgan's men at Lexington[93]

By midsummer 1863 Edmund Shurly had nearly recovered from his wounds and was yearning to return to duty. One day, as Edmund steadily improved, his daughter Edna complained of a sore throat and a cough. A hand to her forehead indicated high fever. Soon a gray membrane began to form in, around, and over Edna's sore throat and the worst possible diagnosis was certain. She was suffering from diphtheria, one of the most dreaded of childhood diseases. Doctors had no clue in those days what caused diphtheria or how to treat it. They had not yet learned of the microbes that formed the toxin that killed its victims or, of course, the antitoxin that would soon enough eradicate diphtheria from most of the developed world.

In five days the powerful diphtheria poison spread throughout Edna's tiny body, causing severe heart damage and paralysis of the breathing muscles. Her neck swelled to twice its normal size and her throat closed. She could no longer breathe. For all practical purposes, she was dead of asphyxiation. It was an immense tragedy for the family, especially for Augusta, who had relied on Edna for love and comfort while Edmund was away. She had always assumed it would be Edmund who would depart.

Captain Edmund Shurly in 1863. Picture courtesy of the Reuther Library, Detroit.

Augusta Shurly in about 1863. Author's file.

Edna Shurly with her favorite doll shortly before she succumbed to diphtheria
in 1863. This print was copied from a small photo album her father carried with him
while out west on the Bozeman Trail. Author's file.

Arthur Shurly, less than one year old. Author's file.

Arthur Shurly in 1866. With the departure of Edmund for combat on the
Bozeman Trail and the passing of daughter Edna, Arthur was now Augusta's little
"man of the house." Author's file.

So Edmund sought a position with the military that would allow him to keep the family together. In July he submitted an application to join the Veteran Reserve Corps (earlier known as the "the Invalid Corps") and included several personal recommendations with his application, including a strongly worded letter of recommendation from Gilbert Jennings. Having recovered from his wounds at Fredericksburg, Jennings was now a major in the Veteran Reserve Corps.

August 15, 1863
To: Major A. S. Diven, A. A. P. W. Genl.,
Headquarters, Fort Porter:
Sir

I would most respectfully commend to you, the application of Capt. E. R. P. Shurly, late of the 26th N. Y. Vols., as one every way worthy, your warmest recommendation. I know him well, and it is such men as him, we need, in the Invalid Corps.

He served in my regiment, nearly two years, and always bore the highest reputation as an officer, and a gentleman, as the papers he forwards will show. And if you would ask for his appointment, and also request to have him ordered to report for duty to you, when appointed, it would be greatly to the advantage of the corps—and I would esteem it a very great favor, personally, and I am sure when you come to know Capt. Shurly, you will feel pleased in doing so much for him.

I do not mean to ask you to do such a thing again, nor would I now, but that I know Captain Shurly so well. He was severely wounded at the Battle of Fredericksburg, in December last, and has been unable to do duty since, and is now recovering. He forwarded his application, some time since, and has heard nothing from it—and at my urgent request, he has obtained several letters from influential men, who know him well, and cheerfully recommend him, because he is every way worthy of it.

You will pardon my troubling you, but my own knowledge of the man, and his deservings, and the necessity of such men in our corps, forced upon me every day, by my experience, is my apology.

Very Respectfully,

Your Obedient Servant

G. S. Jennings

Major, Invalid Corps[94]

These recommendations had their desired effect. On August 28 Shurly was appointed adjutant general with the rank of captain in the 8th Veteran Reserve Corps and assigned to the staff of Colonel Benjamin J. Sweet at Camp Douglas, a prisoner-of-war camp in Chicago. Augusta moved with him from Buffalo to Chicago and now the couple was happily together again. Within a year a baby son, Arthur Eugene, would join the family.

CAMP DOUGLAS WAS NAMED after Senator Stephen Arnold Douglas, who had debated Lincoln before the recent presidential election, and who had died on June 3, 1861, in Chicago at the early age of forty-eight. The camp was located four miles south of downtown Chicago[95] on open, flat land surrounded by pleasant family residences. On one side was the University of Chicago campus.[96] The camp fronted on Cottage Grove and ran west four blocks to Kankakee Avenue (now named Martin Luther King Drive). On the north it was bounded by East 31st Street (Ridgely Place) and on the south by East 33rd Street (now College Place). In total it encompassed eighty acres of land. Two hundred yards to the east was a section of the Illinois Central Railroad, convenient for transporting prisoners to the camp. Beyond the railroad was Lake Michigan. As many as eleven thousand Confederate prisoners of war were held at the camp at any one time.

Camp Douglas was a grim facility consisting of wooden buildings located on low ground surrounded by a six-foot-high wooden board fence with platforms for the guards. The grounds inside the stockade often flooded, turning the area into an expansive quagmire. The camp was reported to reek with a terrible stench and the prisoners were belligerent, "suffering [as they were] from Chicago's arctic cold, the open latrines, sickness, [and] death."[97] It was not uncommon for as many as two hundred prisoners to die in a month.

Conditions inside the buildings were even more wretched, the result of a purposeful policy of the government in Washington, and of General Montgomery C. Meigs, quartermaster general, in particular, to reduce rations and supplies for the prisoners in retribution for the inhumane treatment of Union prisoners held by the Confederates. In March 1864 Secretary of War Stanton personally approved the reduction of rations despite pleas for more supplies from the Camp Douglas staff. The Washington government, however, did not relent until late in the war.

IN 1863 CONFEDERATE GENERAL JOHN HUNT MORGAN'S RAIDERS invaded the North and ravaged large areas of Ohio, Indiana, and Kentucky before being captured and imprisoned at Camp Douglas.[98] This was a particularly rambunctious bunch, and many escaped at various times. One grim yet humorous incident they caused was recalled in a newspaper article appearing in a Chicago newspaper after the war.

> As the autumnal winds of 1864 began to put on the wintry temperature of that latitude and sweep into Camp Douglas prison from out on the lake, and the hope of escape or exchange began to die away, a feeling of despondency hitherto unknown seemed to pervade the entire prison....
>
> The rations had been exceedingly short during the summer, and many of the prisoners had become desperate on the subject. Fried rats had been regarded as a dainty dish for several months, but after the barracks were raised five feet above the ground, to prevent tunneling, the rats had no place to hide and sought refuge in the sewer, out of reach of the hungry prisoners. Occasionally they crept cautiously out of the sewer in search of "strange adventure," and they seldom failed to find it, for not one ever succeeded in getting back to its underground home. They were closely watched, and after one left the sewer it was an easy matter to cut off its retreat, and then it was only a question as to which mess would feast upon it. The writer retains a vivid recollection of a breakfast of fried rats which he relished very much, but the meat tasted

so much like squirrel that he never had been able to eat squirrel since on account of the memories that mastication of the last-named animal revived.

One raw, windy afternoon, when even rats were hard to obtain, an incident occurred which created considerable stir, not only among the prisoners but among the members of the Illinois legislature. This was the sudden and mysterious disappearance of a sleek and fat black-and-tan dog that belonged to the legislature, or rather, to a member of that body.

Governor Oglesby and the members of the legislature were on visit to Chicago, and Colonel Sweet, who was in command at Camp Douglas, invited them out to the prison to show them how well the prisoners were cared for; and on the afternoon referred to they filed through the gate in two's, led by the governor and Colonel Sweet. The news of their arrival soon spread through the prison and the Confederates began to flock to the point of entrance to take a peep at them.

A member of Duke's 2nd Kentucky Cavalry was strolling around with his blanket thrown over his shoulders when the visitors began to enter, and he stopped and squatted down against the corner post of the barrack to take a good look at them as they passed. The ends of his blanket reached the ground on both sides of him and lay in folds at his feet. The dog had accompanied its master on the tour of inspection, and, being a guest, it was allowed all the privileges necessary to enable an animal of its inquisitive nature make a thorough inspection. It bounded through the gate as if perfectly at home, and began to scout around at will, running first one way and then another, wherever its nose led it. In one of these promiscuous sallies it ran right up to where the Confederate squatted, and, as he had been a great admirer of canine sagacity in ante-bellum days, his old affection for the species warmed up as his memory wandered back to the fox hunts of happier times, and as he spoke to the dog in a kind tone it ran up to him and stopped. He stroked it caressingly a few times, and, finding that it was not only good natured but fat, he instantly formed a bold determination to see how it would taste cooked. It seemed to enjoy his caresses, and remained with him until the legislative column had passed, and, finding that it was disposed to stay with him, he raised his blanket and lowered it over the dog's body, and, putting his arm affectionately around the animal, he arose and walked away with the dog under his arm, and not a member of that august body of legislators knew that one of their attendants had been kidnapped.

He hurried to his barrack with his gain, and found the building nearly empty, the prisoners having gone out to see the visitors. Fortunately for his plans, he found that two occupants of neighboring bunks, who felt no desire to see the lawmakers, had remained indoors, and he whispered to one to bring the spit-box into the aisle between the bunks, and requested the other to sharpen his knife as quick as possible. Both did as requested, though totally ignorant of their comrade's intentions.

The dog was perfectly docile and made no resistance while its friendly captor was preparing to carry out his desperate resolve. He raised the blanket, showed his comrades what he had under it and, directing them how to assist him, he placed the dog's neck across the spit-box and while they held it in position he cut its throat and the crimson canine gore gurgled into the receptacle prepared to catch it.

Kitchen discipline was very exacting and had required great caution to get it cooked without the sergeant's knowledge. There was not, however, a hitch in the entire act, and before the gloom of night had surrounded the prison that dog had been devoured.

Several legislators and some of the guards were certain that the dog had entered the prison, but no one saw it go out, and a vigorous search was made for it, but in vain. Its head, skin and feet had been thrown into the sewer. The legislator advertised for it in the Chicago papers and offered a large reward for it.

The guards tried for several days to get on the track of it, and one of them interrogated the man who cooked the dog, as the answers were not satisfactory the cook received a clubbing, but he never gave up the secret. The feral brain that conceived this bold stroke of policy was greeted by hundreds of his old comrades at the recent reunion and asked if he had tried dog meat since the war.[99]

After Shurly arrived in the camp he received weekly reports of conditions from a subordinate. These reports and the many other problems he saw there made him furious and he bitterly complained to his superiors, often in writing. It was not unusual, for example, for prisoners to be released through political influence, expedited in at least twenty instances by a law firm from Kentucky with ties to President Lincoln. The law partners had the audacity to actually send business cards to the inmates, offending Captain Shurly to the point that he complained directly to the Commissary General of Prisoners, Lieutenant Colonel William Hoffman. Hoffman did not reply.[100]

Chapter Nine

CONSPIRACY

A GENERAL SACK OF THE CITY INTENDED—PLUNDER, RAPINE—
FIRE—BLOODSHED IN THE STREETS OF CHICAGO.

—Headline in the *Chicago Tribune* November 11, 1864, three days
after Lincoln's reelection, reporting on the intent of the captured terrorists
attempting to release thousands of Camp Douglas prisoners[101]

BY EARLY 1864 THE CONFEDERACY WAS DESPERATE to relieve military pressure on Richmond and Atlanta and was open to almost any conceivable plan to exploit the war-weariness in the North. President Lincoln was increasingly unpopular and faced the real prospect of losing his reelection bid to the Democratic nominee, General George McClellan. If the South could succeed in truly embarrassing the president, they could expect an end to the war on their terms.

For some time, the Confederate Secret Service had held in place an extensive spy network in the northern states and Canada and had chosen for their director of operations in the North none other than a former member of President James Buchanan's cabinet, Jacob Thompson, a past U.S. secretary of the Interior. He was an active, aggressive manager, precisely the right man for the job.

Thompson and his cohorts decided that nothing less than a gigantic insurrection of prisoners of war held in Northern camps would end Lincoln's chances on election day. The extent and seriousness of the insurrection has been argued in newspapers and history books ever since November 1864, when it was uncovered. But many historians who dismiss the conspiracy as a hoax may have missed a detailed account of the plot by Major Charles H. Cole, a member of the Confederate Secret Service and one of the major participants. The story appeared in the *Philadelphia Press* on January 28, 1882, and in the *Chicago Tribune* on January 29.[102] Doubters, furthermore, may not know of Edmund Shurly's rebuttal to parts of the article as a result of conversations he would have years later with another of the participants during his days fighting Indians out west on the Bozeman Trail.

According to Major Cole:

> The northwest was selected as the basis of our operations [to embarrass Lincoln] because there was a rebellion there against conscription and the people were generally tired of the war. Then, too, we had older and stronger friends in that section than in the east—those who were willing to do and dare more to aid us. The four thousand men we had in Chicago at the time the convention met were not all regular Confederates, but many of them were northern friends ready to assist the Confederate authorities commissioned to do the work.[103]

The Confederate spy network was well funded. Thompson had $800,000 deposited in the Bank of Toronto to work with, and he used it to finance operations in most of the Northern states, including Illinois, Indiana, Ohio, and Michigan. His organization in Illinois was headed by Major Thomas Henry Hines, a man with an exciting past. In July 1863 he had ridden with General John Hunt Morgan's cavalry. Captured near Salineville, Ohio, Morgan, Hines, and others were imprisoned in Columbus, Ohio, but tunneled to freedom in a daring escape. Morgan and Hines reached Confederate lines safely, and Hines was reassigned to Jacob Thompson in Canada for undercover work in Illinois. Hines was able to recruit many influential Southern sympathizers in Chicago to assist him, either knowingly or unknowingly. One of his cohorts, Brigadier General Charles Walsh, would figure importantly in the days to come. Walsh, the father of ten children, operated a prosperous business and was active in politics. When Lincoln signed the Emancipation Proclamation Walsh was embittered and began to collect arms, which he stored in his small home. In later years Captain Shurly would enthrall his listeners with stories of this intrigue.

Chicago was home to numerous secret Copperhead organizations of Southern sympathizers such as the Sons of Liberty. One of the leaders of the Sons of Liberty, Clement Vallandigham, had gone so far as to visit Thompson in Canada and promise him three hundred thousand men for any disturbance he might concoct to bring down Lincoln and elect McClellan. Thompson certainly must have realized this number was preposterous since the population of Chicago at the time was just over one hundred thousand, but he would have been heartened by the offer. If three hundred thousand were promised, he felt he could, at the very least, expect help from four thousand sympathizers and infiltrated Confederates.

Thompson's man in Indiana was Major John B. Castleman, living near Camp Morton, a prisoner-of-war camp outside Indianapolis. Charles H. Cole was Thompson's commander in Ohio and was a remarkable man, one whose interview, appearing in Philadelphia and Chicago newspapers in January 1882, would provide many details of the gigantic, desperate plot against the Union.

Thompson estimated that Camp Douglas held eight thousand prisoners; that Camp Morton held four thousand Confederates; that Camp Chase near Columbus, Ohio, held eight thousand men; and that, most important, a prison on Johnson Island in Sandusky Bay, Ohio, contained 3,200 Confederate officers, who could command the other twenty thousand Confederate soldiers if they were freed from their prisons. Twenty thousand escaped Confederate soldiers raging through the streets of Chicago, Cleveland, Columbus, Indianapolis, and other large Northern towns, burning and looting as they went, would end any chance of Lincoln's reelection. But how could this prodigious feat be accomplished?

The answer sounded as far-fetched as the goal. Thompson knew that each of the prison camps was garrisoned by fewer than eight hundred soldiers recruited from the Veteran Reserve Corps, that is, made up of soldiers who had been seriously wounded and were unfit for regular army duty, then assigned to lesser posts after their wounds had healed. Thus, the camps were vulnerable to concentrated and coordinated attacks from the outside, assuming that reinforcements for the prison's staff were unavailable from the Federal Army. Thompson's superiors in Richmond assured him that when the breakouts occurred they would schedule an attack by General Jubal Early[104] on Union lines near Washington, D.C. That would hold

Union Army regiments in Virginia and prevent their diversion to the north. The optimum date for these breakouts would be July 4, when the Democrats were to hold their party convention in Chicago. If all went as planned, the attack would cause a fatal humiliation for Abraham Lincoln, McClellan would assume the presidency, and the war would be settled on Confederate terms. It was, they thought, a plan that just might work, and even if only partially successful, would still doom Lincoln's presidency.

Thompson, by necessity, left it to his lieutenants, Hines in Illinois, Cole in Ohio, and John Castleman in Indiana, to work out details for the attacks in their respective geographic areas of responsibility. Even the date of the attack seems to have been left to his people in Chicago. When the Democrats postponed their convention to August 29, Hines convinced the Copperheads to delay their attack to July 20, when there was more likelihood that Jubal Early's Confederate Army to the south would attack Washington to divert Union troop reinforcements away from the north. Still, even on July 20 there was no detailed planning for an assault on Camp Douglas. Soon Hines was informed that the July 20 date would have to be set back first to August 16 and finally to August 29, the revised date for the Democratic Party Convention in Chicago. Hines now insisted that there be no further delays.

INDIANA

IN INDIANA THE PLANS OF JACOB THOMPSON began to unravel with the June 30 publication of an exposé of the Sons of Liberty in an Indianapolis newspaper, charging them with conspiring to establish a northwestern confederacy. Detectives hired by Brigadier General Henry B. Carrington, a gentleman who would figure prominently in Edmund Shurly's life after the war, gathered the information used for this exposé. The information exposed a Mister Harrison H. Dodd, owner of a small printing company in Indianapolis, who had printed documents and booklets implicating himself and the Sons of Liberty in treasonable activities. The exposé did not discourage Dodd, however, and in July he accepted funds from Thompson's people in Canada and continued to try to recruit friends and Democratic Party officials to participate in his plans for insurrection in Indiana—plans that horrified most but not all of these officials.

All that summer Dodd was in continuous contact with the Confederates and, for example, knew of the August 16 date for a coordinated release of prisoners. After intercepting a shipment of arms to Dodd's company on August 20, General Carrington had Dodd and several of his accomplices arrested, tried, and convicted for conspiring to seize arsenals at Indianapolis and Columbus and then to release and arm Confederate prisoners at Camps Douglas, Morton, Chase, and Johnson Island, and flee south back to Confederate lines.[105]

Any plans Major Castleman and Jacob Thompson may have had to assist the Sons of Liberty in the insurrection evaporated with the Dodd arrest. Security around Camp Morton in Indianapolis was strengthened, and Major Castleman was soon in Chicago assisting Tom Hines with his plans.

OHIO

A MAJOR PIECE OF THOMPSON'S PLAN was developed and carried out by Major Cole, who was far more resourceful and devious than Hines and Castleman. It was Cole who conceived the plot to commandeer the sole armed naval ship deployed on Lake Erie, use it to free prisoners held on Johnson Island near Sandusky, and use them to create havoc and panic in that part of the United States.

Immediately after reporting to Jacob Thompson for duty, Cole received $60,000 in gold deposited in a bank at Sandusky, and additional funds deposited for his use with Drexel & Co. in Philadelphia under the name of John Dell, and another account at Belmont, New York. With these funds, Cole established a fictitious Mount Hope Oil Company out of Titusville, Pennsylvania, to give him a cover for his activities. Judge Fillmore[106] of Buffalo was elected president of the company and Cole was secretary and manager.

The Confederate Secret Service was aware that the Union's only man-of-war on the Great Lakes was the 167-foot USS *Michigan,* at anchor in Lake Erie off Johnson Island, near Sandusky, Ohio. An impressive ship in its day, it was a three-masted barkentine commissioned in 1844. It had an iron hull, the first built in North America, and was equipped with auxiliary steam power that turned side paddle wheels. She displaced 450 tons and her fourteen thirty-two-pound guns in broad-side and two eight-inch guns on pivots gave her plenty of firepower, enough to convince the Union forces on Johnson Island to capitulate. Once these Confederate officers escaped, they would assume command of the prisoners released from the other camps and lay waste to the Northern cities. Meanwhile, the captured ship would sail unopposed around the Great Lakes to bombard Detroit, Chicago, Cleveland, Toledo, and Buffalo. It was a daring plan and one that only a desperate enemy would attempt.

Cole was friendly and gregarious and, with unlimited funds to spread around entertaining the military officers, quickly befriended the crew of the *Michigan* when it was docked at Erie, Pennsylvania, and later at Sandusky, after it moved there to guard the camp at Johnson Island. Once the ship moved to Sandusky, Cole set up an office there for the Mount Hope Oil Company, complete with an office manager by the name of Miss Annie Davis, and was able to meet and befriend officers from the camp as well. He even purchased a small vessel, *The Georgian*, which he used on Lake Erie to transport and store small arms for the Confederate cause. At the same time Cole managed to enlist and infiltrate many Southern sym-pathizers into the U.S. Navy as sailors on the *Michigan* and into the army to serve as garrison in the camp.

Cole found it easy to obtain information from the Union military people and later said:

> There were of course very many ludicrous, interesting, thrilling inci-dents attending the days, weeks and months of our preparations for the assaults. It would take a volume to record them all. We had to keep up constant communication with Mister Thompson, the representative of the Confederate government in Canada from whom we received all our orders. This was most important as each Confederate commander in the states acted independently of the rest. Thompson was a man of great nerve—just such a bold, aggressive spirit as Secretary Stanton. If he had been secretary of war, as Stanton was, he would have given you just the same kind of an administration.
>
> Not long before our plans were completed, Mister Thompson, at one of our conferences in Canada, said he should like to visit and look over

the steamer *Michigan* before we attacked her, and also personally inspect the details of my plans upon the ground.

"If you think it's safe, Mister Thompson, I should be exceedingly glad to have you do so."

He didn't reply and we parted without my knowing what his intentions were. A few days after, while sitting in my room at the West House, Sandusky, the servant came up and said, "Your aunt is in the parlor and would like to see you."

I asked Miss Annie Davis, my secretary and assistant, to go down and invite her up. Of course I knew it wasn't my aunt, but I was never taken by surprise at anything and was always on my guard. I supposed it was a female courier with orders or information. Miss Davis went down to the parlor and in a moment returned with an elderly lady nicely dressed in a style that well became her age. When her veil was removed there stood Jake Thompson. I was wholly taken aback as the disguise was perfect and the assumption of the character easy and graceful.

I promptly reported to the *Michigan* that I had a lady relative who had stopped over from Lorain to visit, that she had never seen a man-of-war, and that I should like to bring her aboard. They returned a cordial invitation and that afternoon Thompson and I went out to the ship. Mister Thompson went all over the ship, and [he], in a squeaky voice, put such questions about her construction and arrangement as a rural female of well advanced years and small opportunities for gleaning information would be likely to propound. No one suspected him and the officers were exceedingly polite to the one they afterwards spoke of as my "country aunt."

It was of course a great risk for Mister Thompson to run. It took a man of nerve and tact to succeed. He felt a great interest in the capture of the *Michigan* and it was his intention to board her soon after she was captured and make her the headquarters of the civil power of the Confederacy in the northwest.[107]

By early summer 1864 Cole had recruited more than enough Southern sympathizers in Detroit, Canada, and Ohio to carry out his plans. He was as ready as he ever would be and needed only a start date to begin the operation. The original July 4 date, however, had slipped past because the Democrat Party convention was delayed to August 29. Then for reasons unclear to Cole the attack date moved again, this time to September 19, a date that does not agree with the dates fixed for the attack in Chicago. September 19 may have been just another of the slippages that occurred because of the planning problems in Chicago.

Nevertheless, Cole was anxious to get started, and on Saturday, September 17, he departed for Detroit to begin the operation. On Sunday morning he came aboard the *Philo Parsons*, a small passenger ship plying the Great Lakes, and greeted Captain Atwood, whom he had befriended many months before, then spent most of the evening socializing with him. Cole had made it a point to cross Lake Erie on Atwood's ship many times over the previous months in order to gain his confidence and friendship.

Just before departing on the morning of the 19th, Cole went ashore and telegraphed to Brigadier General Charles Walsh in Chicago:

> Detroit, September 19, 1864: Close out all the stock in the Mount Hope Oil Co. before three o'clock today. Be prompt. C. H. Cole[108]

This message was written in a code all the conspirators understood, and it conveyed to the Chicago group that an attack would be made on the *Michigan* at five o'clock that evening. It was understood that all dispatches relating to their military activities would be related to the Mount Hope Oil Company. This message is of particular importance because it connects the Ohio and Chicago conspiracies and shows the true dimensions of the Confederate plans to disrupt the North.

Cole's operation was now under way. The *Parsons* made its first stop at Windsor, Canada, just across the river from Detroit. There a number of Cole's men boarded the ship and it departed for Malden (a landing on the Detroit River just north of Amherstburg, Ontario), where more of Cole's men boarded. By this time Captain Atwood had noticed the unusual number of men boarding his ship and remarked to Cole who had, as Atwood's friend, been invited to join him on the bridge, "[Look] how many skedaddlers are coming on this morning. These fellows are all well off. They ran out of the United States to escape the draft, and are now returning. They look hard, but all of them have means and are men of position."

"Yes, poor fellows," replied Cole, "They have had a hard time."[109]

When the last of Cole's men were on board, the *Parsons* pushed away from the dock and began heading south down the Detroit River toward Lake Erie and Put-In-Bay Island. A man by the name of John Yates Beale was Cole's second in command, and seeing Cole's signal to begin, moved his men to their assigned positions around the boat. When Beale saw that everyone was ready he signaled Cole in the pilot house.

Cole then pulled out his pistol, put it to the head of Captain Atwood, and said, "Captain, you are my prisoner!"

"What's the matter, Cole?" he asked in total surprise.

"You are my prisoner. I have possession of this ship in the name of the Confederate States Government. Go below."[110]

Immediately, Cole's men pulled their weapons, surrounded the ship's crew, sent them to the hold of the ship, and closed and locked the hatches. The ship's passengers were assured they would not be harmed, and, finally, the American flag was hauled down and replaced with the Confederate stars and bars.

"This flag is a guarantee of protection to women and children,"[111] said Cole. This assurance was maintained, although with some difficulty. According to Cole, the Confederate soldiers were gentlemen, but some of the sympathizers hired from Philadelphia, New York, and elsewhere were not and had to be severely disciplined.

By twelve thirty that afternoon, everything was running smoothly and Put-In-Bay was sighted in the distance. There at the wharf, unloading cargo, was a small ship by the name of the *Island Queen*. Among its passengers were three hundred unarmed Union soldiers, heading for Cleveland to be mustered out of the army. The *Parsons* moved up, tied up to the *Island Queen*, and Cole's men scrambled aboard to capture her without a struggle. Its passengers were given assurances of no harm as well, and with that the two ships departed Put-In-Bay and headed to Fighting Island (what may now be named Kelly's Island, or possibly Pelee Island) to disembark the passengers where they would be unable to warn authorities.

Now came the climax to the operation: the capture of a Federal man-of-war while lying at anchor in sight of a Union encampment. Having gained the confidence of the officers of the *Michigan* over the past several months, it did not seem unusual to them when Cole told them he planned an "entertainment" for them on their ship on September 19 at five o'clock sharp, including wine and other fine beverages.

All was calm in Sandusky Bay as the *Philo Parsons* and the *Island Queen* steamed slowly into the bay and set anchor. Nothing unusual could be seen when several small boats departed the two ships for shore and other places. Then more small rowboats drifted out from shore and from the two Confederate ships, apparently fishing in the bay and aimlessly drifting toward the *Michigan*. Finally, a small boat carrying Cole delivered him to the *Michigan* precisely on time so the "festivities" could begin. Only Cole knew the small boats surrounding the *Michigan* contained not fishermen but armed Confederate soldiers ready to attack.

Cole was to descend the steps to the ship's wardroom, with its officers following to lure as many of the crew as possible down below. Then he would step back up above and signal his men to climb aboard and close and lock the hatches to trap the crew below. Given the goodwill he had earned mingling with the ship's crew over the past several months, his plan could work.

As Cole stepped aboard the *Michigan*, his thoughts raced to his two other ships anchored in Sandusky Bay, and to the thirty-two hundred Confederate officers imprisoned on shore with fifteen hundred revolvers distributed among them, well informed of the plan and awaiting release, with but eight hundred guards holding them. With this capture, he would hold the only armed vessel on the Great Lakes. Commerce on the entire lake system would be absolutely at his command. According to plan, another vessel, sailing on Lake Michigan and based in Chicago, was about to be captured by Hines and his people. The towns and cities around the Great Lakes then would be at the mercy of the Confederacy. With twenty thousand Confederate prisoners freed this day, added to this maritime advantage in a part of the Union where the South had so many friends and where so much hatred of the war was felt, they would be invincible. So it was with a feeling of near euphoria mixed with trepidation that Cole stepped onto the ladder leading down the hatch of the man-of-war.

No one noticed the small boat depart Johnson Island and row steadily toward the *Michigan*. There was nothing unusual about this.

Reaching the bottom of the ladder, Cole announced it was time for the party to begin, and the wine bottles were opened. The crew was ready to relax and enjoy the evening. Cole joined in, perhaps for just moments too long. But how could he find an excuse to break away from the conviviality to jump topside to give his men the signal to attack?

The small boat that departed Johnson Island now reached the *Michigan*, tied up to it, and several officers clambered aboard. In a moment they had joined the party below, and, walking toward Cole, one said, "Captain Cole, you are my prisoner!"

"Captain of what?" Cole asked with a chuckle. "Certainly no man will accuse me of being a soldier!"

"No," replied the officer whom Cole well knew, "but here is a telegram saying you are a Confederate spy and are in a conspiracy to capture Johnson Island. It orders your arrest. We must at least take you into custody."

"Oh that's all right," Cole answered lightly, but he knew it was all over.[112]

Cole was searched and his commission from the Confederate States found. He was arrested on the spot. Nothing, however, was amiss as far as the men waiting in the boats nearby could tell, and they were beginning to wonder why Cole had not come topside to signal them. Below decks, unknown to them, Cole was being vigorously questioned, and he quickly thought of a way to get word to his friends. He confessed that a dozen prominent but entirely innocent citizens of Sandusky were involved in the plot, including a Mister West, the manager of the hotel in which he had his office, and where Annie Davis would be awaiting news of the insurrection. Word went out promptly to arrest Mister West, and when Annie Davis saw him being led away, she immediately rushed to a small boat, rowed out to the men awaiting their signal, and warned them off. John Beale, Cole's second in command, scuttled the *Island Queen* in full view of the *Michigan* and escaped with many of the men on the *Philo Parsons* to Canada, where he then scuttled that ship near the mouth of the Detroit River. None of Cole's men were caught. Annie Davis was arrested several days later when she returned with a Confederate message that said the Confederates were holding two Federal officers for execution if Cole was treated other than as a commissioned soldier.

Cole was confined on board the *Michigan* until Generals Dix, from the Department of the East; Heintzelman, in charge of the Department of Ohio; and Hitchcock could arrive to investigate the affair. Then he was transferred to Johnson Island where he would endlessly explain what happened, in detail, to its mortified thirty-two hundred Confederate officers.

Cole was told and believed, probably to the end of his life, that he and his enterprise had been compromised by a Colonel Johnson who accidentally or on purpose dropped an incriminating piece of paper on the Malden dock at Amherstburg, Canada, when the *Parsons* stopped there to take on passengers. The Federal government, wanting to protect Colonel Sweet's informants in Chicago, could well have invented this story. It seems far more likely that Sweet's people found evidence of the Ohio conspiracy and warned the Veteran Reserve Corps garrison on Johnson Island.

Sweet was actively investigating the activities of the Copperheads and Confederate spies in Chicago and had penetrated their ranks with four detectives and one turncoat prisoner, John T. Shanks of the 14th Kentucky Cavalry. By early September, Sweet and Shurly were getting solid information about the conspiracy. According to Shurly, "The work of watching these conspiracies was simply a matter of hiring spies. We kept a number of them among the prisoners and were well informed of all their doings."[113] It was tainted information coming as it was from the unsavory characters Sweet had recruited, but it was enough to proceed with preventive action.

Shurly states positively that credit for Cole's arrest belongs to Colonel Sweet,[114] who arrested one of Thompson's agents in Chicago two days before Cole's adventure began and forced information about it from him. Sweet immediately telegraphed the information to Secretary of War Edwin Stanton, who would have quickly acted to warn those at Johnson Island. Shurly, as Sweet's adjutant, would know of Sweet's communication to Stanton. Sweet also gained information about a Confederate plan to capture an iron steamer docked in Chicago named the *Merchant*, but thwarted the takeover by placing armed guards on the ship.

ILLINOIS

MEANWHILE, IN EARLY SEPTEMBER, Hines, using the home of Charles Walsh near Camp Douglas, at last entered into serious planning of his attack. Walsh's home was located on Ellis Street, just one block east of the fragile wooden fence surrounding Camp Douglas.

Hines, making extremely detailed drawings of the camp and its approaches, decided that there would be a night assault against three sides of the camp, with the prisoners inside coordinated to rush the board fence enclosing the camp as soon as the exterior attacks began. After the prisoners were released, telegraph lines would be cut, banks would be looted, and the city set afire. Then, bribed railroad employees would carry the escapees by train to a prison camp at Rock Island to release still more prisoners and to further disrupt the North. Hines was in contact by coded messages with a committee of prisoners in the compound, the Supreme Council of Seven, who were developing plans of their own to break out of the camp. As early as the spring of 1864 they had hatched plots to make a mass breakout so they were receptive to any ideas Hines might offer.

Hines had to know that escape of these prisoners to Rock Island or anywhere else by railroad was far-fetched, but for him and Jake Thompson simply unleashing eight thousand prisoners on Chicago and setting it ablaze during the Democratic convention was success enough to hurt Lincoln's reelection. Combined with the results of simultaneous attacks by their Ohio and Indiana friends, the plot would inflict huge damage and embarrassment in the North and surely affect the war effort.

The plans for Illinois began to unravel when Vallandigham withdrew his people from the venture and returned to Ohio, then went further awry at the very last minute when it became obvious that the thousands of civilians pledged by Charles Walsh to risk their lives freeing the Confederate soldiers, who then would descend on their own city and burn it down, did not exist. A day before the scheduled attack, only some twenty-five men could be found for this duty. To make matters worse, coordination of the attack with a simultaneous attack by Cole in Ohio had broken down. Cole was proceeding on his own timetable for an attack later in September under the false assumption that Hines would follow his lead.

As Hines worked on his scheme, and without the knowledge or approval of their Supreme Council of Seven, a number of Camp Douglas prisoners made separate plans for a mass breakout. On October 28, Colonel Sweet was out of town and Captain Shurly was in temporary command of the camp. That day there was an unusual amount of activity and agitation in the camp, a good sign that something big was going to happen soon. Finally, he learned from sources inside the camp that a mass escape was planned for that evening "to be spearheaded by one hundred prisoners, with eleven thousand to follow."[115]

Edmund Shurly took quick and decisive action. He positioned the 8th Veteran Reserve Corps outside the western fence just after dark. They were armed with rifles loaded and aimed at the camp stockade walls where the breakout was expected. Another regiment was posted four city blocks farther west as a backup. They did not have long to wait.

At 8:00 p.m. the prisoners assembled outside their barracks and tore through the flimsy wooden fence surrounding the camp. Seeing this, the 8th Veteran Reserve Corps fired a volley, driving them back into the camp. In the confusion, about eighteen prisoners got past the 8th Veteran Reserve Corps but were rounded up by the regiment positioned to their rear. Fortunately, casualties were light: ten prisoners were slightly wounded. As it turned out, the prisoners were extremely lucky to have had Shurly in command at the time, as Colonel Sweet would certainly have used cannon instead of rifles to quell the escape. There had been a number of attempted breakouts earlier in the year, many successful, and Sweet was anxious to punish the prisoners trying to get out. Shurly did not even consider using artillery as it would have shredded the escapees at such close range, including some still in the barracks who were not involved in the attempt.[116]

By late October Colonel Sweet and his adjutant were obtaining more and more information about these plots from their spies and detectives. These sources told them Thomas Hines was persisting with his plans and had targeted election eve for his attack. Moreover, the attackers in Ohio had been arrested by this time and questioned, so Sweet and Shurly now knew details of the plans Thompson and Cole had developed for Ohio and that they were solidly linked to the Chicago activities.

On the night of November 7, the evening before election day, Colonel Sweet stationed riflemen on a University of Chicago tower overlooking the camp to deliver deadly rifle fire to prisoners attempting a breakout. Additional riflemen were positioned around the camp. Then, units of the Camp Douglas garrison moved into Chicago and, along with the help of the Chicago police, arrested 106 "bushwhackers, guerrillas and rebel soldiers."[117] Shurly himself was part of a contingent that arrested some of the conspirators, including General Vincent

Marmaduke and an Englishman by the name of Moffam. In 1882 Shurly told a newspaper reporter:

> There is no doubt that Jake Thompson of Mississippi was the head of the whole affair, for after Moffam was released and I had gone into the regular army, I saw him in Omaha, and he told me that Thompson furnished him with all the money. This Moffam was the coolest, smartest man I ever saw. He was no more excited than a man in church when I arrested him, and he was a sort of paymaster and head financier for all the people.... I don't know what became of him, for I have never seen him after we parted at Omaha.[118]

Captain Hines was staying at the Morris home when the police raided it and escaped capture by hiding between two mattresses on a bed occupied by two ladies faking sleep. Hines, after the war, would serve on the Kentucky Court of Appeals in Bowling Green, Kentucky.

With these arrests mass hysteria descended on Chicago, generated in part by *Chicago Tribune* headlines that appeared on November 11, such as: "A GENERAL SACK OF THE CITY INTENDED—PLUNDER, RAPINE—FIRE—BLOODSHED IN THE STREETS OF CHICAGO."[119] The U.S. Army had to send in more troops to quell fears of the citizens that insurrection was imminent. A newspaper in Chicago favoring peace with the Confederacy, the *Chicago Times* considered it all a hoax.[120]

Of the eighty-one suspects held at Camp Douglas for trial, twelve died of smallpox and all but eight of their remaining number were released for lack of evidence. Of the eight who went to trial in a military tribunal in Cincinnati the following spring, one committed suicide in prison, one escaped, one went insane before the trial, two were acquitted, and three were convicted. Of those convicted, two were later pardoned and the other, Colonel George Saint Leger Grenfell, a colorful English soldier of fortune who had spent time in the Confederate Army, was reportedly drowned with a thirty-pound ball and chain attached to his leg attempting to escape captivity in a small boat off Dry Tortugas, the outermost of the Florida Keys.

Shurly did not believe this report. "Grenfell, they say, committed suicide, but my later correspondence with the commander at Dry Tortugas, where he was confined, leads me to believe that he made his escape. I rather pity him. He was purely a soldier of fortune, and a most elegant refined gentleman. What his career may have been [before the war], I cannot guess, but once our war here was over there can be no doubt that he sold his sword to the next government that needed it without much hesitancy about a matter of principle."[121]

In 1882 a Chicago newspaper reporter filed this story of Colonel George Saint Leger Grenfell:

> The revival of George Saint Leger Grenfell's name brings again to the front one of the most mysterious and romantic characters of the closing months of the great Civil War. What was absolutely known of him at his trial in Cincinnati after his arrest here appeared in the public prints at the time. From this it appears that he was the illegitimate son of a wealthy English gentleman, who sent him to France to be educated early in his youth. When he approached manhood a boyish escapade brought him into disgrace, and he joined the French army as a private. His splendid fighting qualities in Algeria brought him a promotion to one of the lower commissioned grades, which he held until an army scrape led to his dismissal from the service.
>
> He next appeared at Gibraltar, where, probably through his father's influence, he was appointed to a lucrative position in the consular service. This furnished him with a livelihood until a crusade against smugglers brought out the fact that Grenfell had entered into an alliance with them to defraud the customs officials, and he was again dismissed in disgrace.
>
> The investigation shows that he [Grenfell] returned to military life again, and passed through the greater part of the Crimean War in connection with some irregular British troops. It is known that later he was connected with the petty wars arising from the small revolutions in one or two of the South American republics, and then found his way into the heart of the Southern Confederacy, where he served with General Morgan first and later with General Joe Wheeler, now a congressman from Alabama. There can be no doubt that he was selected and duly commissioned for his work with the conspirators in the Northern states.

He was in all respects the typical cavalry officer—tall, dark complex-
ioned, with black hair and whiskers, but a nervous, flashing, and unreliable eye. With his work laid out for him he succeeded in running the
blockade to Nassau and next appeared in New York. Going directly to
Washington he secured an interview with Secretary Stanton and boldly
revealed what he claimed to have been his sole connection with the
Southern Confederacy. He denied that he had ever been commissioned
but had served merely as a gentleman volunteer. He claimed that he had
grown weary of Morgan's methods, and had quarreled with Wheeler,
and then determined to leave the country. Having some private business
in the Northern states, he told the great war secretary that he would be
out of the country in a very short time, and wanted a safe conduct that
would protect him from annoyance while he was attending to his private affairs. So well and so boldly did he tell his story that even the acute
secretary was convinced, and the necessary papers were given him.

The next thing he turned up here in Chicago under arrest, and was
sentenced to death at the military trial at Cincinnati. The sentence was
afterwards commuted to imprisonment for life at Dry Tortugas, and
the soldier of fortune was sent there. The reports bear the record that
he committed suicide, but as seen above Captain Shurly does not think
so. The facts are that Grenfell, with just the cool daring that would
be expected of such a man, secured an open rowboat and one evening
boldly paddled out to sea toward the nearest West India island. That
was the last seen of Colonel George Saint Leger Grenfell, but whether
he lives again with another name or was drowned in the first smart gale
is only a matter of conjecture.[122]

Thus ended part three of the Confederate Secret Service plot to disrupt the
1864 presidential election. In the years to come Shurly would share with friends
and newspaper reporters alike his conviction that the conspiracy was huge, the
Chicago arrests were entirely justified, and that Chicago had escaped the fate for a
time that eventually befell the city: the Great Fire.

The outside plotters were in communication with the prisoners [Shurly later said], for when the latter were finally released and sent home I talked with many of the more intelligent ones, and they said that the entire number imprisoned in the stockade was organized into companies, regiments, and brigades, and could have fallen in and marched out like an army. There were nearly fifteen thousand of them inside the stockade as I recollect, and we were guarding them with about seven hundred men. If they had once succeeded in gaining the advantage of the officers and men in charge of the camp, Chicago would have been sacked and burned and they would have torn this country all to pieces from here to Saint Louis.[123]

After the Civil War, as we will see in the next chapter, Edmund Shurly joined the regular army and fought Indians on the frontier. There he met one of the Confederate officers captured in Chicago and had a long conversation with him about the Confederate conspiracy. According to Shurly, the officer (whom he would not name because the officer was living in Chicago) said:

Some of our best officers were detailed to take command of the troops [prisoners of war] upon their release. They were to capture the [Camp Douglas] garrison, take possession of their arms and others concealed in the vicinity of the camp, then possess themselves of all the serviceable horses, raid the [Chicago] banks and other places where there were articles of value, secure all the arms and ammunition, and then fire the city. A part of the plan was to make a forced march to Rock Island, release the prisoners, thence to southern Illinois and Missouri. They hoped to have possession of Saint Louis for a base. I can assure you that if it had not been for General Sweet[124] they would have succeeded.[125]

Shurly had high regard for General Sweet. "General Sweet," he said, "is really the man who frustrated a scheme on the part of the rebels that would have been fraught with mischief. He did this too when suffering, as few men suffer, from wounds received at the battle of Perryville. I have known him to be up night after night during that exciting time, shattered as he was—in fact, he died from wounds received in battle the same as though he had been killed on the field."[126]

After the conspiracy to release prisoners at Camp Douglas was suppressed, Shurly continued on as adjutant and was brevetted major of volunteers, to date from March 13, 1865, for "gallant and meritorious services in the battle of Fredericksburg, Virginia," and then raised to the rank of brevet lieutenant colonel of volunteers, the same day, for "gallant and meritorious services during the war."[127]

General Sweet resigned from the Veteran Reserve Corps on September 19, 1865,[128] and Brevet Lieutenant Colonel Shurly commanded the camp for another two weeks, working to dismantle the facilities and auction off supplies and property. He was mustered out of the 8th Veteran Reserve Corps on October 7, 1865, and was replaced by a Captain E. C. Phetteplace, who became the last commander of Camp Douglas.

By the end of its terrible existence, over four thousand Confederate prisoners had died from various causes.[129] When the camp was decommissioned, 655 Confederates and twelve Union soldiers who had succumbed to smallpox within its walls remained in a small cemetery on the site of the camp, a ghostly reminder of the suffering and death that went on there during the war. The others were exhumed and relocated elsewhere.[130]

AFTER THE WAR BENJAMIN SWEET was appointed pension agent for the Chicago district. He continued to suffer from his wounds and, in 1868, hired his daughter, Ada, as his secretary. In 1871 she became chief clerk for Mister David Blakely, who succeeded her father when he could no longer carry the burden of the office. Ada did a fine job helping the office survive the Chicago fire and was appointed pension agent in 1874 by President Grant after her father died. This was unusual because women in those days rarely were given so much responsibility. She was a fine young lady who had much younger sisters and a ten-year-old brother to support with her salary from this job.

By 1882, however, her father's Democratic political enemies, acquired during the Camp Douglas conspiracy days, found ways to pressure her superiors to have her removed from this office. Shurly helped as much as possible to prevent this from happening, including writing vigorous letters to Chicago newspapers to arouse the public to the unfairness of the issue. He wrote:

> [Sweet] left a family of small children; the eldest, Miss Ada Sweet, the present pension agent, has had the care of the family. The boy who will inherit his father's honor and spotless name is about ten years of age. This young family are dependent upon the exertions of their sister for a living. In view of these facts, is it possible that any soldier who ever faced an armed foe in the field or that ever battled for the flag could seek this girl's place? I've heard so, but "believe it not." To turn this brave soldier's daughter with her little sisters and brother dependent upon her from the office of pension agent, a place she has filled such intelligence, fidelity, and honesty that no fault can be found, would indeed be a wrong.
>
> [Signed] E. R. P. Shurly, late Captain and A. A. G., Camp Douglas.[131]

Shurly was intent on remaining in the army after the war, and Chicago papers reported that he was asked to join the staff of Captain Andrew Sheridan Burt, commander of Company F, 1st Battalion, 18th Infantry Regiment, Regular Army, at Chattanooga, Tennessee. Andy Burt was a genuine army hero, having distinguished himself in bloody battles around Chattanooga, Chicamauga, and Missionary Ridge. To have served under such a man at this time would have secured Shurly's position in the army, but this would not occur until much later under far more difficult circumstances. On September 22, 1865, the following telegram was received at Camp Douglas:

> To: Brigadier General B. Sweet, Camp Douglas
>
> Captain Shurly will remain at Camp Douglas until the meeting of General Court Martial at the place of which he is Judge Advocate, by command of Brigadier General Cook.[132]

By 1895 the animosities between the veterans of the North and the South had cooled, and a huge reception honoring Civil War veterans of both sides was prepared in Chicago for May 30. It was called "Chicago's Peace Festival and Reunion of Confederate and Union Commanders" and was held in the Palmer House. Among the fifty-four invited guests from the Confederate Army were Generals Longstreet and Wade Hampton, South Carolina's ex-governor.

An article in a Chicago newspaper dated May 30, 1895,[133] describes the affair and lists many of the attendees, including Edmund Shurly. It also describes how the antagonists were now friends who joked and laughed about the happenings at Camp Douglas and became involved in "long arguments as to the days of the Golden Circle conspiracy and the exact location of certain tunnels and stockades in the old Camp Douglas."[134] One gathers from this newspaper article that the participants were not arguing over *whether* the conspiracy existed but, rather, just how close it had come to success.

Chapter Ten

THE BLOODY
BOZEMAN TRAIL

"Which is the next place, to hell, to send a regiment?"
"To the Powder River country," was the prompt reply.
"Then order the 18th Infantry there at once."

—Edwin M. Stanton, Secretary of War. From a story, possibly apocryphal,
circulating among the soldiers attached to the
18th U.S. Infantry Regiment at Fort C. F. Smith[135]

AT THE END OF THE CIVIL WAR an even more vicious war loomed on the horizon. The Oglala Sioux nation in Wyoming Territory, under the leadership of chieftains Sitting Bull and Red Cloud, was becoming extremely agitated by the continuing intrusion of immigrants into the last, best hunting grounds along the Big Horn Mountains north of the Oregon Trail. They had wrested these grounds from the Crows a short time before and meant to keep them.

In 1862 gold was discovered in Montana Territory, and immigrants flooded to the gold fields near Virginia City, in what is now southwestern Montana. To get there they took the Oregon Trail across the western Wyoming border to Idaho, then headed north to the gold fields. One year later, John Bozeman, an adventurous man of twenty-six years, along with an obscure frontiersman by the name of John N. Jacobs and Jacobs' twelve-year-old half-breed daughter, found a shortcut.

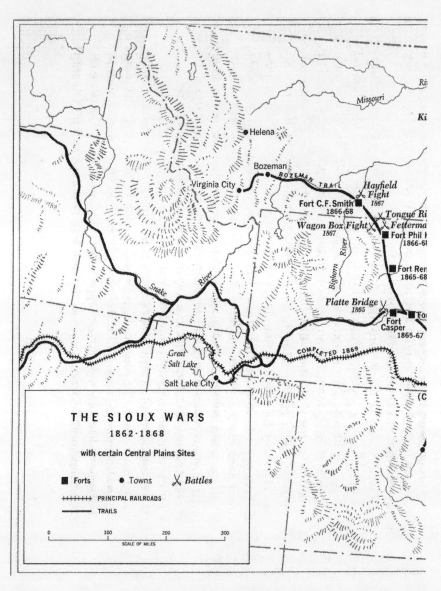

THE SIOUX WARS

1862-1868

with certain Central Plains Sites

■ Forts   ● Towns   ✗ Battles

┼┼┼┼┼┼┼ PRINCIPAL RAILROADS

──── TRAILS

0   100   200   300
SCALE OF MILES

Courtesy, Robert M. Utley, from his book *The*

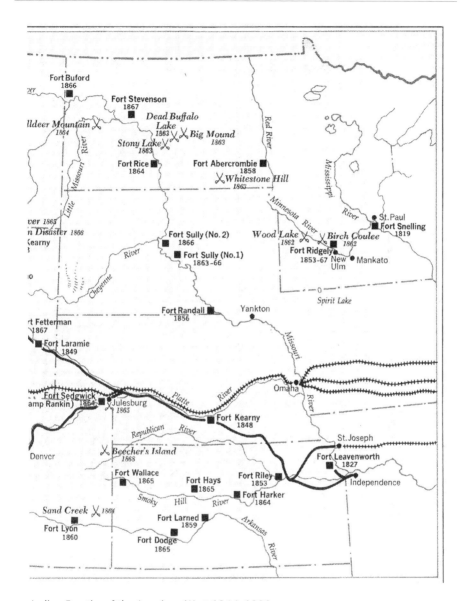

Indian Frontier of the American West 1846–1890.

In the spring of 1863 Bozeman and his two companions set out from the settlement of Bannock, in the Montana Territory, where gold had first been found, traveled east past the Big Horn Mountains to eastern Wyoming, then south to the Oregon Trail. Their route took them through the favorite hunting grounds of seven thousand Sioux who had convinced themselves the land was protected from trespass by a treaty solemnly signed with the United States government.[136] During the trip they were surrounded by seventy-five hostile Crow and warned that, had Sioux captured them, they certainly would have been killed.[137] They continued on after this encounter, however, and finally, in early July, reached Deer Creek Crossing (now Glenrock, Wyoming), nearly starved. Rather than heed the warning, Bozeman immediately began to promote travel along this route to save the wagons more than four hundred miles of weary travel over the Oregon Trail.

The first wagon train to attempt this new trail left Deer Creek Station on July 6, 1863, with forty-six wagons, eighty-nine men including John Bozeman, ten women, and several children. Ten days later they were camped at Clear Creek, a branch of the Crazy Woman's Fork of the Powder River, where so many wagon trains and soldiers would be ambushed in the coming Indian War.

On the morning of July 20 a war party of 150 Cheyenne and Sioux approached the train for a meeting. The old chief leading the Indians politely but firmly laid down an ultimatum to the white invaders. His message was simple and clear: Turn back or be annihilated. This was the only hunting ground left to his people, and that it was theirs by treaty with the U.S. government.[138]

Government records show that the Sioux did *not* have a treaty right to keep immigrants from passing through this territory. Present day authorities Glenn Sweem and Robert A. Murray[139] point out all treaties concerning access to this land had been negotiated with the Crow, whom the Sioux subsequently forced from the land. Nevertheless, this was indeed the last of the good hunting grounds for the Indians, and they could see only dispersal and death if the white man were to invade the territory and drive the game away.

Rights or no rights, the ultimatum confused the immigrants, and they argued among themselves for ten days, during which time they sent riders back to the Oregon Trail, asking the U.S. Army to escort them to the gold country. To their disappointment, the army command at Fort Laramie agreed with the Indians and refused the request for an escort. In the end, the army refusal and the U.S. treaty with the Indians had less influence on the settlers than the Indians' promise to annihilate them if they continued on. On July 31 the Bozeman wagon train turned around and headed back to the Oregon Trail.

Subsequent wagon trains, however, began to get through to Montana and reported Bozeman's trail to be a much shorter and easier trip. Soon traffic on the trail increased, and in 1865 many wagon trains, often consisting of upward of 150 wagons, passed through to Virginia City. With this increase in traffic came the Indian raids promised by Sioux Chieftain Red Cloud. Torture and murder of civilians became commonplace. In 1865 some vicious massacres of civilians by Sioux were reported in the Eastern press and before long the army was assigned to protect the travelers. By 1866, with the Civil War over, the army began to focus its full attention on the Indian problem and decided that an army regiment would be needed along the Bozeman Trail to quell the uprising.

MEANWHILE THE TRANSFER TO CIVILIAN LIFE after his adventurous Civil War service had not gone well for Edmund Shurly. It probably was not exciting enough to suit him, and, to make matters worse, when the war ended the economy plunged into depression. Jobs could not have been easy for Shurly to find. After seven months of civilian life, he received an appointment back into the army to an assignment so arduous and harrowing that his family could not accompany him. For Augusta and their two-year-old son, Arthur, this was heartbreaking news.

Winter had barely ended when Shurly said his final good-bye to his wife and son, left his home in Chicago, and traveled west to old Fort Kearney in Nebraska to enlist in the Regular Army. When he arrived at the fort, it was at the height of its importance to westward expansion, acting as the last outpost of civilization on the Oregon Trail for immigrants pouring into the western plains. Heavy Concord stagecoaches, pulled by six horses and filled with tired and thirsty passengers, freight, and mail, pulled into town from points east and west. Blacksmiths, restaurants, hotels, and saloons labored to keep up with the demands of the droves of raucous people passing through town. Two miles to the west of Kearney lay Dobytown where whorehouses and more saloons could satisfy the wildest dreams of the lusty traveler. Few there imagined that their prosperous world would end in less than six months when the Union Pacific Railroad and its terminus advanced past their town, effectively bypassing it on the other side of the Platte River.

The 18th U.S. Infantry Regiment, ordered to fortify and guard the Bozeman Trail against Sioux attacks, had wintered at Kearney, taking on supplies and recruiting experienced Civil War veterans and raw recruits alike in preparation for an expedition that would take them deep into hostile Indian territory.[140] On May 11, 1866, along with eight other young men that day,[141] Shurly joined as a second lieutenant. He was assigned to its 2nd Battalion.

Brigadier General Henry B. Carrington, commanding the expedition, had organized it into a small army of seven hundred men, some of whom were accompanied by their wives and children. About two hundred of the men, particularly the officers, were experienced veterans from the Civil War, but the rest were raw recruits armed with obsolete muzzle-loading Springfield rifles left over from the Civil War. There were to be sure some newer, though limited-range, Spencer breech-loading carbines available; but ammunition for all weapons was in very short supply. Some of Carrington's men were mounted on worn-out horses acquired from a cavalry regiment that had recently passed through town heading east to be mustered out. Accompanying the expedition were 220 wagons drawn by six-mule teams; four mountain howitzers; a steam sawmill; mowing machines; shingle and brick-making machines; carpenters' tools; rocking chairs; churns; primitive washing machines; turkeys; chickens; a couple of hogs; and a forty-six-piece marching band![142] Some called this train "Carrington's Overland Circus," perhaps because it included so many untrained recruits carrying so little ammunition for their arms.

Edmund Shurly had only four days to absorb this extraordinary scene. On May 15 the expedition picked up and left Kearney, heading west along the Oregon Trail en route to Fort McPherson, Fort Laramie, Fort Reno, and points north on the Bozeman Trail. The marching band played music for the first three miles, until the unit was past Dobytown,[143] where bartenders, brothel madams, and whores lined the road to wave good-bye to the affluent customers they had been fleecing for the past six months.

By joining the 18th U.S. Infantry Regiment, Shurly stepped into the pages of history alongside men who were to become legends of the West—men such as Sioux chiefs Sitting Bull, Red Cloud, and Crazy Horse; Cheyenne Chief Dull Knife; military officers Henry B. Carrington, William J. Fetterman, James Powell, Andrew Burt, and Henry B. Wessells. He would hear, firsthand, stories of John Bozeman who discovered and then was killed by Indians on the trail named for him; and of cattleman Nelson Story who in 1866 brought the first large cattle drive from Texas to Montana. Shurly was closely associated with famous scout Jim Bridger; with scout Mitch Boyer, later killed in the Custer massacre; and John "Portugee" Phillips.

SHURLY JOINED THE ARMY AT A CRITICAL TIME in the crisis that had developed along the Bozeman Trail. The U.S. Interior Department policy was to mollify the Indians with beads and trinkets in the hopes that gifts would turn them to peaceful pursuits. The department had sent representatives to Laramie to establish peace talks with the Indians and to convince them that the white man had no intention of invading their hunting grounds. With complete disregard for Interior Department policy, the War Department at the same time was proceeding to send troops to the area, intent upon protecting settlers regardless of the outcome of any peace talks that might take place.

The talks opened in Fort Laramie on June 5, 1866. Less than three days later the 18th Regiment marched into view. As might be expected, Red Cloud, who had been reluctant to attend the "Peace Conference" in the first place, saw this bureaucratic blunder as the white man's intention of taking their land, regardless of whether it meant peace or war, or as they put it, again speaking with a "forked tongue." Furious, he stormed out of the meeting on June 13, and war with the Sioux was now inevitable.

CARRINGTON'S WAGON TRAIN left Fort Laramie June 17 and reached Fort Reno in Wyoming Territory on June 28, after a strenuous march. At the time, Fort Reno was the only fort on the Bozeman Trail. Carrington's mission was to strengthen that fort and establish a military presence, not only to guard the wagon trains traversing the Bozeman Trail but also to draw the attention of the Indians away from the transcontinental railroad being constructed to the south. The result was the strengthening of Forts McPherson, Bridger, and Reno, and the construction of Forts Phil Kearny[144] and C. F. Smith in the summer and fall of 1866.

Work began immediately on Fort Reno. Then, eleven days later on July 9, Carrington, with a reduced force, set forth northward to find a suitable location for the southernmost of the two new forts, Fort Phil Kearny. The first day out they marched twenty-three miles north to the Crazy Woman's Fork of the Powder River, a small, swiftly running creek with muddy, yellow water. Banked with soft sand and lined with trees and underbrush, it was ideally suited for Indian ambushes. It was named, so legend has it, for a woman driven insane by Indians who forced her to watch as they tortured her husband and daughter to death.[145] It was here that Shurly was "schooled in the tactics of Indian warfare. He learned to read the fire signals by night, a system of telegraphy [Indians] used to signal to one another details of the strength and movements of the column. At other times, on well traveled trails, hieroglyphics on flat stones would serve the purpose of the fire signals."[146]

Carrington's force was strong enough to discourage any trouble by Indian marauders, but nine days after Carrington crossed the Crazy Woman, First Lieutenant George M. Templeton, commanding a smaller, ill-protected wagon train, was attacked there and seriously wounded. One of his men, Lieutenant Napoleon H. Daniels, was captured, then viciously tortured to death by his captors.[147] Templeton was lucky to escape with an arrow in his back and a jagged cut across his face.[148] His wagon train had seen a warning of Indians ahead in the form of a body stripped, scalped, and bloody some miles back on the trail, but was determined to cross the creek before dark. As they did so, about fifty Indians attacked, and it was only through superhuman effort that the train completed the crossing and corralled the wagons for defense. Trapped in its small corral, the tiny band of travelers faced certain death if help did not come soon. But help was a day's ride from Fort Reno, and no one knew of their trouble. Then, in answer to their prayers, as dusk was approaching, a smudge of dust appeared on the horizon to the north. It turned out to be a train of thirty-four wagons escorted by forty-seven soldiers under the command of sturdy Captain Thomas B. Burrowes, a man who would later figure in the rescue of Edmund Shurly and a work party under Indian attack in a hayfield in Montana Territory.

Meanwhile, Carrington's train continued north and reached a spot he felt was ideal for building the proposed Fort Phil Kearny, a place roughly twenty miles south of present-day Sheridan, Wyoming. Construction of the stockade that would surround the fort began immediately, and by early August progress was to the point that it was safe to send Captain Nathaniel C. Kinney, with two companies, ninety miles farther north to establish Fort C. F. Smith. It would be located on the Big Horn River at a point where the river emerges from the Big Horn Mountains through the steep-sided Yellow Tail Canyon.

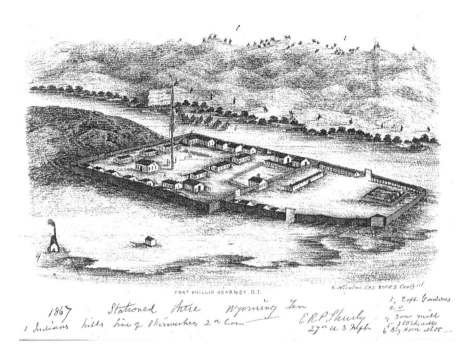

Fort Phil Kearny when Shurly was there. This is Shurly's copy of the
Nicolai sketch of the fort. Shurly marked and signed it to show various features
in the scene. Courtesy of the Reuther Library, Detroit.

Soon after the failed peace conference concluded its work, Sioux attacks on wagon trains increased. By the end of the summer of 1866 the Sioux were attacking the Bozeman Trail wagon trains and the forts guarding them up to five times a day. Meanwhile, wagon trains were flooding the trail, and one report had as many as three hundred wagons waiting in line to cross the Big Horn River near where Fort C. F. Smith was being constructed. Troops defending these trains were equipped with muzzle-loading rifles and too little ammunition to adequately carry out their mission. At one point even target practice by new recruits was prohibited because there was not enough gunpowder for defense of the forts. From August 1866 until the end of that year Red Cloud's warriors killed 154 soldiers and civilians and wounded another twenty. They attacked almost every wagon train passing along the trail and in the process captured 306 oxen and cows, 304 mules, and 161 horses. Congress, intent on a presidential impeachment and a harsh Southern Reconstruction, reported to the nation that "all was at peace in the Big Horn country."[149]

When winter arrived it was one of the coldest in memory. Temperatures reached thirty degrees below zero, blizzards seemed almost continuous, and contact between Forts Phil Kearny and C. F. Smith effectively ceased from December to March. During that time the Bozeman forts were left on their own to fight the elements and the Indians.

THE INDIAN EDMUND SHURLY FOUND himself fighting in 1866 was a cruel, vicious savage who lived a precivilized life. They had a tradition of torturing their prisoners, red man as well as white, to an agonizing death, quite unlike the "gentle and benevolent"[150] "custodians of nature"[151] so fashionably portrayed by late-twentieth-century academia. During his visit to America in 1831, Alexis de Tocqueville recognized this inhuman characteristic of the Indian, later writing in his widely read book, *Democracy in America*:

> Mild and hospitable when at peace, though merciless in war beyond
> any known degree of human ferocity, the Indian would expose himself
> to die of hunger in order to succor the stranger who asked admittance
> by night at the door of his hut; yet he could tear in pieces with his
> hands the still quivering limbs of his prisoner.... The Indian could live

without wants, suffer without complaint, and pour out his death-song at the stake.[152]

In a June 1904 letter, teamster R. J. Smyth, who accompanied Carrington to the Fort Phil Kearny site, described typical Indian depravities:

> I was with the hay-making party down the Big Piney during a part of the summer of '66. During one of our trips to the hay field, we were accompanied by a man who represented Frank Leslie's *Illustrated Weekly* as an artist. This man rode with me a part of the way. He intended to do some sketching near there but I advised him to stay with our outfit. However, he insisted on stopping by the way. On our return we found him dead, a cross cut on his breast, which indicated that they thought him a coward who would not fight. He wore long, black hair, and his head had been completely skinned. Probably it was the work of a band of young Cheyenne bucks; they could cut the scalps into many pieces and thereby make a big show in camp. [I] was very sorry for this man; he appeared to be a perfect gentleman. His thought was, that if the Indians found him they would not hurt him, as he intended to show them his drawings and also explain to them that he was not armed.
>
> Later on the Indians got so thick that we had to abandon this hay-making [camp]. The day that we broke camp we had a great deal of fighting with the Indians. I remember a soldier named Pete Smith who borrowed a revolver from me that day. This man was mounted. He rode too far ahead of the outfit, the Indians cut him off. Later we heard from the Crows that the Sioux caught him [and] skinned him alive.[153]

On one cold December day in 1866, one of the more spectacular examples of the danger Lieutenant Shurly could expect when attacked by Indians occurred less than five miles from Fort Phil Kearny. Shurly watched from the stockade of the fort[154] as Red Cloud, a chieftain of the Oglala Sioux, and almost three thousand of his warriors, enticed a poorly armed contingent of cavalry from the fort to chase down a small band of Indians that appeared threatening. As soon as they had decoyed the cavalrymen out of sight of the fort, masses of Indians appeared and massacred every one, torturing to death those who surrendered.[155] The eighty unfortunate soldiers were led by Captain William J. Fetterman, an officer foolishly determined to make a name for himself. According to reports obtained from Indian squaws in 1867, his soldiers killed some three hundred of their attackers in the battle before the last of the cavalrymen surrendered. If General Custer had not bettered his record a decade later, Fetterman today would be the household name Custer became.

In his report of January 3, 1867, Colonel Carrington described the fate of these men:

> I give you some of the facts as to my men, whose bodies I found just at dark, resolved to bring all in.... Mutilations: eyes torn out and laid on the rocks; noses cut off; ears cut off; chins hewn off; teeth chopped out; joints of fingers; brains taken out and placed on rocks with other members of the body; entrails taken out and exposed; hands cut off; feet cut off; arms taken out from sockets; private parts severed and indecently placed on the person; eyes, ears, mouth and arms penetrated with spearheads, sticks and arrows; ribs slashed to separation with knives; skulls severed in every form, from chin to crown; muscles of calves, thighs, stomach, breast, back, arms and cheek taken out; punctures upon every sensitive part of the body, even to the soles of the feet and palms of the hand. All this doesn't approximate the whole truth.
>
> The great real fact is that these Indians take [prisoners] alive when possible, and slowly torture [them to death]. It is the opinion of Doctor S. M. Horton, post surgeon, that not more than six were killed by [gunfire]. Doctor Samuel M. Horton examined these bodies and said many of these mutilations were performed on living men.[156]

The Sioux had stripped these live prisoners of their clothes in the frigid weather, mutilated them, and then shot hundreds of arrows into them. Most bodies were found in this condition after capture by the Sioux. Lieutenant Shurly now had witnessed far more horror than he had seen in the entire Civil War.

After the massacre, Carrington dispatched John "Portugee" Phillips to ride the 235 miles south on the Bozeman Trail, through country infested with Red Cloud's warriors, to Fort Laramie. His legendary ride past ambushes, and in blizzard conditions reaching twenty-five degrees below zero, has been told many times, and today he is still a hero in the Wyoming-Montana area. He is said to have reached Fort Laramie on Christmas eve, almost dead of exposure, with Carrington's report and request for troops and Springfield breech-loading rifles. When reports of the Fetterman massacre reached Washington there was widespread indignation, a hunt for scapegoats, and a decision to send the forts seven hundred new Allin-modified .50–70 caliber breech-loading Springfield rifles[157] and a hundred thousand rounds of ammunition.

Troops, including Edmund Shurly, were detached from all of the western forts to form a supply column commanded by Colonel John Eugene Smith. On May 2, 1867, this expedition left Fort Sedgwick (Colorado) for the Bozeman forts, with a combination of seasoned officers and 350 raw recruits, much needed supplies, and the new Springfield rifles. It arrived at Fort Phil Kearny on July 2. A smaller contingent of men and supplies under the command of Lieutenant Colonel Luther P. Bradley was now formed and directed to proceed farther north to Fort C. F. Smith. Lieutenant Shurly and his company were ordered to accompany this column.[158] Bradley would assume command of Fort C. F. Smith upon arrival. The wagon train arrived at C. F. Smith on July 23, 1867. Shurly, second in command of Company H, 27th Infantry Regiment, was assigned to be post commissary and quartermaster.[159]

Chapter Eleven

FORT C. F. SMITH

Wyoming Territory,
Headquarters 2nd Battalion, C. F. Smith,
September 15, 1867:
Detail for Tomorrow; Officer in charge of wood detail Lt. E. R. P. Shurly;
Detail to report at 5 a.m.;
By Order of Brigadier General L. P. Bradley, Commanding;
George Templeton, *1st Lt. 27th Infantry, Post Adjutant*

—From a scrap of paper from Shurly's days at C. F. Smith, carefully saved in
Shurly's scrapbook in his archives in the Reuther Library. Written in Shurly's
penmanship at ninety degrees to the orders on the paper: "Fort C. F. Smith was
situated on the Big Horn River one hundred four miles away from Fort Phil
Kearny, Wyoming Territory—near the mouth of the big canyon."[160]

IN 1866, ACCOMPANIED BY THE FAMOUS SCOUT JIM BRIDGER, Captain Kinney
had left Phil Kearny with 165 men to establish Fort C. F. Smith on the Big Horn
River, near what is now Billings, Montana. The fort was named for General
Charles Ferguson Smith, a thirty-five-year army veteran, hero of the Mexican War,
and Commandant of Cadets at West Point when Ulysses S. Grant and William
Tecumseh Sherman were there. Smith was a division commander under Grant at
the Battle of Fort Donelson in the Civil War and was a big reason for the Union

118

victory. Smith, a great fighting general, died of wounds sustained in the battle of Shiloh. The new outpost was appropriately named.

Kinney's column of soldiers marched north over rugged rolling hills covered with plains grass and tumbleweeds until they reached a serene valley formed by a river gushing from a narrow opening in the majestic Big Horn Mountains.[161] The Big Horn Mountains, richly covered with pine woods teeming with all manner of game, rose abruptly to the west. When within eight miles of the site picked for the fort, the men found themselves on the edge of a steep descent. From there they could see the Big Horn River burst from the canyon, then become a docile silvery ribbon wandering off to the northeastern horizon. The bluff down which the wagon train struggled would later serve to warn the fort's sentries when Indians approached.

Kinney located the camp on a plateau, just a few hundred yards from the river, affording lookouts over a mile of visibility in all directions. Beyond the plateau the ground sloped down toward the river into a wide grassy flood plain extending as far as the eye could see. It would be a plentiful source of hay, crucial for the oxen, horses, and pack animals.

Almost immediately, Kinney's men began constructing log buildings to house the troops and store their supplies. In the very center of the parade grounds the soldiers planted a flagpole to fly the stars and stripes. Each morning, to the sound of drums and bugles the men raised the American flag, and in the evening lowered it to the sound of one cannon blast.

On October 3 the men began to build the stockade. It would be roughly square, approximately 375 feet on a side, and made of logs dragged from the mountains and placed upright, side-by-side, in trenches. When earth was packed around the log ends in the trenches a palisade was formed that Indians could not penetrate. At the southeast and northwest corners of the enclosing walls blockhouses extended outward, and cannon were placed there to rake each of the fort's walls when under attack. One wall of the stockade would be constructed of adobe brick.

No sooner was the stockade completed than Sioux war parties attacked the fort and the wagon trains attempting to supply it. Shurly would later recall: "Processing lumber to build the post was a service of great danger—as the Indians, in force, hurry around the fort to catch all small detachments. We had to go up in the mountain to procure the pine logs."[162]

On November 28 C. F. Smith had its last contact of the year with civilization when Second Lieutenant Horatio Bingham arrived with the mail and twenty-four enlisted men. When they left to return to Phil Kearny, the post had only friendly Crow Indians for company. As winter set in not even the Sioux bothered them, and for two months the fort was completely isolated. This was, of course, only a lull in the fighting, for the Sioux were using this time to plan their attacks for the coming spring and summer and were recruiting as many braves as they could find. By the summer of 1867 over four thousand Sioux were camped on the nearby Little Big Horn River, ready to attack the garrison or starve it out. Making matters worse, conditions for the men in the fort had become so cruel that the post surgeon went mad and had to be restrained.[163]

Thus it was with real relief for everyone at the fort when Luther Bradley appeared on July 23 with two companies of the 27th Infantry Regiment, a wagon train of supplies, new Springfield rifles, more ammunition, and a new post surgeon. These reinforcements brought the garrison strength up to something around three hundred men organized into five companies.[164]

SOON AFTER ARRIVING WITH BRADLEY, Shurly found the Crow in the area to be friendly, and often as many as four hundred of them camped near the small fort. They were mortal enemies of the Sioux and often provided grim entertainment for the troops in the fort. An example of how Indians visited their barbaric cruelties on *all* enemies, not just the white man, occurred just after the reinforcements arrived at the fort.

Shurly watched incredulously from the C. F. Smith stockade as Iron Bull, the Crow chief, spotted a war party of fifty to seventy-five Sioux and, with permission from the fort commander, attacked them. A witness, Private James D. Lockwood, described the appalling outcome:

> The little band of Crows hastily mounted and rode out within arrow shot, and then began a parley; a war of words and abuse followed. The soldiers lined the walls of the fort under arms and prepared themselves for a surprise, at the same time eager to see the fight.

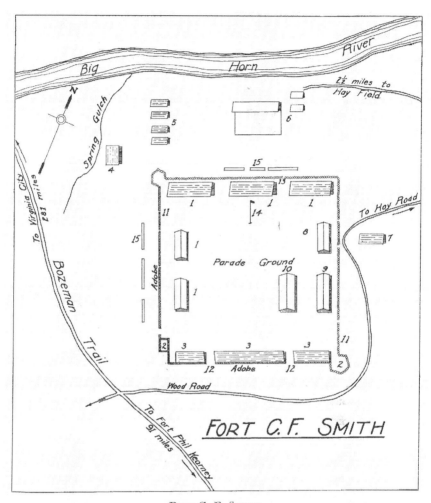

FORT C. F. SMITH

Drawn from information furnished by Vie Willits Garber and F. G. Burnett.
(1) Officers' quarters; (2) Block and guardhouse; diagonal corner also a blockhouse; (3) Barracks; (4) Sawmill; (5) Teamsters' and employes' log cabins; (6) Stable and corral; (7) Sutler's store; (8) Office; (9) Storehouse; (10) Quartermaster's department; (11) Port holes situated at several points in the four walls of the stockade; (12) Wagon gates; (13) Small gate; (14) Flag staff; (15) Rifle pits.

Reprinted by courtesy of the University of Nebraska Press.

The Indians shouted and gesticulated in an amusing manner for some little time; at length each band, in a twinkling, arranged themselves in a circle, riding furiously, one following another in an endless chain, looking like two large moving wheels with their edges together, the warriors of each band lying along their horses, on the opposite side from his enemy, which they were enabled to do by braiding the mane of their ponies so that it formed a loop, through which the rider thrust one arm in such a manner that the bow could be used to discharge arrows underneath the neck of the horse at the respective enemy, the leg being kept in place upon the back of the pony by a strong hair rope, which encircled its body. As soon as the order of battle was arranged, the arrows began to fill the air, each warrior being careful not to hit the horse of his enemy—for they understood that [a dead or wounded horse] would be useless to either side after the battle.

This spectacle had endured some ten or fifteen minutes when Iron Bull, arising to a bold, upright position upon his pony, rode bravely at the Sioux chieftain, and with lasso in hand skillfully threw the noose of it over the head and tightened it around the neck of his foe; then suddenly wheeling, rode for the fort, dragging the unlucky Sioux over the ground at the heels of his horse in a rapid rate. This practically ended the battle, and the Sioux retired, in a demoralized condition.

Iron Bull returned to the fort with his hapless captive dragging behind him and invited the garrison to watch what was to follow, but Colonel Kinney refused and only a few soldiers crept out of the fort, including Lockwood, to view the horror that was to follow. Iron Bull decided to turn his prisoner over to the Crow women.

The tribe was assembled in a level flat of land, from which arose abruptly a high, rocky cliff. The squaws, with their prisoner, were in this flat, the poor wretch in the center, and the tormentors in a circle around.

The chief's warriors and children lined the cliff, from which they could obtain a full view of the entertainment. There was a small fire burning near. The prisoner was entirely nude. A large strong rawhide rope was about his neck, with four or five squaws grasping the opposite end. Occasionally they would jerk the poor wretch to his knees or flat on the ground, and then he would be [forced] to rise [back to his feet] by a woman running up with a piece of bark with hot ashes and coals of fire, which she would place upon his reclining body; no sooner would he regain his feet than he would be jerked this way, that way, slapped, beaten and kicked; burning fire brands were thrust into his ears and, in fact, outrages too shocking and horrible to narrate, were perpetrated.

This treatment was prolonged until, thinking that death would soon relieve the poor victim from their hellish cruelty, they began dismembering him; cutting off his toes, fingers, ears and nose; no part of the miserable being's human anatomy escaped their horrible attentions, and they were constantly encouraged and directed to greater cruelties by the warriors and children.

[James Lockwood], having been trained from boyhood among scenes of war and bloodshed, found that this was too much even for him, and with a feeling of sickening faintness he rushed from the spot and returned to the garrison. Not long afterward, a party of warriors came riding up, dragging the armless, limbless trunk of the poor prisoner, by means of the rope which was still fastened around his neck. The commandant, shocked and disgusted, drove them from the place.[165]

Shurly later wrote[166] of Fort C. F. Smith and his life on the trail:

Old Fort C. F. Smith was situated on one of the most pleasing sites in Wyoming [now a part of Montana]. It was built on a [river terrace] five hundred yards from the Big Horn River, and a mile above the great canyon that extends westward one hundred miles to the Shoshone River. Fort Smith was one of the three posts built to hold the Indians in check. It was a stockade post, and once stood an assault against a force of Indians twenty times the strength of the garrison. After our arrival, the old wooden barricades were replaced by ... adobe [construction], the [adobe] bricks being made [on the fort site] by the men, the lumber [for the doors and window frames] sawed at the mill.

The Indians were bad. The government did not mean war, but the Sioux, Arapahos and [Cheyenne] did. They lost no opportunity to let us know it. We were then considered out of the world, and were, so far as getting news from the east was concerned. Months intervened between mails. Wagon trails were closely guarded, and even then there was constant fighting with the large bands of Indians, who took advantage of any inattention of the escort to "jump the train."

The garrison at the fort was most of the time in a state of siege. A man going from the stockade to the river took chances. Occasionally our friends, the Crows (Absarakas) to the number of three or four hundred would camp near us. Then we had lively times. Their old enemies, the Sioux, would come in to give them a fight, and the garrison would look on.

Old Fort Smith was a monotonous post. The sun would rise out of the plains and disappear over the mountains. Slowly the days passed. Game was abundant. From the top of the stockade could be seen buffalo, elk, antelope, and sometimes bear. Small game was equally plenty, but it was risking one's life to hunt. Many took chances, however, so we were usually provided with game. The country was fruitful in season, with wild plums, grapes, and berries, and the streams were alive with trout. During the winter of 1866, however the garrison lived mainly on corn. No trains came through, while the Indians, numbering thousands, had their winter quarters on the Little Big Horn.

That this post was an isolated and desolate one is best shown by the following story: Our colonel was after a "soft snap" in the east, but he was not in the best graces of Secretary of War Stanton. The 18th Infantry at that time was stationed at Louisville [Saint Louis] enjoying peace. Apparently our colonel had been pestering Stanton to be sent farther east than Saint Louis, for, upon opening another letter from the colonel, Stanton turned to his clerk and demanded: "Which is the next place, to hell, to send a regiment?"

"To the Powder River country," was the prompt reply.

"Then order the 18th Infantry there at once," commanded Stanton. And so we were sent to Fort C. F. Smith![167]

Very soon Shurly would discover that life at Fort C. F. Smith was anything but "monotonous."

Chapter Twelve

THE HAYFIELD FIGHT

First private: "Sergeant, how many Indians do you think
our squad here could lick with these 'ere new guns of ours?"
Sergeant {Norton}: "We can wallop the devil out of
all the Indians that could stand between here and that hill"
(which was about three hundred yards distant).
Second private: "By jinks, I should like to try them a crack,"
sighting over his rifle and then resuming, "I have an idea that I could make
some of them scratch where they didn't itch."
Third private: "So cud I, aisy enough, be jabers; fur it wud be
on the ground that they's be afther scratchin."

—Private James Lockwood, *Life and Adventures of a Drummer Boy*

ALL DURING THE SPRING AND SUMMER OF 1867, the Sioux, Cheyenne, and Arapahos had been strengthening their forces in preparation for an all-out assault on the Bozeman Trail forts. Several thousand of their warriors had assembled fifteen miles to the east of Fort Smith and were quarreling among themselves over the best strategy for annihilation of their enemy. Which fort should be attacked first? Finally, in late July, in a fateful compromise, the arguing chieftains decided to divide their forces and attack Forts Smith and Kearny simultaneously. Small bands of friendly Crow reported this to the soldiers at Fort Smith, but the soldiers could not bring themselves to believe that the Sioux could actually assemble the thousands of braves described by the Crows. So no special preparations were made for the coming battle.

To begin their assault on C. F. Smith, the Sioux planned to overrun a tiny outpost near a shallow creek about three miles from the fort. A. C. Leighton, the post sutler, had constructed it to store the hay before delivering it to the fort. The corral was roughly one hundred feet on a side, with vertical posts located every six feet around its perimeter. The only improvement to security was a single heavy log laid on the ground between each of these posts to protect riflemen from assault. Willow branches and collected underbrush covered the logs to hide the defenders from view but were little protection from bullets and arrows. The corral was intended to provide reasonable protection from the casual Indian attacks that occurred as often as four or five times a day but was not intended for defense against an all-out attack. Usually, a war party of Indians would scare the civilians and soldiers into the corral and then burn the hay they had collected. This time the Indians intended to overrun the outpost and massacre the defenders. Completing this, they would proceed on to the destruction of the fort.

But they were unaware that the soldiers defending the corral had been supplied with new, rapid fire, breech-loading Springfield rifles and generous supplies of ammunition. In addition, the civilians in the camp had Spencer, Henry, and Model 1866 Winchester repeating carbines. Zeke Colvin, one of the civilians, had his favorite Enfield muzzle-loading musket, one he had found on a Missouri battlefield during the Civil War.[168]

On the morning of August 1 the hay party consisted of twenty soldiers and six civilian workers,[169] including Private Lockwood and F. G. "Finn" Burnett, who would both, in the years to come, write varying stories of the fight.[170] Back at the fort, 260 troops were on duty. Lockwood recounted the scene just before the Sioux attacked:

> The mowers [had] rattled on for some time without interruption, and there had been a quantity of hay cut, and the boxes had been taken off from the wagons ... they being replaced upon the wagons by racks, for the drawing of the hay.

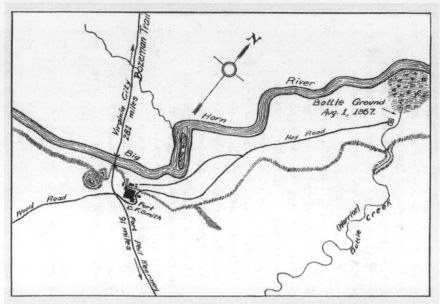

PART OF THE RESERVATION OF FORT C. F. SMITH
Scale, 2 inches to the mile.   Redrawn from a map made January 27, 1881, by Capt. Edward L. Hartz, Twenty-seventh U. S. Infantry.

Reprinted by permission of the University of Nebraska Press.
From Hebard and Brininstool, *The Bozeman Trail, Volume II.*

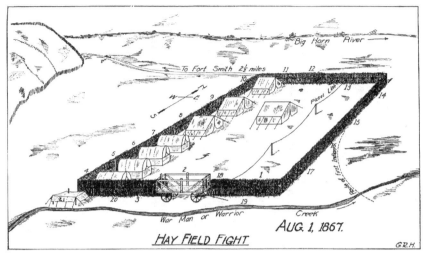

FROM DATA FURNISHED BY F. G. BURNETT
Figures indicate positions of fighters.

(1) Capt. Colvin; (2) Lieut. Sternberg killed; (3) Al Stephens; (4) F. G. Burnett; (5) George Duncan; (6) Man located here who lost his nerve and never fired a shot during the battle; (7) Bob Little; (8) Holister, wounded; died next day; (9, 10, 11) Soldiers; (12) Soldier killed; (13) Soldier stationed here who lost his nerve and threatened to commit suicide; (14) Soldier wounded with arrow; (15) Zeke Colvin; (16) A sergeant; wounded in shoulder; fought bravely throughout battle; (17) Billy Hanes; (18) Soldier; (19) Sioux chief killed here by Capt. Colvin; (20) Soldier known as "Scotty," wounded; fought desperately through engagement; (21) Cook tent at lower left, outside corral.

Reprinted by permission of the University of Nebraska Press.
From Hebard and Brininstool, *The Bozeman Trail, Volume II.*

While these arrangements had been progressing, the soldiers had been lounging around the encampment, playing cards, wrestling, pitching horseshoes in lieu of quoits, and striving to pass time pleasantly, as soldiers usually do at remote stations where there is no society aside from their own.

Upon the day of which we write, the following conversation was held at the camp among them in reference to their estimation of the value of their new breech-loading arms:

First private: "Sergeant, how many Indians do you think our squad here could lick with these 'ere new guns of ours?"

Sergeant [Norton]: "We can wallop the devil out of all the Indians that could stand between here and that hill" (which was about three hundred yards distant).

Second private: "By jinks, I should like to try them a crack," sighting over his rifle and then resuming, "I have an idea that I could make some of them scratch where they didn't itch."

Third private: "So cud I, aisy enough, be jabers; fur it wud be on the ground that they's be afther scratchin."

Sergeant [Norton][171]: "Well, boys, we shall have no such good luck, I fear, for damn them, they won't fight fair, and they never come when you are ready for them. But now I think of it, some of you loosen the screws in the lids of those ammunition boxes, so that if we do need them, we can get at them quick. I am of the opinion that if they come and stay long enough to have those five thousand rounds pumped into them, there will be a number of them in need of the doctor."

Fourth private: "An by the same token, there will be a pile of them that divil a docther wud be only good to."

The sergeant wound up, musingly, with the remark, "I wish that 'boss' hay maker had taken this grass up from around the camp here, as I requested him to do—a fire here would play the devil with us."[172]

A short time after this conversation shots rang out in the direction of the mowing machines and minutes later the mowing crew appeared at full gallop toward the safety of the corral. A small band of Indians was chasing them and circling, hoping to entice the soldiers to follow after them. A few soldiers wanted to follow the Indians but the wiser Sergeant Nolan put them to work digging trenches around the perimeter and using the dirt to form protective barricades.

With defensive preparations complete, they could only watch now as Indian squaws and children climbed a bluff nearby and settled themselves comfortably to watch what they were sure would follow: massacre of white men. In the distance the defenders could see an Indian chief urging his braves to attack.

Finally, and with suddenness, a band of five hundred to six hundred warriors formed and headed straight toward the fortified corral, screaming their war whoops and yells. All the defenders were now flat on the ground, breech-loading rifles loaded and aimed out from between battlements, ammunition heaped beside them.

As soon as the Indians were within rifle range, Lieutenant Sigismund Sternberg stood up and shouted, "Fire!" Instantly, the defender's guns opened up and scattered the Indians in all directions. When the volley ceased, the Indians, believing they were facing muzzle-loaded muskets, rose up and attacked again only to find the guns already loaded, ready, and blazing away. Again the Indians attacked and there was more slaughter and disarray. The guns of the defenders encircled the corral in fire and lead and sounded to some like "the rumbling of a mill, or the hum of machinery."[173] The Indians had to withdraw.

When the Indians saw they could not take the corral in a frontal attack, they set fire to freshly mown hay upwind from the corral, and flames shot into the sky, only to peter out, to the dismay of the Indians, within twenty feet of the barricades. The smoke from the fire, however, allowed the savages to pull some of their dead and wounded away from the perimeter of the corral. Lockwood later reported:

> There was one body which they could not get, as it was too close to the camp for them to venture; this was the body of an Indian, who had actually crawled up to the wagon-box containing the provisions of the party, and had extracted therefrom a mess-pan full of molasses, during the battle. He was seen by a teamster, who, still having one of the old Springfield muzzleloaders, and being short of ammunition for it, had loaded into it a handful of thirty-two caliber pistol cartridges, copper

shells and all. It is hardly necessary to state that this dose did the business for the brave who possessed such an inordinate fondness for sweets.
After the battle, he was still lying "taking his rest," with his pan and
molasses around him.[174]

Soon after the fight started, piles of dead Indians littered the ramparts of the
outpost, and only two of the defenders were dead, both because they foolishly stood
up and ordered the others to stand up and fight like men. The others remained
on their stomachs behind the log barriers with their rifles wounding or killing
attackers with almost every bullet.

After the first mass attack the Indians withdrew and pulled as many of their
wounded away from the perimeter of the corral as best they could. Then they
organized a second mass attack, flinging themselves against other sections of the
corral walls, only to be stopped by more withering fire from the breech-loading
Springfields and Zeke Colvin's favorite Enfield. Similar in intensity to an attack
that took place the next day ninety miles south at Fort Phil Kearny, the Indians
were packed so closely together that the bullets from the Springfields passed
through multiple attacking Indians as they rushed the ramparts. Indian casualties
were fierce, and they soon broke off the attack and withdrew.

By midday the Indians had pulled back far enough to allow a party from the
corral to bring water back from nearby Warrior Creek without forcing a single
shot. Soon after, the Indians returned to bring sniper fire to bear on the corral.

Just before the battle resumed after noon, a Sioux chief rode up to the east bank
of the creek to reconnoiter. He had not realized he was within rifle range, and an
accurate shot knocked him off his horse and into the creek. There he struggled
with his wound until he drowned. This provoked the next charge by the Indians
from the slopes west of the compound. A civilian named George Duncan brought
down the leader of the attackers, and he was dragged off the battlefield and revived
some distance away by warriors in the face of steady fire from the defenders. After
this the attack lost its punch and the braves retreated to plan their next move.

The next attack came from the south and on foot. It was led by a chief said to
be a Minneconjou Sioux. Al Colvin (Zeke Colvin's brother) guessed correctly that
the attack would come from this direction and had moved most of the men to the
south side of the corral just in time. To attack from the south, the Indians had to

wade across the shallow Warrior Creek, move through willow bushes, then rush across yards of open ground before reaching the corral. Colvin ordered the men to hold their fire until he signaled.

The attack opened with a mass of Indians rushing down the far bank of the creek, their chief in the lead. When the Indians emerged from the willows, the chief was easily cut down by a volley from the defenders. Volley after volley from the defenders cut into the attacking Indians who, despite heavy casualties, tenaciously rushed the enclosure. Time and again the Sioux attackers bravely tried to retrieve the body of their fallen chief but were never able to get to him and lost many men in the attempt. Finally, the warriors broke off the attack, retreating across the creek with the dead and wounded they had been able to retrieve. Other than sporadic sniper fire from long range, this was the last big attack from the Sioux. Not long afterward, bands of Indians were seen riding away to the east.[175]

The fight could not be seen from the fort, but the sounds were unmistakable. Lieutenant George Henry Palmer, in command of forty soldiers from Company E and a small supply train, passed within view during the battle and estimated that eight hundred to a thousand Indians were involved in the fight at the hayfield and saw that the tiny band of defenders was holding out, although in desperate straits. Palmer quickly returned to the fort and asked for reinforcements to be sent to the outpost. But post commander Bradley refused his request, possibly because he feared a repeat of the Fetterman disaster. On into the afternoon the fight continued, but Bradley ordered the fort gates closed and locked, a performance that, ever since, has had little comment by the army.[176]

Finally, around three in the afternoon Bradley relented and allowed Lieutenant Shurly out of the fort with twenty men to scout the area. Shurly soon attracted Indians, and in the distance he saw someone desperately riding toward him under attack by four Indians. It was a white man and, as Shurly watched, they knocked him off his horse into a dry creek bed. Shurly and his men galloped to his rescue, scattering his attackers just in time to save his life. All this was seen from the fort and finally energized post commander Bradley into sending out Companies G and H, under the command of Major Tom Burrowes, along with a small field howitzer, to reinforce Shurly. The stricken man turned out to be Private Charles Bradley (no relation to the camp commander) who, during a lull in the fight at the corral, sometime after noon, had volunteered to ride to the fort for help. Bradley bravely dodged arrows and bullets, evaded capture, and made it as far as the dry creek where Shurly found him.[177]

Burrowes' two companies proved to be enough to disperse the Indians and rescue the men trapped in the corral.[178] In the encounter, Shurly was slightly wounded in the hand.

The official report submitted by Major Burrowes, three days after the attack, provides a harrowing, firsthand account of the rescue mission:

> Fort C. F. Smith, M. T.
> August 3rd, 1867
> To: 1st Lieut. George M. Templeton
> 27 US Inf.
> Post Adjutant
> Fort C. F. Smith, M. T.
> Sir:
>
> I have the honor to report that at 4 o'clock P.M. August 1st, 1867 I was ordered with "G" Co., 27 US Inf., to go to the relief of Lieut. E. R. Shurley [*sic*], 27 US Inf., who was in charge of twenty mounted infantry and citizens and sharply engaged with Indians whilst reconnoitering the ground between the garrison and the hay field.
>
> I proceeded with my force until I formed a junction with Lieut. Shurley, when the Indians with whom he was engaged retired out of range. When I had secured Lieut. Shurley from danger, I was about to return to the post when I received a reinforcement of a detachment of "H" Co., 27 US Inf., 1st Lieut. R. N. Fenton comdg., one mountain howitzer and its gun squad; with orders from Brevet Brig. General L. P. Bradley, Lieut. Col. 27 US Inf. [commanding the] post, to move forward with my command to the hay corral, relieve them, bring back the killed and wounded, and do whatever I might deem best after I arrived there and discovered the exact status of affairs.
>
> In obedience to these instructions I moved forward throwing out Lt. Shurley and his mounted party to protect my flanks and guard against surprise. The mounted men were supported by an infantry skirmish line, Lieut. Fenton in charge.

When I arrived at the hay ground I found the following casualties to have occurred—viz:

Lieut. Sigismund Sternberg "G" Co. 27 Inf. killed

Pvt. Nevins "H" Co. 27 Inf. killed

Sergeant Norton "I" Co. 27 Inf. wounded—left shoulder.

Pvt. Henry C. Vinson "G" Co. 27 Inf. wounded—both legs—right leg fracture.

Pvt. Francis M. Law "E" Co. 27 Inf. wounded—knee.

Citizen J. G. Hollister wounded—chest—since died.

Upon surveying the position I found it untenable from its nearness to a thickly brushed creek from which the enemy could come very close and deliver their fire unseen, without great sacrifice of life.

I immediately threw out a line of skirmishers, Lieut. Fenton in charge, and ordered the dead and wounded to be loaded at once and all the available mules to be harnessed. I then discovered that out of twenty-two mules two had been killed and seventeen wounded, many of them severely, having from three to nine arrow wounds each. With this limited and inefficient motive power I found I could not transport all the property. I therefore ordered all heavy articles to be left such as wagons, wagon beds and the mowing machines and the wagons loaded to the utmost capacity of the mules with more valuable property, judging that the enemy would not disturb the property thus left. The result has proven its correctness for today these articles were recovered uninjured. I was obliged for want of transportation to abandon some wagon sheets and articles of like description as the owners preferred to save lighter articles of more value. The articles so abandoned I burned to prevent them falling into the hands of the enemy.

I made these dispositions as rapidly as possible for the wounded men were sadly in want of medical attendance. During this time quite a lively skirmish was kept up with the Indians.

They appeared on the bluffs all around me in numbers which I estimate at from 450 to 500 whilst on the bluffs in rear a party of about 300 more were within supporting distance of the main force. Upon conversing with the contractors and men on the hay detail I found my estimate considerably lower than theirs.

When ready to return I opened on the Indians with the artillery and cleared the bluffs under cover of the fire. I ordered Lt. Shurley to take possession of the bluffs and Lieut. Fenton to support him with his skirmishers whilst I with my company and the train moved toward the garrison by the river road. I moved forward after these dispositions were made in the manner heretofore described, only being obliged to halt once and clear some Indians off a bluff round the base of which I was obliged to pass with the train. Here the howitzer was again called into use. I arrived at Fort C. F. Smith at 8:30 o'clock p.m. Aug. 1st, 1867. The distance marched was about seven miles. I lost neither men or animal. Lieut. Shurley was slightly scratched on the hand in the action. My command in going to relieve the hay party was eighty men; in returning it aggregated about one hundred.

Credit is due both Lieut. Fenton and Lieut. Shurley for the zeal displayed and the fidelity with which they carried out all my instructions.

I deem it proper to add that from personal inspection of the corral (which was but a brush screen, rifle pits having been constructed after the first dash of the Indians was made) that the fight was a success to us. The Indians were certainly very determined and the number of arrows in and around the work shows that they came very close.

When I arrived I found one Indian lying dead within fifteen paces of the work. I am fully convinced that the number of Indians killed must be from eighteen to twenty-two or three, with a goodly number wounded.

All agree in this that the men behaved exceedingly well, that they were calm and deliberate seldom wasting a shot although their commanding officer, Lt. Sternberg, was killed at the first onset and Sergeant Norton, the second in command, placed "hors de combat" shortly after.

The new breech-loading musket gave the men an opportunity to fire much more rapidly when the occasion demanded and with less exposure of the person than the Springfield rifle, whilst the superiority of the sights gives more accuracy to the aim. The confidence which it gives the men from the rapidity with which it can be fired and the telling effects of the shots tends to keep them calm, composed and confident under fire.

The Indians engaged were Sioux, Cheyenne, and Arapaho.

I am, sir, very respectfully your obt. servt.

T. B. Burrowes, Capt. 27 US Inf., Brevet Maj. USA.[179]

Private Lockwood reported that:

Before leaving the ground they scalped the dead Indian in the latest and most artistic western style, then beheaded him, placing his head upon a high pole, leaving the carcass to his friends or the wolves. The general verdict was "that he came to his death on account of his extreme fondness for government molasses," the soldiers, of course, making due allowance for the ignorant savage's perverted tastes.[180]

Besides the heroic efforts of Lieutenant Shurly, Major Burrowes, and their men, much credit for the survival of the men in the hayfield corral must go to the Springfield rifles with which they were supplied. These were single-shot rifles, loaded from the breech rather than from the muzzle of the barrel. Moreover, the cartridge was a single entity rather than a combination of ball, powder, and percussion cap. The action of reloading thus allowed the rifle and the soldier to remain hidden while he opened the breech, emptied the weapon, and reloaded with a fresh cartridge. One could easily discharge four to six shots per minute from these breech-loaders, rather than perhaps two shots from the earlier muzzle-loading Springfields.

If the old muzzle-loading Springfield muskets had been used, these defenders would have been easily overrun and massacred. The Indians had learned early on that they could provoke a volley from defenders using the old muskets, then rush them and overcome them before they could reload. This had been amply demonstrated in the battle with Fetterman. Now the tide had turned in favor of the white man, and at both this battlefield and one near Fort Phil Kearny, called the Wagon Box Fight, huge Indian casualties were to teach them a renewed respect for U.S. Army firepower.

Estimates of enemy dead vary widely, from seven or eight as admitted by the Indians, to statements by Finn Burnett, a participant in the battle, that dead Indians were "piled up" around the corral. Burnett wrote that Al Colvin took charge of the soldiers after Lieutenant Sternberg was killed, and believes Colvin killed more Indians that day than any man before or since.

> He was armed with a sixteen-shot Henry repeating rifle, and had a thousand rounds of ammunition. He was a dead shot, and if he missed an Indian in that fight, none of us ever knew it. He fired about three hundred shots that day, and after the fight the ground out a little way from where he was lying was simply covered with dead.... As to the Indian loss in this fight, it would be impossible for me to make a correct estimate, but I would swear ... that Captain Colvin himself killed and wounded more than 150 of the Indians.... [He] was one of the best rifle shots I ever saw, being absolutely steady under fire. As he did most of his shooting at distances of from twenty to seventy-five yards, it was almost impossible for him to miss a target as big as man at such short range.[181]

One has to question the estimates of all the witnesses except Finn Burnett as being too low. If the Springfields were as good as claimed, if the Indians were truly surprised by the rapidity of their fire and attacked in waves as reported, if the battle lasted from nine in the morning until rescue arrived around five in the afternoon,[182] and if the "rattle and roar" of the breech-loading rifles was indeed "as steady and continuous as the rumbling of a mill or the hum of machinery," as reported by Private Lockwood,[183] then Indian casualties must have been extraordinarily high.

The Indians were skilled at retrieving their battlefield dead and wounded and managed to remove all but one by the time the battle ended. So it would be reasonable and prudent for Major Burrowes to report no more than eighteen to twenty-three had been killed since he personally had seen only one Indian body. He had no way of knowing otherwise. If no more that twenty-three had been killed, the corral defenders would have had to have been very poor marksmen and the battle nowhere near as significant as reported.

AFTER THE HAYFIELD FIGHT, Shurly continued his duties. As quartermaster he was always in a search for supplies in and around the countryside that surrounded the fort. In 1897 a newspaper reporter for the *Chicago Daily Inter-Ocean* wrote:

Lumber in abundance could be found for the new post, but nowhere could any lime be discovered. The Crows, who were friendly, reported that the Sioux had gone to the lower country. Vigilance at the station was accordingly relaxed, and Major Shurly made repeated excursions alone in the neighborhood in search of limestone.

He was one day at the mountain foot riding along a natural road, which the soldiers named the "backbone." He saw some stones which looked like limestone, and he dismounted to investigate. As he was stooping over the specimens he looked up the mountain bluffs, and about sixty feet above he was dazed to see the grinning, painted faces of about twenty Indians. To remount took only a moment, and before the horse's hoofs clattered on the road the wild, savage whoops of the Sioux echoed along the mountain.

When his horse's head turned from the curving road to the plateau, which separated him from the post, the lone rider met with even a greater surprise—the plain was full of Indians. Thought and action were coincident. Major Shurly dashed into a deep ravine, an old water course, about a quarter of a mile long, which led to the river. His horse seemed to move like the wind. The race was a series of springs, for the bed of the ravine was like a huge, rugged stairway, some of the steps being over fifteen feet high. The maddened Indians clambered over the banks as thick as flies, some rolling down the boulders and others speeding across after the fleeing fugitive. Some charm protected the soldier and the ever-changing yells lent nerve and energy to the plucky horse.

A garrison, aroused by the war whoops, watched the strange scene, but, seeing only part of it—the central figure being hidden in the gulch—did not understand it. When horse and rider plunged from the ravine's mouth to the deep river, a cheer went up from the stockade that for the moment silenced the yells of the Indians. The frenzied warriors had missed their prey, and a few minutes later Captain Shurly stood surrounded by his comrades.[184]

Finally, in late October, it was Edmund Shurly's turn to take command of a wagon train. Records show that Edmund Shurly commanded the military escort of just three wagon trains, and that two resulted in some of the bloodiest fights on the Bozeman Trail. This was to be Edmund's first escort command, and it would be a train of empty wagons bound for Fort Phil Kearny.

Chapter Thirteen

LIEUTENANT E. R. P. SHURLY'S FIGHT

"I saw the situation at a glance. I told the driver of the gun to make for the corral, save the gun at all hazards! Those mules flew!"

—E. R. P. Shurly, while under attack, November 4, 1867[185]

IN CHAPTER ONE WE LEFT LIEUTENANT SHURLY wounded and dazed as he and his men battled seven hundred Sioux for the supplies in his wagon train on a snow-covered battlefield on November 4, 1867. The Indians had made off with wagons containing their ammunition and warm blankets, which would have protected them against the winter cold. Two brave soldiers had just slipped out of camp after dusk to ride to Fort Phil Kearny for help, but chances of them getting through were very slim.

Luckily, Shurly never really lost command of his senses after he was wounded, and it was never necessary for him to turn over command to his wagon master. When his wound was cleaned and bound, Shurly's mind cleared and he organized his troops and the civilians for a long engagement. Huge bags of corn, intended for the soldiers of C. F. Smith, were pulled off the circled wagons and pressed around them as protection against arrows and the weather. The howitzer would not be fired without explicit approval from Shurly and then only in an extreme

141

situation. The men were warned to drastically conserve their remaining ammunition and other supplies. Fires were lit to warm the men and allow them a sparse dinner. At this point all were certain help was days if not weeks away.

Shurly now had time to review the events leading up to the predicament he was in. The trip south had been pretty much uneventful until the train got within about six miles of Phil Kearny, whereupon they heard sharp reports of a cannon and could see a wagon train ahead of them, corralled and fending off an attack. Shurly and his men immediately charged into the melee and, along with elements of the 27th Infantry now arriving on the scene, scattered the attackers. When calm returned, Colonel John E. Smith, commanding the infantry contingent, ordered Shurly to assume command of the northbound, heavily-laden Wells-Fargo train and escort it to C. F. Smith. As an afterthought, Smith decided that perhaps Shurly should take along the 12-pound field howitzer. After all, these Sioux were known to be Red Cloud's warriors and were desperate for the warm blankets and ammunition carried by the train. Spare ammunition for the howitzer was secured in the lead wagon with the other ammunition, and the cannon and its caisson pulled by mules brought up the rear of the train.

Weather conditions steadily deteriorated as all of this was going on, and Shurly wondered if it was possible to continue. It was snowing on and off, and a frigid, howling wind was causing the oxen to rebel. But they started out anyway and advanced for a day and a half over the treacherous ground, progressing no more than four miles because of the weather.[186] As they struggled with their wagons and oxen, he and his men saw small bands of Indians all along their path watching their progress, but it was not until they found themselves at a particularly awkward position on a steep ravine near Goose Creek that their enemy gathered up a sizable force and attacked.

The conclusion of this fight, now known either as Lieutenant E. R. P. Shurly's Fight, or as the Battle of Goose Creek,[187] is probably best described by Shurly himself in his 1888 letter to James S. Brisbin, a soldier who had since become a writer of western history.[188]

> I was suffering fearfully with my foot; the arrow had passed through
> so that the point protruded through the sole of my boot [but there was]
> no time for a surgical operation. I caused the sacks of corn to be unloaded

and piled under the wagons, [and] the mouth of the circle to be closed so that it just [left] room to operate the gun. [Now was the first opportunity for the] wounded [to be] attended to. The Indians kept up their fire but did not come close. We could see about a hundred of them inspecting the wagons left [outside the circle on] the other side of the ravine. They were a prize more precious than diamonds to Indians.

I was very weak but had pulled out, or rather pushed through, the arrow and bandaged my foot with my necktie.

I said, "Bring some ammunition for the guns. Let the men fill their cartridge boxes."

But you may be the judge of my dismay when I learned that the ammunition wagon and its mules [were] gone. [It had] in fact run right into a lot of Indians [at our front] coming from the direction of Goose Creek. [This was the lead wagon. It carried ammunition for the troops' guns and for the howitzer. The wagon driver had abandoned the wagon and the mule team bolted in panic as soon as the gunfire began. The Indians had their prize.]

Our command consisted now of thirty-one soldiers with about forty rounds to each man left, twenty-six drivers, one wagon master, William Harwood, brother of Lieutenant Harwood now in the service, with a few revolvers amongst them—it seems they did not expect [that their situation would come to this]—and a small [twelve] pound howitzer with all of six rounds available for it.

We had scarcely our arrangements made when we saw the Indians descending from the bluffs in large numbers. The [war] party [consisted of] about seven hundred [braves] under [the command of] Red Cloud.

I told the men that the first one that fired without my order I would shoot. I told them the enemy would know that we only had a few rounds of ammunition; on they came as gallant as I have seen in the Army of the Potomac. I did not want to use the [howitzer] if possible except in a great extremity, but saw this charge was too formidable as a reserve was forming to back up the first. So I concluded to use a shell. Mister Harwood served the gun and [was] most effective.[189]

After an interview with Shurly in 1889, Brisbin wrote:

The first shell fired burst directly over the Indians and greatly terrified them—they went off that part of the field as fast as their legs could
carry them. They soon returned, however, and as if ashamed of being
beaten by a handful of men renewed the fight with great fury. They
got in the bush along the creek and from this cover greatly annoyed
the little garrison. Shurly surprised them by making a charge into the
brush with a party of men and run them out at the point of the bayonet
almost. They made frequent charges during the day but were always
repulsed, the gun did good service and whenever it was run out they
gave way. Once when they came too close Shurly put a solid round shot
in the howitzer and fired it into the mass of Indians. It killed several of
them and then went on plowing up the ground and bounding into the
air until it came across a squaw and child and killed them both. The
Indians at once got out of the way of this bad medicine gun. The mere
presenting of it and pointing of it at them would cause them to take to
their heels. At length the Indians gave up their charges and resorted to
their favorite method of attack by stealth and circling around hoping
to pick off the little garrison in detail. But the soldiers lay close and let
them ride and whoop and howl to their hearts content. Only occasionally when a young buck braver than the rest and wishing to show his
courage came too close, would [the soldiers] fire, and then generally
with fatal effect. From the bluffs a corps of Indian archers continually
showered the fort with arrows until Shurly sent out a volley and almost
his last shell, when they left. (It is a fact that after this battle a wagon-
load of arrows was picked up on the battlefield.)

The day wore slowly away ... but at last the sun went down and
night closed in—dark as pitch. It is seldom Indians will attack at night;
they are not fond of hand-to-hand conflict in the dark, which is nearly
always the result of a night attack. Shurly knew this and the men had
little fear of being disturbed until morning. The Indian loves to sleep
and will always take a good nights rest when he can get it.

So the little garrison began to make themselves comfortable. There were but two horses left with the command—the captain's horse and the one the wagon master rode. Shurly called for volunteers to try and reach Fort Phil Kearny and acquaint General Smith of their desperate condition. He thought by following up the ravine to the mountain the men could get through. Most of the Indians were still on the bluffs or had gone down the stream. The night was dark as pitch. Two men volunteered to try it, and ... started out. A strong guard was posted and the rest of the tired men lay down to sleep as well as the groans of the wounded would allow them.

At early light the Indians were on hand again and the fight was recommenced. They seemed to have resolved during the night to be very brave and wipe out the white men that day. They charged with a yell but the deadly rifles of the soldiers and the awful shells from the howitzer soon changed their minds and they fell back in confusion. [By now] most of the poor oxen had been killed or wounded and many of the men had slight wounds, six men [were] seriously wounded, and three were dead.

In the afternoon when the fighting was again becoming lively a soldier called out, "Look up there, Captain—on the mountain toward Phil Kearny. There comes another lot of Indians!"

The captain did look and then gave a great shout of joy as his heart came up into his throat. The men approaching did not ride like Indians and his experienced eye at once made them [out] to be United States Cavalry coming to his relief. His messengers had got through safely and there were the yellow-legs riding for dear life.

"Saved—we are saved!" went up from a score of throats and even the poor dying [and] wounded soldiers raised up and strained their fading sight to see the troopers while tears of joy ran down their cheeks.

The Indians saw the relief at hand, too, and as if realizing their prey was about to escape them rushed down upon the fort and began a terrific attack, attempting to carry it by storm before the cavalry could get up. It was a perilous moment for the cavalry was still a mile off and five minutes in that fort would suffice to murder every man and take his scalp. But the Indians might as well have charged a stonewall; every man stood true and fired fast and accurately, for this was their [enemy's] last charge and the result was life or death to the little garrison. Even the old howitzer chimed in and sent its last two shells into the thickest of the enemy. The sound of the conflict grew heavier and heavier; the smoke rose and enveloped the combatants and from out of it came the shouts of men, shrieks of pain, and the cries of the wounded and dying.

Suddenly there was great confusion among the Indians; the gleam of sabers was seen at their backs and they fled over the hills. Major David Gordon, 2nd Cavalry, with his troops had [arrived] and the troubles and perils of Shurly and his men were over.

Said he to Shurly as he rode up, "Old man when I saw the Reds around you from yonder mountain I could not hold back and just cut loose and came for all that was out to get a whack at them."

Very soon after Gordon's arrival Major Nelson B. Switzer, of the 2nd Cavalry, with [three] more companies of Cavalry came up. The horses were very much blown for they had been riding hard ever since they heard of Captain Shurly's peril and had arrived just in time in all probability to save him. Shurly likely will not admit this for with all his clerical appearance and mild ways he is a man who knows not the meaning of the word fear and thinks he could whip the world with a very small army.

Singularly enough a part of the cavalry that came to the relief of Shurly and his beleaguered men had passed the day before within three miles of him and heard the firing, but thought it was some men out hunting antelope and went on to Phil Kearny. They had been on a scouting expedition to Fort C. F. Smith and had not seen any Indians.

The battlefield where Shurly had fought presented a terrible appearance after the conflict was over. Men, horses, oxen, broken guns, and the debris of the battle lay mangled together. The corn sacks bristled with arrows and the corn was filled with bullets.

Red Cloud, the famous Sioux chief, commanded the Indians in this battle, and Shurly was one of the few if not the only officer in our army who ever came off victorious in a set-to with the greatest Indian warrior and general of the plains.[190]

According to Shurly's official report, written three days after the battle, the relief force consisted of "three companies of cavalry, Major Gordon with his company as additional escort, a surgeon and ambulance for the wounded, and a bale of blankets for the use of the men."[191]

The names of the dead and wounded, from Shurly's official report were:

Killed

Corporal Peter Donnelly, Co. H, 27th Infantry

Private Harold Partenheimer, Co. G, 27th Infantry

Wounded

Corporal Gordon Fitzgerald, Co. I, 27th Infantry

Private James McGeever, Co. E, 27th Infantry [since dead]

Citizen Wm. Freeland, Driver, Howitzer[192]

In his report Shurly strongly complements Corporal Peter Donnelly, Company H, Corporal Gordon Fitzgerald of Company I, and William Freeland for their bravery. Shurly was promoted to brevet captain for his heroism in this fight.

ALTHOUGH SHURLY'S FIGHT PALED in comparison to Crooks' Campaign or Custer's fight a decade later, it was a perfect illustration, for anyone interested in the question, of the hopelessness of the army's strategy for controlling Indian aggression with statically defended strong points. Within a year this strategic weakness would become obvious to army commanders, and the Bozeman Trail forts would be abandoned in favor of a strategy of armed incursions into Sioux territory to attack them at their base camps.

Chapter Fourteen

SHURLY'S BATTLE AT
FORT RENO

The Red Warriors aimed to spring from the ground. The woods were alive with them,
and they yelled like demons, as they thought the extermination of the little band certain.
Famous Red Cloud was in command of the Indians.

—Edmund Shurly

BY THE SPRING OF 1868, the United States War Department, many if not most
of the troops defending the Bozeman Trail, and the American public as well had
come to the conclusion that the Bozeman Trail forts were nearing the end of their
usefulness. Civilian traffic on the trail had dropped off to a trickle. The transcontinental railroad had now pushed almost to Salt Lake City and immigrants seeking
gold in Montana were finding it easier and safer to travel west by train in relative
comfort to Ogden, Utah, then due north to the gold country around Virginia City,
Montana, by stagecoach, entirely bypassing the Sioux hunting grounds.

IN MARCH LUTHER BRADLEY LEFT FORT SMITH and Captain Andrew Sheridan
Burt assumed command of the fort. Burt and his wife, Elizabeth, and their
two children had arrived at the fort just weeks after Shurly was wounded in his
November fight. "Andy" Burt, considered one of the best Indian fighters in the

army,[193] would continue a brilliant career with the army, retiring in 1902 as a brigadier general.[194]

In April a conference was held at Fort Laramie with elements of the Crow and Sioux nations, and rumors began circulating that the Bozeman Trail forts might soon be abandoned. In mid-May orders went out to secure bids for the sale of stores and other goods at the forts, and on June 16 the first soldiers, under the command of Captain Edward L. Hartz, departed Fort Smith for old Fort Kearney in Nebraska.[195]

BY THE END OF JUNE EDMUND SHURLY'S FOOT HAD PRETTY MUCH HEALED and in early July he was ordered back to C. F. Smith. There he finally met Captain Burt and in the years to come they would become close friends. His wife, at the suggestion of General William T. Sherman, kept a diary of their life on the frontier, and it would survive to become one of the few records of life at C. F. Smith.[196] The diary often mentions Shurly.

On July 7 Captain Burt called Shurly to his office and handed him Special Order 81. Burt informed him Lieutenant Albert John Neff, commanding officer of Company A, 2nd Cavalry, unconscious and in no pain, had died of dysentery at five that morning. Company A had been ordered to depart C. F. Smith and take up residence in one of the new forts along the Oregon Trail, Fort D. A. Russell, built to protect the new railroad that would eventually extend all the way to California. Now Company A needed a new commanding officer. "Lieutenant Shurly, you will replace Lieutenant Neff as commander of Company A, and relocate your men and equipment to Fort D. A. Russell. With you and your supply wagons will be paymaster Brevet Lieutenant Colonel Robert D. Clarke and the body of Lieutenant Neff. Private Michael Quarters will be with him as his bodyguard. You have one day to prepare for the move."

This was only the third wagon train that Shurly had escorted, the second nearly costing him and his men their lives. This one would prove to be every bit as hazardous.

Early on the morning of July 8 Shurly had the bugler call assembly, and Company A fell into ranks and came to attention. When the last of the baggage was loaded into the wagons and all was secure, the assembled men marched out of Fort C. F. Smith, never to see it again. It was a cloudless day and the train was able

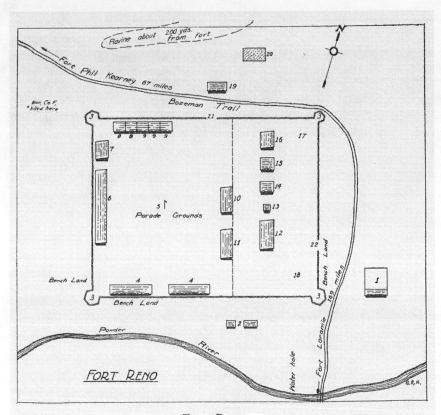

FORT RENO

Prepared from information furnished by A. B. Ostrander, Vie Willits Garber, F. G.
Burnett, and Edward Parmelee.

(1) Corral and teamsters' quarters; (2) Sawmill; (3) Blockhouses; (4) Barracks; (5)
Flagstaff; (6) Storehouse; (7) Commanding officer's quarters; (8) Officers' quarters;
Eastern 9) Post headquarters and Adjutant's office; (Middle 9) Post headquarters,;
master's headquarters; (Western 9) Officers' quarters; (10) Hospital; (11) Laundry;
(12) Storehouse; (13) Guardhouse; (14) Barber shop; (15) Bakery; (16) Mess room;
(17) Wood storage; (18) Place for wagons; (19) Sutler's store; (20) Cemetery; (21,
22) Gates.

Reprinted by permission of the University of Nebraska Press,
from Hebard and Brininstool, *The Bozeman Trail, Volume II.*

to pass the distant ridge to the south overlooking the Big Horn Valley before temperatures topped one hundred degrees. The trip south to Phil Kearny was thankfully uneventful, and they arrived there intact on July 12. After three days of rest and resupply, Shurly's train departed Phil Kearny, again in blistering heat. But now there was reason for worry. Shurly, an experienced Indian fighter by this time, saw signs of hostile Indians everywhere. Despite assurances of peaceful intent from the "Indian Peace Commission," he was "uneasy."

On the afternoon of July 18 the sight of decrepit Fort Reno rose into view, beyond it, gently flowing, the winding, shallow Powder River. The fort's stockade had been rudely constructed in 1865 of cottonwood logs "of uneven lengths, leaning and generally frightful,"[197] by its original garrison, men only too glad to be mustered out of the army by General Carrington when he arrived in 1866. Inside the stockade were rough stables and a warehouse, and crude, earthen-roofed buildings with dirt floors. Although this construction was common to most forts built at this time, what was not common was the slovenly upkeep obvious everywhere one looked. The fort did not have the spit and polish Shurly was used to seeing at the two Northern forts.

The fort had been renamed in 1866 for popular General Jesse L. Reno who, Shurly well remembered, had been killed in the battle of South Mountain less than a mile from Shurly's regiment as it chased Colonel John M. Steedman's South Carolinians from the north slope of South Mountain. Shurly would note several adobe-walled buildings had been added since he had passed through the fort on his way north.

A gentle slope of about one hundred yards separated the fort from the Powder River. Surrounding the fort was a rolling terrain of scrub weeds and cactus and a pattern of shallow, rugged ravines leading erratically toward the river. On each side of the river was a thin line of cottonwood trees that could not rescue the land from an overpowering monotony. About two miles upstream, to the southwest, was a grassy plain ideal for pasturing the tired and hungry stock that had pulled Shurly's wagons in the sweltering heat. There, Shurly decided, his men would camp for the night. They could cool off in the muddy waters of the river before bedding down, but they would have to be vigilant. Captain Green, who had rescued him from his trap on Goose Creek six months earlier, had lost seventy-five horses to Indians not far from there just days before.

Fort Reno, when Shurly arrived, had a complement of ninety-seven men, just two companies, down from five companies that had garrisoned the fort only a few months before. First Lieutenant Jacob Paulus, 27th U.S. Infantry, commanded the fort now after the recent death of Major Benjamin Franklin Smith, its third commander in two years. Paulus had been in the group of young men with Shurly who had joined the army at Kearney four days before moving west with Carrington and would himself be replaced with a permanent commander in the weeks to come. According to Shurly:

> [Sunday, July 19:] About two o'clock in the morning, the sergeant-of-the-guard awoke me and said a large herd of buffaloes was crossing the river. I immediately got up and sure enough there was a large train moving across the river—but it [was not] buffalo. They were Indian ponies, and quite a number of them. I ordered the teamsters to "hitch up" and we returned to the stockade, arriving there about daylight.
>
> As day broke, we could see across the river a couple of Indians driving an ox up and down in the open. The Powder River at this point was about twice the width of the Chicago River [but shallow]. I knew at once that the Indians whose ponies I had seen during the night had captured the [garrison's] stock of beef. The solitary ox was paraded as a taunt—and for another purpose, which will appear presently....
>
> Soon after sunrise, as I was viewing the antics of the Indians on the opposite bank of the river, [Paulus] came to me and said, "Captain you will take some of your cavalry and recapture that ox."[198]

Shurly refused, seeing this as a crude Indian ruse to draw his soldiers into an ambush, as he had seen two years before in the Fetterman massacre. Paulus, unconvinced this was an Indian trap, ordered his own men, the soon to retire First Sergeant William L. Day and seven privates, to cross the river on foot and search for cattle. Horrified, Shurly watched as they crossed the river and marched upstream half a mile looking for the lost animals. Soon, Day's men came across five Indians that appeared friendly. But then they spied twenty-five more warriors laying in wait for them in a ravine. The fire fight began.

Meanwhile, Shurly, realizing Paulus had ordered Sergeant Day and his men into mortal danger, ordered fifty of his men to saddle up and prepare for action. When the gunfire broke out, Shurly's men climbed on their horses and raced to engage the Indians. They crossed the river, galloped along the river bottom to a ravine beyond Day's men, then turned and fired at the flanks of their enemy to distract them. Day's eight men quickly scampered back safely to the fort.

The Indians now turned to Shurly's men, gathered about the soldiers' flanks, and prepared to send in a dangerous fire. Shurly, seeing more Indians appearing all around him, feared the trap was about to be sprung and ordered his bugler to sound recall. As the men turned to head for the fort, Private George F. Peach was encircled and pulled from his horse.[199] By now as many as three hundred Indians were all around Shurly's men, and they had to dismount and take up positions in a ravine. Mixed into the crackle of rifle fire and Indian war whoops now were the screams of Private Peach in agony as the Indians dismembered him there on the battlefield. The screams of Private Peach were sounds the soldiers would long remember.

In the ravine the soldiers and their mounts were well protected by the rocks and dirt, and they set up a deadly fire with their breech-loading rifles. Shurly remembered years later: "The Red Warriors aimed to spring from the ground. The woods were alive with them, and they yelled like demons, as they thought the extermination of the little band certain. One of the fiercest fights of my life followed."[200]

The battle raged for almost an hour before Shurly felt it possible to remount and get safely back to the fort. Other than Private Peach, only Private George Miller was wounded, but he too made it back to the fort on his wounded horse. Shurly later wrote: "The loss to the Indians, I think, was severe. I saw many ponies without riders. I think it will be a low estimate to place the loss of the Indians at fifteen killed and wounded."[201] The attackers were identified as a band of Man-Afraid-of-His-Horses, Indians the soldiers had thought were friendly. Shurly thought Red Cloud was in command of the Indians.[202]

Returning to the fort, Shurly found the fight was far from over. Paulus and his men were heavily engaged in a fire fight of their own along one side of the stockade. Shurly's men joined in, and the Indians scattered. Later, Shurly and Paulus realized they had witnessed new Indian tactics. Standing and fighting was unusual for the Indians, one the Bozeman Trail military had not seen before.[203]

After the Indians disappeared, soldiers rode out to the battlefield and found the butchered remains of Private Peach and returned him to the fort. He was buried at Fort Reno, the last soldier to be buried there.[204]

Within days the Shurly wagon train, resupplied but much subdued with the grisly loss of their man fresh in their minds, left Fort Reno for good and soon enough arrived in Cheyenne. There at Fort D. A. Russell, Edmund Shurly, possibly with relief that his tribulations on the Bozeman Trail were over, transferred the wagon carrying Lieutenant Neff and his guard to the fort commander. Neff's body would continue on to Fort Laramie.

Chapter Fifteen

CHEYENNE

*It was a fearful night—a perfect reign of terror. But it will tend to quiet the place.
It was exceedingly dangerous before, with garroting, robbing and shooting.*

—Reverend Joseph Cook, *Diary and Letters205*

WHEN HE ARRIVED IN CHEYENNE on that hot, dusty summer day in 1868, Edmund Shurly could see much had changed since he had last been there. The Union Pacific railroad had advanced west from Fort Kearney, Nebraska, along the Platte River to Julesburg, Colorado, and Fort Sedgwick. Then, following the Lodgepole Creek to a point south of Fort Laramie, the route left the Lodgepole and crossed over the divide to Crow Creek. The railroad had brought with it a whole new town ... and new problems.

General William T. Sherman, commander of the Department of the Missouri, had visited this area of his command in 1866 and ordered a depot be established near the eastern base of the Black Hills, sufficient for a regiment of infantry and storage of supplies for twenty-five hundred men to guard the new railroad.[206] The depot would be named Cheyenne and the fort named D. A. Russell in honor of Brigadier General David A. Russell, who had been killed at the Battle of Winchester on September 19, 1864.[207]

On July 4, 1867, as Shurly was moving north with Bradley's reinforcements for C. F. Smith, railroad engineers and company officials met at Crow Creek Crossing and agreed on the site for the depot and fort ordered by Sherman. Already it was a bustling town with military personnel and civilians there to take part in the Independence Day festivities, and more were arriving every day to establish stores, saloons, and other businesses. It was a tent city for now, and Elizabeth Burt writes of how difficult conditions were as she passed through the town in October en route to her husband's assignment at Fort C. F. Smith. Conditions improved rapidly, however, especially after November 13, when the tracks of the Union Pacific reached town. By January 1868 wooden barracks were completed for the enlisted men, and in February the officers were able to move into permanent structures. Now conditions had improved so much that even a military band was assigned to the fort.[208]

On July 4, 1868, exactly one year after the decision to establish the town and fort at Crow Creek Crossing, its freshly minted newspaper, the *Cheyenne Daily Leader*, declared:

> This post, occupying the position it does, employs a great number of men and teams, and annually expends millions of dollars, all of which operated in favor of this city.... Fort Russell is pronounced the best arranged and one of the most important military garrisons in the United States.[209]

EDMUND SHURLY HAD A HUGE SURPRISE awaiting him when he arrived in Cheyenne. His wife, Augusta, was there to meet him. She had traveled all the way from Chicago to be with him and to plead with him to resign his commission and return home with her. She had read in the Chicago papers many lurid tales of death and Indian atrocities on the Bozeman Trail and was sick with fear. Some newspapers reported the Bozeman Trail to be a "graveyard," others reported thousands of Indians descending on C. F. Smith to annihilate the garrison. So it was with immense relief as well as tears of joy and happiness that Augusta finally hugged her man and found him recovered from his wound. Only later would she see the noticeable limp as he walked, a condition that made him no longer fit for infantry duty and ended his military career.[210]

The town folk also welcomed the arrival of Shurly and his contingent from the north. Fears of Indian attack had reached a new high in July 1868, and most of the town's army garrison had left the fort for field duty, leaving it largely unprotected. On July 18 the *Cheyenne Daily Leader* reported:

> Yesterday a party of about two hundred Indians of assorted sex and sizes came up Crow Creek to within about three miles of this city where they erected their lodges, and are now ready for anything from matrimony to manslaughter.[211]

These Indians turned out to be friendly but, nevertheless, disconcerting as revealed by a follow-up story in the paper three days later:

> The Indians who are encamped below town appear to be doing a lively business in the sale of bows, arrows, quivers and moccasins. Now is the time to secure Indian trophies. Perhaps a few white mens' scalps may also be for sale by the precious scoundrels.[212]

Augusta Shurly was profoundly uncomfortable in Cheyenne. She was a "city girl" by nature, and the town, while much improved from the previous year, was, by any measure, no match for Chicago. She saw the countryside as desolate and windswept, without color or definition. Sagebrush and scrub grass extended as far as the eye could see and tumbleweeds littered the town. The gently rolling hills in the distance did nothing to break the monotony of the landscape, as far as she was concerned. She was appalled by the presence of Indians so close to town, and to her ultimate horror, white outlaws, literally the scum of the earth, had taken over. Murder and robbery were everywhere day and night, and the only control of violence was a murderous vigilante gang. Reverend Joseph Cook wrote of one of the more violent actions by these vigilantes. On October 16, 1868, while the Shurlys were in town:

> The vigilantes started out about supper time to clear the town of the worst of the rogues, and the whole town was in excitement. They hung three men that night and the next morning in broad daylight they hung another. Two innocent men were shot in the melee and have since died and another is wounded in the arm. It was a fearful night—a perfect

reign of terror. But it will tend to quiet the place. It was exceedingly
dangerous before, with garroting, robbing and shooting.[213]

No, this sort of thing was not for Augusta; she would soon leave Cheyenne, and
Brevet Captain Edmund Richard Pitman Shurly would be with her.

ON JULY 29 THE LAST WAGON TRAIN departed Fort C. F. Smith, and Andy Burt,
his wife, and children were in the lead wagon. Elizabeth Burt, ever the prolific
writer, was able to capture the poignancy of their departure in her journal, as they
returned to what for her could be considered normal life:

> To gain a parting glimpse of our last winter's home the command
> halted upon the crest of the hills overlooking the post from the south,
> while the wagons made the ascent. In spite of the trials experienced in
> the nine months of our sojourn there, the feeling arose that if in the
> years to come a post might again be built upon this beautiful site we
> would be glad to return, that is, provided hostile Red men be gone for-
> ever. Day and night the dread of their attacks had been hovering over
> us; time and again the sentinels had given the call, "Indians!" so that at
> the moment of departure nothing but gladness filled our hearts; still,
> while bidding a last farewell to this region the beauty of the scene was
> vividly impressed upon us. The mountains to the west, the Big Horn
> River sparkling in the sunlight to the north and bordered by undulat-
> ing slopes of green, the post set in the grassy plain between us and the
> river—all combined to make a beautiful picture.
>
> Indians, innumerable, taking possession of all surroundings and rev-
> eling in their untrammeled rights, gave the one touch of sadness to the
> moment. Although my husband had tried to impress upon them the
> sanctity of the little graveyard on Cemetery Hill where several graves
> told the sad tale of lives lost in the struggle of the past year, we could
> not but feel that we were leaving comrades to the hostilities of those
> savages.[214]

As had Shurly three weeks before, the Burts made their trip south to Fort D. A. Russell. Elizabeth's diary records the scene at their reunion with friends from the recent past:

> We were welcomed at Russell by many officers and ladies of our regiment who were unknown to us. However, among those we did know, General Bradley and his bride greeted us warmly. Major Burrowes and his wife, whom we had learned to love before meeting her, were already near and dear to us. It was a great pleasure to join so many old friends.
>
> Where we had slept in a tent a year ago a comfortable house stood. Frame quarters for a regiment had sprung up, as it were, into a small village; but the surroundings were destitute of any green to relieve the eye, and the wind, constantly sweeping the parade ground bare, drove the garrison almost to despair with its monotony. They longed for the quiet of some sheltered eastern post....
>
> We were here joined by Lieutenant and Brevet Captain Shurly and his wife. He had been badly wounded at Fort Smith in an Indian fight. Covering himself with glory he won a brevet but the wound cost him his health and he was soon retired for disability.
>
> The regiment was now to be divided and scattered along the railroad. Our company was assigned to Oglala Station. What this would turn out to be I had not the most remote idea, but had the satisfaction of knowing that it was east of Cheyenne and that much nearer home....
>
> On the day of departure for that town we [and the Shurly's] drove to the station to take the evening train and for the first time in years saw a dazzling headlight, our first pilot toward civilization. The cars were new and seemed very handsome to us who had lived the very simple life for three years. Our ex-Mormon nurse, Christina, was lost in admiration of such grandeur. We rested very little, for the run to Oglala was only a few hours. Arriving there that same night, we were hurried from the train to the loneliness of the prairie with nothing in sight but the stars overhead. At length the station was discovered, the only building within reach, a tiny frame house used by the telegraph operator, who kindly placed it at the disposal of the ladies.

Mrs. Shurly, my sister and I, my two children, and the nurse were to be the occupants of the one sleeping room. The soldiers brought hay and laid it on the floor. Upon this we placed our wraps and on this bed tried to finish the night in sleep. Early in the morning our fitful slumbers were disturbed by loud cries and talking. Upon peeping out of the window, what appeared to our astonished eyes but two soldiers carrying a tent pole from which was hanging a line of horrible rattlesnakes—yes, veritable rattlers that had been killed on the site where our tents were to be placed. This was on the banks of the Platte River, where the high grass had to be cut before camp could be made. In doing so this terrible array of snakes had been killed. A pleasant prospect, indeed, to be camped among such poisonous reptiles!

When we were at Leavenworth the older officers who had been stationed on the frontier before the war had told us such thrilling stories of the probability of our finding snakes in our beds, or on the ridge pole of the tent, or creeping under the edge of it, that our fears were roused lest all kinds of terrible creatures would disturb our peace of mind. My husband took the precaution at that time to purchase two buffalo hair ropes long enough to lay on the ground around our tents. Snakes would not cross the hairy surface, we were told. Through several years this proved to be true in our case and we now rejoiced in their protection.

Mrs. Shurly was here introduced to camp life and it naturally gave her a very disagreeable impression of the frontier. I believe that she needed nothing further to convince her that Chicago was a more desirable home than Oglala Station, especially as her husband was soon to retire.[215]

Later, Elizabeth Burt would remark in her diary:

Our dear friend Captain Templeton [had contracted tuberculosis[216] and] was visibly failing in health as the result of his life of exposure in the two years spent at Fort Smith. From a strong man of robust appearance, day by day his strength failed until the hollow cheeks and sunken eyes told too clearly his days were drawing to a close. Every care that was possible was given by the surgeon and many friends. Finally, upon our arrival at Fort Russell, after our twenty-one days trip [from Fort C. F. Smith], he started east with a nurse but only lived to reach home. So passed away another fine soldier lost in his effort to do his duty for our country.[217]

On December 2, 1868, to the relief of his long-suffering wife, Captain Shurly finally retired from active duty.[218] For the rest of his life, Shurly would regale friends and acquaintances alike with stories of his years in the military service. And, each day until he died, he would be reminded of his adventures by the chronic pain of his battle wounds suffered at Fredericksburg and Goose Creek.

BY AUGUST 1868, ALL THREE FORTS guarding the Bozeman Trail—Reno, Phil Kearny, and C. F. Smith—were abandoned and the bodies of the hundreds of soldiers and civilians killed by the Indians in the vicinity of these forts were moved for reburial elsewhere. Red Cloud had won this war with the white man.

The Sioux would be successful again a decade later in a fight with General Custer, but their time was nearing an end ... an end that finally arrived at the battle of Wounded Knee in Dakota Territory on December 29, 1890. They, along with most of the other Indians of North America, were never able to accept the inevitability of the white man's occupation of the North American continent nor comprehend his concept of land ownership until it was too late. They fought bravely and hopelessly to near extinction for the free use of this vast land; all the while immigrants by the millions from overseas were pouring into the cities of the east and west coasts, and the white man's government of the United States was spreading westward across their land, staking out towns, counties, states, and territories from the Atlantic to the Pacific. No power on earth could have stopped this unrelenting westward movement.

Had the Indian shown even a modicum of mercy to their captives, perhaps it would have been possible for the American government and its people to have shown sympathy for their cause. But the Indian's cruelty seems to have been inbred, and every firsthand account of life on the frontier contains vivid descriptions of their depravities. Linda Slaughter, wife of a doctor living on the frontier during the Indian wars, put it succinctly when she wrote in 1893:

The Indians suffered wrongs, but these were inflicted through the government by the entire people. Yet so mercilessly did they revenge these wrongs upon the innocent and helpless captives who fell into their hands that they extinguished in all feeling hearts the pity and sympathy that otherwise would have been theirs, and were regarded by all who dwelt near them as wild beasts (less merciful, to be sure) whom it would be a blessing to humanity to destroy.[219]

Chapter Sixteen

THE GREAT
CHICAGO FIRE

Everyone about me likened the awful scene
to his fancy of the Judgment Day.

—Joseph Medill, publisher, the *Chicago Tribune*, 1871

WHEN EDMUND SHURLY RETURNED HOME from his military service, Chicago was a boomtown, growing faster than any other town before or since. Grain, cattle, railroads, machinery, lumber, furniture, and a host of other industries were expanding and contributing to the wealth of the city. He recognized this explosive growth and resolved to take advantage of the opportunities that surrounded him. In 1869 Shurly established a business as a watchmaker in the center of town near the Chicago River at Number 6½ Clark Street, and a home five or six blocks away at 892 Madison Street,[220] where he, Augusta, and five-year-old Arthur could settle comfortably into a normal civilian life—or so they thought.

Edmund was a voracious reader of newspapers and now, with more time for himself, responded to them with articles of his own whenever he saw misinformation and injustice. He had developed skill in writing and expressed himself well in print. He never hesitated to reply to newspaper statements to which he objected. Many of the newspaper articles he authored have helped to round out his story.

In 1869 the *Chicago Times* printed an article sympathetic to the Indians by the Episcopal bishop of Minnesota, Henry B. Whipple. For the previous ten years Whipple had been an outspoken champion of the Indian cause and would continue his influence on public opinion for another thirty. His comments infuriated Edmund, who had seen, firsthand, what the Red Man did to his enemies. Shurly, of course, saw the Indian Question through the eyes of a soldier, ordered by his superiors to defend wagon trains against attack, to support and garrison the army outposts, and to save the lives of innocent civilians whose only thought was to start a new life for themselves. Granted, not all of these civilians were model citizens, but laws were in place to handle the lawbreakers.

Shurly had seen too much barbaric torture and killing of captured men, women, and children, irrespective of their race, to allow Bishop Whipple's sympathy for the Indian to go unchallenged. He replied in a letter to the paper that it was "not possible to find one full-blooded Indian at any of the agencies that can be trusted. Moral suasion had been tried, and the 'Quaker policy' has cost the lives of hundreds of those who have been struggling on the borders for a home."[221]

He pointed out:

> There is not a savage tribe in existence but what holds the lands it roams over by conquest—having driven some other tribe of Indians from it. It is singular that the bishop and those of his kind have not a word for the one hundred fifty men, women, and children who fell under the scalping knife of these fiends last summer—women dying by the most revolting means; children tied up and slowly tortured to death. There is no more treacherous kind in existence than the American Indian on the Plains, and how the bishop's sense of justice can allow him to say one word in favor of the Cheyenne is more than I can imagine. It was the duty of the troops at all hazards to recapture them. There is not one of them whose hands were not dyed with the blood of the settlers of Kansas.[222]

Shurly was writing about what he had seen with his own eyes. Close friends had suffered similar fates at the hands of the Indians. These comments were not from someone who had merely read about Indians in books or newspapers.

Shurly was very concerned that the reading public not get their impression of the Indian from "Cooper's novels, Indian agents or Bishop Whipple."[223] He was not reflecting on Whipple alone when he wrote, "the same mawkish sentimentality is shown toward condemned murderers in our prisons. Not a thought for the murdered ones, for the bereaved friends, fatherless children."[224]

On the Fourth of July, 1871, another son joined Shurly's family. He was a healthy, alert baby with curly locks and a bright smile, and his parents named him after Edmund's good friend, Andy Burt, and after Fort D. A. Russell where Edmund and Augusta were happily reunited after his service on the Bozeman Trail. To the delight of his parents, their new son, Burt Russell Shurly, would find his life to be every bit as challenging and successful as had been his father's.

The joy of this new addition to the family drew Edmund's attention away from plight of the Indians for the time being and from another developing concern for the city of Chicago. The summer of 1871 had been unusually hot and dry in the Midwest, and smoke from distant prairie fires filled the Shurly home almost every day. By fall the wooden buildings surrounding the town center were tinder dry. Edmund and Augusta read in the papers of fires occurring almost daily in the Chicago area. On October 7 a particularly serious fire burned out a part of Chicago just north of a cow barn owned by Catherine and Patrick O'Leary. Over sixteen city blocks were consumed before the exhausted fire fighters could control the flames. That, however, was only a harbinger of what was to come.

The firemen went to bed that night tired and with lungs burning with the residue of smoke and flame but triumphant knowing that they had prevented fire from torching the entire city. The next morning they awoke to the dreadful news that two thousand people had just perished in a holocaust 275 miles due north of them in the small town of Peshtigo, Wisconsin. Huge walls of flame and smoke had encircled the drought-ravaged town and created a firestorm that pulled oxygen and its human victims into its vortex. The country had never before experienced a peacetime disaster this huge. The relief these tired Chicago firefighters felt from having prevented a similar catastrophe in their city lasted less than twenty-four hours.

The Great Chicago Fire ignited at about nine o'clock in the evening on October 8, this time inside the O'Leary cow barn. The barn was located at 137 Dekoven Street, and the fire rapidly spread past the burnt-out section of town that had been consumed the night before.[225] A steady, bone-dry wind had been blowing all day from the southwest, and it directed the flames toward an Irish section of Chicago called Conley's Patch. This part of town consisted mostly of tinder-dry wooden buildings and it was consumed in minutes, killing many of the fire's victims. Soon the fire reached the south branch of the Chicago River. By this time it was generating its own draft and quickly jumped over the river. Now a firestorm, it raced toward the municipal gas works where a huge fuel storage tank exploded, causing many of the city street lights to slowly flicker out. The entire population of the city now knew this was not just another of the many bad fires that had plagued them over the summer and fall.

Before the gas works explosion, the Shurly family and all of Chicago could only look in wonder at the dull red glow in the southwest section of the city and the vivid shower of sparks and blazing embers that all accounts of the fire describe. The Shurly home was located south of the Chicago River on West Madison Avenue, where it should have been safe from the fire. But it wasn't. When the fire jumped the river the Shurlys were directly in its path. After the gas works explosion, it was clear that the fire would not stop until it reached the main body of the Chicago River, well beyond their home.

The Shurlys now had less than three hours to escape the flames. They had to gather their two children and personal belongings into their horse-drawn wagon, along with valuables from Edmund's jewelry store on Clark Street, and then push their way north through the frenzied mob. Night had fallen and the town, now illuminated only by the ghastly, distant glow and firebrands of the approaching fire, were clogged with huge throngs of humanity. By a miracle, the Shurlys reached the Clark Street bridge and somehow crossed the river. By two o'clock in the morning the fire had reached the river they had just crossed and was consuming the "fireproof" stone and brick buildings that made up downtown Chicago.

Edmund, Augusta, and their two children fought their way north through what one writer described as a "panorama of human behavior" in the streets. As the fire bore down on the terrified citizens, panic-stricken people on foot, horseback, and in carriages and wagons jammed the streets and bridges leading over the Chicago River. The mass of humanity pressed relentlessly forward; horses and wagon wheels rolled over people who could not wedge out of the way; children screamed in terror, and fights broke out at street intersections where no one could control traffic. Where the pathway narrowed at the approach to bridges, people were pushed off the embankment to land on boats or into the cold river water to drown. Mourners carrying caskets or the dead bodies of their loved ones could be seen at times, and the sick and infirm, rescued from hospitals, were brought along on chairs, litters, and wagons. Men ran into burning buildings to save valuables and business records, often only to be next seen at second-and third-floor windows jumping to save themselves from the advancing flames. Behind the mass of people, urging them on, was the horrid red-orange glow in the night and what sounded to many like a huge waterfall and the occasional crack of thunder as another building exploded or collapsed.

By three in the morning the fire had jumped the Chicago River and was consuming whole city blocks on the near north side. The Shurlys continued to push their way north through the human glut and finally reached the outskirts of Highland Park, a northern suburb of Chicago. There Edmund, along with Augusta, Arthur, and infant Burt, could rest for a moment and watch as the fire smoldered, then slowly burned itself out at the northern boundaries of the city in a light drizzle, some twenty-four hours after it had begun.

By the standards of the twentieth century and to those readers with senses dulled by descriptions of Nanking, Tokyo, Hiroshima, London, Hamburg, and Dresden, this scene might be considered no more than a microcosm of the horrors that would come soon enough to the world; but for the inhabitants of Chicago at the time, it was sufficient for a lifetime.

Edmund Shurly was financially ruined. His home and business had literally gone up in smoke. Over one hundred thousand people were burned out of their homes and three hundred had perished. Bad as it was, though, Edmund had faced worse many times before. His past adventures had fully prepared him to survive and reestablish his family in the Chicago area. He would persevere and proceed on.

Chapter Seventeen

THE BEAUTIFUL BANKS
OF THE CRYSTAL SEA

"All is not lost.... Chicago still exists....
We have lost money,
but we have saved life, health, vigor and industry."

—Joseph Medill, publisher, the *Chicago Tribune*

MANY PEOPLE, DISCOURAGED BY THE RUIN OF THE CITY after the Great Chicago fire, left town, but Edmund and Augusta stayed on to help the city recover. Edmund saw the fire as an opportunity for the city to start over and, as he expected, the next five years were indeed a challenge. Soon after the fire, the family found living quarters in Highland Park, a small town just north of Chicago. Damage to Chicago, though extensive, was largely repaired within a year or so and the city population soared, much of it because of the work available to people assisting with the rebuilding effort.

Tragedy, however, had not ended for the Shurly family. After the fire, disease spread rapidly through the makeshift housing available to the refugees from the fire and struck hard at the Shurly family. In 1872 eight-year-old Arthur, just as Edna had years earlier, began to complain of a sore throat and a cough. Soon the enlarged neck and gray appearance in the throat appeared and confirmed Augusta's worst fears: It was diphtheria.[226] Within a week Arthur was dead.

Arthur's death was a particularly heavy blow to Augusta. Arthur had taken the place of the departed Edna in her heart, and while Edmund was away from her, fighting his battles on the Bozeman Trail, Arthur had been the brave little man in the house. Edmund had returned and now it was Arthur who was gone. Both Augusta and Edmund turned to the church for help.

In the years to come the Shurlys would become very active in church affairs. Newspaper articles saved by the Shurlys describe their involvement in the Trinity Episcopal Church in Chicago and several others. In Saint Andrew's Church, Edmund served as treasurer in early 1875.

In 1882 a newspaper reporter asked the outspoken Shurly, a vestryman for the Trinity Episcopal Church, to comment on the resignation of Reverend Holland, a popular but controversial minister for the church. Shurly, described in the article as "one of the oldest Episcopal lay members in Chicago," said:

> "Well, the truth is, the church wants a clerical dude. About 290 out of the three hundred members are firm friends and staunch supporters of Doctor Holland. The other ten would be insignificant, but they, alas, possess the wealth. In street vernacular, they have got the money and propose to purchase a religion to suit themselves."
>
> "It was generally supposed that Doctor Holland was one of the most successful clergymen in Chicago." [commented the reporter]
>
> "Well, he was. He came here in April 1879, and during his admin-istration the church has been freed from a very large and embarrassing indebtedness. Doctor Holland has no superior as a man of character, force and thought. His crime, if such it be, for which the almost inap-preciable minority of wealthy great wish to ostracize him, consists of his simple earnestness and [his] power[ful] presentation of unguided truth. He is a power in Chicago, but I suppose he recognizes the ele-ment of discord in his church, and chose to leave the field to the believ-ers in a gilt-edged gospel rather than be the subject of comment and backbiting."[227]

In 1873, despite the economic panic that engulfed the country, Edmund's for-
tunes had sufficiently recovered to permit him to open his own business, Shurly
and Company, Watchmakers and Jewelers. It was located in the newly rebuilt
Sherman House at what is now 418 North Clark Street,[228] on the northwest corner
of Randolph and Clark streets, and remained there for nearly nine years. In 1882,
he sold his interest in this business and organized a new company he named the
Shurly Watch and Jewelry Manufacturing Company, located at 77 State Street, in
the Central Music Hall.[229] He installed himself as president and found a worthy
gentleman, Mister Edwin A. Giles, to serve as secretary and treasurer.

Like Shurly, Giles had been among the first to respond to President Lincoln's
call for troops at the beginning of the war, enlisting in the 27th Massachusetts
Infantry Volunteers Regiment. He saw active service for three years and participated in the engagements of Roanoke, New Bern, Little Washington, and others
of the same campaign. Upon his discharge, he returned to New York City and
went into the jewelry business with Giles, Wales & Company. He remained in
New York until 1868 when he relocated to Dubuque, Iowa, to organize the firm of
E. A. Giles & Company, wholesale and retail jewelers. In 1869 Mister Giles married Miss Lucy Mayor of Pawtucket, Rhode Island, and had two sons, Frederick
and Edwin. In 1880 his health began to fail and he sold his interests and traveled
for two years. He then came to Chicago[230] and joined the Shurly Manufacturing
Company.

According to a noted historian, the Shurly Manufacturing Company, Inc., a
producer of all kinds of jewelry, was, in 1886, one of the leading establishments
in Chicago. The historian's report states: "this business [was] controlled and con-
ducted by Edmund R. P. Shurly, president, and Edwin A. Giles, secretary and treasurer. Both of these gentlemen [were] well and favorably known to the trade, and
it is to their reputation and judgment that the company [owed] its success."[231]

One of the products developed and marketed by the Shurly Manufacturing
Company was a gold or silver thimble, often given to lucky young ladies in those
days as an engagement present or at Christmas. By 1882 Shurly's industrious son,
Burt, was old enough to fill in as salesman and delivery boy for these gifts during
his summer vacations from Douglas School.

Shurly was an active member of national jewelry guilds and associations and
was often mentioned in print commenting on activities in the trade. In 1879 he

helped organize the Watchmakers and Jewelers League of the United States, and on May 15, 1879, as its first president, he called their first meeting to order in the Sherman House in Chicago. His address to the assembled delegates outlined the problems of tightening competition and how it was causing lower prices and reduced quality of goods. Shurly cited plans undertaken by the state organizations and "suggested a plan of organization to unite all the trade in the United States engaged in retailing and repairing."[232] In later years he represented not only the Illinois jewelers but also the Texas delegation to the United States Guild. He was an energetic member and for some years edited the journal published by the Illinois guild.

BESIDES HIS INVOLVEMENT in the Watchmakers and Jewelers Guild, Edmund Shurly maintained close contacts with his many friends from his military days and regularly attended 26th New York Regiment reunions, which began in 1885 in Utica, New York. The first reunion was held in Post Bacon Hall[233] and was followed by a march through town. Speaking at this event were, among others, Colonel E. F. Wetmore and Judge Bacon, an important personage in Utica. Captain Shurly was unable to attend the meeting and instead wrote a letter to be read at the ceremony:

> Nothing in the world would have given me greater pleasure than to have met my old comrades of the 26th, the companions of many a long march, very much hard service, and not a few desperate fights. To have seen them after these many years, not as of old, not the youthful faces of twenty-four years ago, but with the lines of age and its gray hairs upon many. Of all the regiments I ever served in after the 26th I never saw its equal for drill. I think it was one of the finest bodies of men in the army. Certainly its record cannot be beaten. The 26th saw hard service and met the best treatment at the hands of the government.
>
> The men who enlisted at the first call were patriots. No bounty lured them; in fact many did not expect any pay. We enlisted at the sound of Sumter's guns to sustain the Union and the flag. If any body of men deserves honor it is the survivors of those who responded to the first

call. My heart is full of friendship to the members of the old 26th. If alive, I will attend the second reunion.[234]

Shurly attended the second and many additional reunions. Often he was asked to speak, and during the fifteenth reunion, on September 14, 1900, he said that since his wedding day he had not enjoyed an occasion so much as he had the fifteenth reunion of his regiment.

"I don't wish to flatter you," Shurly said, "but the 26th was one of the best regiments that ever went to the war. There were many of us who did not know even that their services were to be paid for. We went simply because we believed in the cause and were ready to go to the front in support of it."[235]

Shurly could not attend the sixteenth reunion and wrote to apologize, saying: "I did hope that nothing would interfere to prevent my attending every reunion while life lasts. My mind is willing, also my body, but unfortunately my Fredericksburg leg says 'no.' I have been having a tussle with rheumatism, and up to date, rheumatism is getting the best of it. Remember me to all, especially those of Company C who I know never lost their appetite."[236]

Neither was Shurly able to attend their eighteenth reunion, probably because of unusually wet weather that diminished attendance. At this reunion the veterans honored their beloved commander, Colonel William H. Christian, by presenting a sepia portrait of him to the Oneida County Historical Society.

Shurly's last reunion for which there is a record was the nineteenth, held in Utica on August 22, 1904. A Utica newspaper, probably the *Utica Daily Press*, reported on the event.

The nineteenth annual reunion of the Fighting 26th Regiment, New York Volunteers, was held today at Utica Park. The first order of the day was the assembling of the comrades at nine o'clock this forenoon in Post Bacon Hall. At ten o'clock they marched in a body to the Munson Williams Memorial Building, where the colors were saluted and an inspection made of the many precious relics, which are kept there. The visit was a very interesting one and the stirring days of '61–'65 were vividly recalled by a glance at the tattered and torn flags and uniforms, the rusty guns and pistols, and the shells and other war paraphernalia.

It will be remembered that some time ago the 26th Regimental Association presented a handsome sepia portrait of its original commander, William H. Christian, to the Oneida Historical Society, and today this was viewed with pride and honor by the men who were under his command....

The committee on nominations was appointed by President Swan as follows: Comrades J. E. Watson, John Kohler, ex-Alderman Joseph Tessey ... Charles F. Cleveland and E. R. Shurly....

Captain Shurly was next called on and said that he never felt better in his life. "We men," he said, "have contributed to help make this country what it is, and we are entitled to some credit."

... It was the opinion of the veterans that E. R. P. Shurly ... was the oldest man present and that Chief of Police Charles F. Cleveland was the youngest.[237]

Such was Shurly's attachment to his comrades that as late as 1904, at the age of seventy-five, he was attending reunions in Utica, a considerable distance from his home.

FOR SOME TIME, Augusta Shurly had suffered from asthma and arthritis, and when the new business began showing signs of success, the family spent one winter in New Orleans in an unsuccessful attempt to alleviate her suffering. Later, they spent numerous winters in Wisconsin, where she seemed to improve.

By 1877 the Shurly family had returned to Chicago, settling temporarily into a home at 695 West Adams Street (now 1854 West Adams). Life was rapidly returning to normal, and even Shurly's prized field glass, presented by friends in Buffalo before he went off to war then lost during the attack on the "Cornfield" at Antietam, turned up. It had been found by a Mister J. H. Palmer, Company I, 26th NYV, who became separated from the regiment and had lost contact with Shurly until a friend gave him Shurly's address. The incident found its way into the Chicago newspapers where it received generous exposure.[238]

For Augusta, however, the loss of her two children was still very real. In 1878, she found a poem that helped her through the pain, and preserved it in her scrapbook.

Waiting[239]

I have two little angels waiting for me,
On the beautiful banks of the Crystal Sea,
Not impatiently wait my darlings there,
For smiles light up their brows so fair,
And their little harps ring out so clear,
So soothingly sweet to faiths listening ear.
And they live in the smile of the Savior's love,
Who so early called my darlings above.

I have two little angels waiting for me,
On the beautiful banks of the Crystal Sea,
Forever free from sorrow and pain,
Spotless and pure from all earthly stain,
Never an erring path to rove,
Safe in the bosom of infinite love,
Ever more, ever more walking in light.

I have two little angels waiting for me,
On the beautiful banks of the Crystal Sea,
When my weary heart is throbbing with pain,
And I fain would clasp my darlings again,
I look away from this earthly strand,
To the beautiful fields of the "better land."
I will think of the angels waiting there,
And offer to God a thankful prayer.

I have two little angels to welcome me,
When I too shall stand by the Crystal Sea,
When the great refiner his image may trace,
In the heart he has won by his saving grace,
And in robes of Christ's own righteousness dressed,
My soul shall seek the home of the blest.
On the beautiful banks of the Crystal Sea,
My darlings, still waiting, shall welcome me.

This poem, discovered in the family scrapbook,[240] has "Edna and Arthur" penned above it in Augusta's handwriting.

In 1880 the family relocated to 3220 Calumet Avenue[241] and life steadily improved. And it had grown. The 1880 census shows the family as Edmund Shurly, age fifty; wife, C. A. Shurly, forty-five, born in Canada; son Burt, nine; nieces Florence Jennings,[242] twenty-four, and Laura Jennings, twenty-one, both born in New York State; one servant; and a fifteen-year-old boy, George Burt,[243] born in Canada, who may have been related to Edmund's close friends, Andy and Elizabeth Burt.

In 1888, with Burt graduated from high school and attending Northwest Military Academy, Edmund decided to ease his workload and reorganized his business as The Shurly Company, Jewelers, at what is now 501 West Randolph Street. His colleague, Edwin Giles, left the company and joined his brother's business. In 1889 Shurly sold their Calumet Avenue home and moved to an apartment above the store.

Ten years later, at the age of seventy, Shurly retired altogether from business in Chicago, and he and Augusta moved to Detroit, not only to be near their son Burt, who by this time had graduated from medical school and was practicing medicine there, but also to be near Edmund's younger brother, Ernest, who had become a prominent, internationally recognized physician in Detroit. In Detroit, Edmund and Augusta lived for a while with son Burt, and later in the Palms Apartment House on East Jefferson Avenue (now 1001 East Jefferson Avenue).[244]

AS THE NEW CENTURY BEGAN, Edmund had time to reflect on all he had experienced. He had lived through extraordinary times, and the world he had entered into was gone. His was the first generation that could look back at truly profound change during their lifetimes. Animals had transported humans since the dawn of history and now were rapidly being replaced by coal-and gasoline-powered machines. Steamboats were replacing sailing ships (although the steamboats were still so unreliable and fuel so expensive that sails remained on many ships and, Edmund thought, probably always would). Horseless carriages appeared on the streets of Detroit—even his son had one—and the Detroit newspapers were reporting that a young fellow named Henry Ford was trying to bring down the price of automobiles to levels that anyone could afford.

Burt Russell Shurly. The youngest son of Edmund and Augusta, and their only child to survive to adulthood, he is pictured here in his Northwest Military Academy uniform in 1888. He attended this school for two years, and then went on to graduate from the University of Wisconsin in 1893. Author's file.

Burt Shurly is pictured here in 1900. After graduating from the University
of Wisconsin in 1893, he attended medical school in Detroit followed by a year of
study at the University of Vienna. He interned at Detroit's Harper Hospital
and went on to a brilliant career in medicine. Author's file.

A very proud Edmund Shurly beams down at his first grandchild,
Viola (Pabby) Shurly in 1906. Author's file.

The Oregon Trail Edmund Shurly had traveled to Wyoming and Montana had disappeared and been replaced by a railroad literally as he was living in "another world" in that now forgotten outpost, Fort C. F. Smith. The West that he had come to know, and helped tame, was completely transformed. The Indian problem had finally dissipated, lawlessness was diminished, and now anyone could go west and many "ordinary" folks were doing just that. Telephones, now found in one out of every ten homes, allowed the human voice to be heard over huge distances; electric lights were eliminating darkness from the night; and central heating and indoor plumbing were beginning to appear.

Everywhere Shurly looked there was change. Medicine was producing miracles, as his son explained many times, and life expectancy had jumped to forty-seven years[245] and was still climbing. Doctors could now see the internal parts of the body with something called x-rays; they could anesthetize patients to eliminate their pain when they cut them open; and many of these doctors (but by no means all) now accepted the latest theory that invisible microbes caused disease. Vaccinations now prevented smallpox, and soon doctors would prevent typhoid fever and diphtheria in their patients. *If only these discoveries had come in time to save his own two children.* As long as the doctors understood all of this new technology and were properly trained (and this was not always the case), one did not have to understand how vaccinations worked. Yes, he decided, this was a good step forward.

Edmund had to admit to himself that it was fascinating to watch from the sidelines as progress leapt forward. It seemed that every few weeks one read in the newspapers of another new discovery or invention. Edison was improving his electric lights, and now George Westinghouse was proposing an even better system than Edison's for distributing electricity—technology known as "alternating current." Edison recently announced he had invented something he called "moving pictures." What do you suppose would come of that? Communication over long distances was being improved, and people were saying that soon voice would travel through the "ether" instead of over wires. What nonsense—or was it?

One day in late 1903 Edmund noted a small article in his newspaper. It reported that two brothers from Dayton, Ohio, had flown a flying machine several hundred yards along a thin strip of land, in a place called Kitty Hawk. This contraption could only hold one man and no baggage so it would likely never amount to anything. But it was something man had never done before and would certainly fire up the imagination of other inventors to work hard to achieve their dreams.

And, at last the country had someone exciting in the White House. Not since Lincoln had a president interested Edmund, and still the country had managed to prosper. Now, with Roosevelt at the helm, the sky was the limit. Teddy was a hard charger.

Nevertheless, this was no longer the world Edmund had been comfortable with. He had mastered that old world's crude technology and flourished in it. He knew how everything had worked in that world. Now, new devices and inventions saved effort and time, if and when they worked as they were meant to. But they could not be depended upon, and it took an awful lot of understanding to use them. This new world was nothing like the old one, where everything was as it had been for as long as one could remember. Why did so much have to change so fast?

Later, when Edmund's thoughts turned to what future wars might be like, he shuddered. Now that the airplane, the submarine, poison gas, and the machine gun had been invented, warfare would be mass extermination; not the kind of conflict he knew. But maybe that would not matter. There had not been a serious war in Europe since Napoleon was defeated at Waterloo. Everyone now realized that war was obsolete. Certainly the kings and queens of Europe were too intelligent to allow warfare to despoil their modern worlds. Granted there were continuing crises after crises over there, but did not Bismarck and the other leaders of Europe always settle their differences in the end? With England's modern dreadnoughts and the instruments of mass death, such as the machine gun available to every country, who but a madman would start a full-scale war in Europe? And even if a war began in Europe it could not possibly affect us in America. Yes, his son Burt had been right to select the medical profession over a military life.

Maybe the world really was now a better place in which to live. But still, Edmund had to wonder whether his fellow man truly understood the implications all these wonderful inventions would have for mankind. His own life had been a mighty fascinating adventure, and in a small way he had helped to fashion this new world. His generation had accomplished all this change, so why should he not feel a little proud? Yes, of course he should, but his generation also would have to accept a small portion of the blame if any of this new technology went awry.

If indeed his world was changing faster than man could assimilate, few recognized it or saw the monumental consequences. Mercifully, Edmund would not live to witness the aftermath: the insanity and butchery of World Wars I and II—wars he would never have imagined. Nor would he live through a Great Depression that would put one quarter of the working population of the United States out of work, nor the scourge of Communism and a Cold War that would take forty years for his country to win.

ORDINARILY, THE SCENE from her fourth floor window overlooking Detroit's elegant East Jefferson Avenue would have mesmerized Augusta. The February morning had dawned cold and crisp and a mantle of freshly fallen snow had given one of America's most beautiful cities a Currier & Ives look. The old veteran of so many of the Civil War battles and gunfights with the Sioux, lying silently on the bed in front of her, had often gazed at the everyday busy traffic of fine carriages on Jefferson Avenue, now intermixed with the occasional automobile belching smoke. It was a scene that always caught his fancy. There, to the southeast, was the Detroit River, frozen with ice solid enough to support the horse-drawn wagons traveling to and from Canada, visible beyond the river's edge. But on this particular morning Augusta was almost trembling with concern. The pain in her husband's chest had worsened and the laudanum, an opiate her son had prescribed for him, was beginning to take its effect. When heavy doses of medicine such as this found its way into his blood stream, his mind often would take leave of its surroundings and wander back in time to another cold morning on December 12, 1862, when pain just as intense had washed over his thigh. He again would hear the sounds of cannon, musketry, and the screams of others in even more pain than he, drowning out his own cries for help. He would think of the slope leading up from the Rappahannock River to Stonewall Jackson's cannons expertly defending the Confederate right flank at Fredericksburg. And he would remember the ride back across the river on the pontoon bridge to the field hospital where a decision might have been made to remove his leg had there been enough of a stump to repair. Ah yes, he was indeed no stranger to pain.

When the medicine was taking its full effect his thoughts wandered even further. The arrow in his foot on that field in Wyoming Territory was further proof that he could withstand pain and continue on. Wyoming was perhaps a closer call than Fredericksburg. There were fewer men to help him in that conflict, and he had faced a foe that delighted in the agony of its captured enemies as they screamed, and yelped, and died under slow torture applied as expertly as could be managed.

He thought of the military reports he wrote of that and other battles, reports he always signed with his initials "E. R. P." before his last name; initials familiar to many of his comrades. As his thoughts drifted he was amused by the possibility that future historians would ponder the names that went with these initials.[246] Edmund Richard Pitman, that's who! But many friends and some relatives just called him "E. R. P." and that was fine with him.

The pain was subsiding now and his thoughts wandered to his huge billowing sails that had remained with him ever since that voyage with his mother and father. The memory of huge billowing sails had soothed his thoughts when a giant wall of flame consumed his home and business along with the city of Chicago, one night in the fall of 1871. Of course his military experience had helped as well. By that time in his life he had learned cool temper was a most valuable commodity in the midst of chaos.

But now he was eighty years old and not quite so sure anymore that he could persevere. The pains in his chest had been particularly intense the last few days, and he had not slept much last night. His son, a highly trained doctor in Detroit, and his brother, a nationally known physician, both assured him that the pain would subside, but he was not convinced. Knowing that Augusta, his dear wife and love of fifty-four years and beside his bed now, would be well looked after by these expert physicians eased his cares far more than their reassurances. Knowing that his son would excel in the years to come was real comfort.

Suddenly, sharp pain stabbed his chest again and he knew now that his billowing sails were about to take him onward to a new adventure. Augusta was tightly gripping his hand, but no one could describe his destination to him as his father had done on his earlier voyage so many years before. The insistent pain in his leg that had been with him since that fateful December morning on the battlefield at Fredericksburg was gone now.

He would be pleased to trust in the Lord.

EDMUND RICHARD PITMAN SHURLY died at his home on Jefferson Avenue in Detroit on February 20, 1909, and was buried in Mount Hope Cemetery, Rochester, New York,[247] near his sister Marian and her husband, Gilbert Jennings, Shurly's good friend and comrade in arms. Edmund was survived by his wife and son, and by his brothers C. J. Shurly, living in Cambridge, Ontario, and Doctor Ernest L. Shurly.

While he was in Chicago, Edmund Shurly had been elected to the Illinois Commandery of the Military Order of the Loyal Legion of the United States[248] and transferred his membership to the Michigan Commandery[249] after moving to Detroit. On March 28, 1909, General J. H. Smith, U.S. Army, Commander of the Michigan Commandery, concluded a moving eulogy to him with these words:

> While Colonel Shurly was justly proud of his adopted country, of the flag of this great republic, and of the service he had seen under the folds of the starry banner, he was exceedingly modest about relating his experiences and his services. In fact, one might be much in his society and would never find out that he was in the company of a veteran who had seen and experienced far more than the average soldier of the republic. Yet he was genial, free and entertaining, and loved the society of those who, like him, had served his country, that his country might be preserved. We mourn the loss of a genial companion, an honored member, a devoted soldier.
>
> To his bereaved widow and son we offer our tribute of condolence and respect.

> "We cannot say, and we will not say that he is dead.
> He is just … away!
> With a cheery smile and a wave of the hand
> He has wandered into an unknown land,
> And left us dreaming how very fair its needs must be,
> Since he lingers there."[250]

Augusta Shurly's health continued to deteriorate after Edmund died, and one grandchild reported that much of her remaining years were spent in a wheelchair.

She remained in Detroit to be near her son and his family and continued to live in her home in the Palms Apartment House on East Jefferson Avenue until her death on September 18, 1918. She was buried in Rochester, New York, next to her husband and two children, Edna and Arthur who, we are sure, were awaiting her on the "beautiful banks of the Crystal Sea."

Acknowledgments

I HAVE HAD A HUGE AMOUNT OF HELP in writing this book from many generous friends, relatives, and acquaintances. My good friend Don Rowland offered sound advice for improvements as well as strong encouragement to continue this project. Another good friend, Homer Henschen, suggested I send a draft manuscript to Carlisle, Pennsylvania historian, Jim Wensyel, who offered further advice, encouragement, and, eventually, a massive editing job of a very rough manuscript. Don Wisnoski, a historian in Utica, New York, added invaluable information regarding the 26th New York Volunteers Infantry Regiment and its founder and commander Colonel William Henry Christian, information that had disappeared from the record books over time. Friends Arlene Lawless, and Jim and Mary Lou Amy also added valuable insight.

On a trip to Wyoming in 1998 Jan and I were literally stunned by information generously offered by Helen Graham at the Sheridan County Fulmer Public Library and by the late local Sheridan historian Glenn Sweem regarding E. R. P. Shurly's exploits fighting Indians on the Bozeman Trail. Glenn Sweem, just five days out of the hospital with a hip replacement, absolutely insisted on showing us portions of the old trail and the location he had found of Shurly's battlefield. For months after our visit, he continued to pass on information and photos of Shurly's time on the trail. Jan and I truly mourned his passing in 2001. I had very much wanted him to see this work in print.

Glenn introduced us to members of the Fort Phil Kearny Visitors Center and museum, including Linda DeTavernier and Bob Wilson who generously offered to allow me to use a diorama he painted of the Shurly Fight that appears on this book's cover. Glenn also showed us how to find the remains of Fort C. F. Smith in

Montana and to contact Leo Plainfeather, who kindly allowed Jan and me onto his property to inspect the site of the fort.

Close friend Lee Grills found E. R. P. Shurly's burial plot in Rochester, New York, which had been lost to my generation, and graciously invited Jan and me to stay with him and his wife, Eleanor, in their home while Lee and I explored the area. Afterward, he continued to pass on ideas and information as they came to him and became impatient with the delay in publishing this work, as did several other friends.

And of major importance to the accuracy and scope of this work, Ms. Pat Bartkowski, at the Reuther Library of Wayne State University in Detroit, kindly opened the library files on the Shurly family to me, although I know she trembled at the thought of the damage an untrained researcher such as I could inflict on the fragile records. Her help in finding these records and directing me to books on the subject that I should consult was absolutely vital in attaining the accuracy I was able to achieve. Without her help the work would have been pathetically incorrect on many levels of fact and inference.

I nearly missed finding this trove of Shurly family information. My family always thought, incorrectly as it turned out, that the Shurly archives had been turned over to the Burton Library in Detroit. On one summer Monday morning, early, I arrived at the Burton to review their files one last time and found to my chagrin they were closed on Mondays. Turning away from the Burton door one sees the imposing Wayne State University Reuther Library just across the street. Knowing my late grandfather's antipathy to labor unions I could not imagine the files being in the Reuther Library, but with time on my hands I decided at least to inquire. I was directed to the third floor and when I told them I was a Shurly grandson, Ms. Bartkowski opened their files to me. She and her staff could not have been more helpful. I was overwhelmed. The files are so vast I invested in a hand-held recorder and spent two weeks recording all the information I felt would fit in the book, much of which is too fragile even to photocopy. As a result of this find I added a new chapter and rewrote four others, a delay of several more years.

My thanks go out to Professor Lawrence Lee Hewitt, a Chicago author of numerous Civil War books, who generously reviewed portions of this work relating to the Civil War and added valuable suggestions and comments. My thanks also go out to Donald Hoert, a history teacher retired from Southfield Michigan

High School, who generously offered to review the nearly finished manuscript and provided valuable comments that enhanced the work.

I must also give special mention to a book that has been of special help in completing this work. The book I refer to is British Army Colonel G. F. R. Henderson's *Stonewall Jackson and the American Civil War*, first published in 1898. It is the story of the Confederate general against whom Edmund Shurly and his companions were fated to fight throughout their two years with the 26th New York Infantry Volunteers.

Finally, the editorial suggestions and encouragement of my loving wife, Jan, who left us in 2004, were invaluable. She was just terrific in putting up with my travels to battlefields and time spent in front of the computer. Without her love, patience, and interest I could not have completed this work.

APPENDIX A

DEPLOYMENTS OF THE 26TH NEW YORK VOLUNTEERS[251]

Organized at Elmira, New York, by Colonel William H. Christian

1861

May 17	Accepted by State of New York for a service of two years.
May 21	Mustered into service of United States for three months.
June 19	Left State of New York.
June 20	Arrived vicinity of Washington, D.C.
July 21	Attached to McCunn's Brigade, Army of Northeast Virginia.
Aug. 4	Heintzelman's Brigade, Division of the Potomac.
Oct. 15	Slocum's Brigade, Franklin's Division, Army of the Potomac.
Nov.	Fort Lyon, Wadsworth Command, Defenses of Washington.

1862

May 11	Ricketts' 1st Brigade, Ord's 2nd Division, McDowell's 3rd Corps, Dept. of Rappahannock. [252]
June 26	Brigadier General Zealous B. Tower's 2nd Brigade, Ricketts' 2nd Division, McDowell's 3rd Corps, Pope's Army of Virginia.
Sept. 12	2nd Brigade, 2nd Division, Hooker's 1st Army Corps, Army of the Potomac.

1863

May 28	Regiment is mustered out of service.

189

SERVICE AND ACTIONS OF THE REGIMENT

1861

June 21	Duty begins at Forts Elsworth, Lyon, Worth, Ward, and Franklin.
Oct. 3 & 4	Expedition to Pohick Church, Virginia.

1862

May 4	Depart Fort Lyon; down Potomac to Aquia Creek.
May 5	Series of marches toward Richmond.
May 11	Vicinity of Fredericksburg.
May 20	Manassas Junction, Thoroughfare Gap, Piedmont Station (left baggage).
June 1	Expedition to Front Royal, Virginia; crossed bridge, occupied Federal Hill.
June 2	Bridge over South Fork Shenandoah River collapses, trapping 26th.
June 19	Depart Front Royal.
July 4	Gainsville, Warrenton.
Aug. 6	Cross Rappahannock at Waterloo Bridge to Culpeper.
Aug. 9	Battle of Cedar Mountain.
Aug. 18	Falling back, destroying railroads and bridges.
Aug. 21	Holding actions at fords of the Rappahannock River.
Aug. 23	Holding action at Rappahannock Station.
Aug. 27	Falling back through Warrenton.
Aug. 28	Delay Longstreet's army at Thoroughfare Gap.
Aug. 29	Falling back thru Haymarket to Gainsville, to Bristoe Station by 9:00 p.m.
Aug. 30	Second Bull Run; "Regiment & Brigade lost heavily."
Aug. 31	Brigade in Centerville.
Sept. 1	Chantilly, Little River Turnpike.
Sept. 2–4	Halls Hill and Falls Church; fall back to Washington, D.C.
Sept. 5	Lee crosses Potomac toward Harrisburg.
Sept. 6–22	Maryland Campaign.

Sept. 14	Battles of South Mountain, Maryland.
Sept 16–17	Antietam, Maryland.
Until Oct. 30	At Sharpsburg, Maryland.
Oct. 30–Nov. 19	Movement to Falmouth, Virginia.
Until Dec. 10	At Brook's Station.
Dec. 12–15	Battle of Fredericksburg.

1863

Jan. 20–24	"Mud March."
Until April 27	At Falmouth and Belle Plains.
April 27–May 6	Chancellorsville Campaign.
April 29–May 2	Operations at Pollock's Mill Creek, Virginia.
May 1–5	Battle of Chancellorsville.
May 28	Mustered out. Three-year men were transferred to the 97th New York Infantry Regiment.

REGIMENTAL CASUALTIES[253]

DATE	BATTLE	KILLED	WOUNDED	MISSING
Aug. 30	Second Bull Run	54	89	25
Sept. 2	Chantilly	1		
Sept. 14	South Mountain		2	
Sept. 17	Antietam	7	39	20
Dec. 11–15	Fredericksburg	46	113	11
TOTALS		108	243	56

During this service the regiment lost 5 officers and 103 enlisted men killed or mortally wounded, and 42 enlisted men by disease.

Total killed, wounded, and missing: 407.

APPENDIX B

The Conspiracy at Camp Douglas

THIS IS A LETTER WRITTEN BY EDMUND SHURLY to the editor of the *Chicago Tribune* in response to an article they published about Major Charles H. Cole, one of the prime instigators of the conspiracy of the Confederate Secret Service to release thousands of prisoners from Camp Douglas and other Union prisoner-of-war camps to rampage through Indianapolis, Cleveland, Chicago, and other Northern cities to embarrass Lincoln before his reelection in November 1864.

The letter is important in two respects. Shurly vigorously maintains that the reason for the failure of the Ohio conspiracy, led by Major Cole, was not the defection of one of the conspirators as reported by government sources probably to protect the real source, but rather the actions of General Benjamin Sweet, the commandant of Camp Douglas, whose men infiltrated Chicago anti-war groups, captured, and interrogated several Confederate agents. This provided the information Sweet relayed in a telegram to the War Department, allowing them to arrest Cole just as he was about to capture a warship on Lake Erie. As Sweet's adjutant general, Shurly would certainly have full knowledge of the telegram. Second, he defends Sweet who has, over the years, received much criticism for his management of Camp Douglas.

At the end of the letter Shurly pleas with the Cleveland administration not to release Sweet's daughter, Ada Sweet, from her badly needed job as a pension agent in Chicago. Politics intervened, however, and she lost her job shortly after the letter was published.

This article appeared in the *Chicago Tribune* on February 3, 1882. A copy is filed in the Walter Reuther Library, Shurly collection, Box 1, scrapbook 1.

Chicago, February 3—I read with much interest the account given by Major Cole of Texas, of the operations of the Rebels in and about Chicago in the fall of 1864. I'm glad to have this witness from the other side rise up at this late day and tell his experience as if it convinces many of old citizens of the fact of the conspiracy to destroy this city and release from Camp Douglas not 10,000, but 16,000 prisoners of war. (Not starved men, such as Andersonville contained, but able-bodied men.) I've no doubt there were 2,000 men from the southern part of the state here to aid in the scheme. We arrested the next day, after capturing the leaders, over 1,000 men in and about the city who came up to cooperate with the prisoners when released—this was the same day that the arms were taken from Walsh's house.

I think, though, that Major Cole is mistaken. The state of Illinois was a separate district, and General Vincent Marmaduke was here to assume command with other officers as celebrated to assist. Major Castleton and Maufam had special details. If you remember, General Marmaduke was arrested here. Now a fate worse than the Great Fire hung over the city; the plans, well laid, would have been consummated if it had not been for the sleepless vigilance of General Benjamin J. Sweet, Commandant at Camp Douglas. He not only saved Chicago but the Northwest, and was the man who thwarted Jake Thompson's plans. Major Cole in his letter says: "How did the Federal authorities get information of your designs?"

"A Colonel Johnson of Kentucky betrayed us, as near as I have been able to understand."

The relatives of Colonel Johnson of Kentucky can rest assured that it was not he; *it was General Sweet's telegram to the Secretary of War that did the business for Major Cole. Two days before the attempt was made {September 17}, General Sweet had Thompson's agent in custody and had wormed enough out of him to find out that fact, also that it was contemplated by the Thompson crowd to capture the iron steamer Merchant. To prevent this, the General placed a military guard aboard the vessel.* [Emphasis added]

I'm no statesman, but it has always been a mystery to me why the government did not wheel one army corps out from the 'Grand

Review'—Logan's or Hooker's would have done—marched it into Canada and taken that country, so as have had control of that fighting-in-the-rear crowd of miserable rebels. While stationed on the frontier after the war I met one of those officers captured here (he has settled down, so I withhold the name). I had a lengthy conversation with him in reference to the conspiracy.

He said: "Some of our best officers were detailed to take command of the troop (prisoners of war) upon their release. They were to capture the garrison, take possession of their arms and others concealed in the vicinity of the camp, then possess themselves of all the serviceable horses, raid the banks and other places where there were articles of value, secure all the arms and ammunition, and then fire the city. A part of the plan was to make a forced march to Rock Island, release the prisoners, thence to southern Illinois and Missouri. They hoped to have possession of St. Louis for a base. I can assure you that if it had not been for General Sweet they would have succeeded."

General Sweet is really the man who frustrated a scheme on the part of the rebels that would have been fraught with mischief. He did this too when suffering, as few men suffer, from wounds received at the battle of Perryville. I have known him to be up night after night during that exciting time, shattered as he was—in fact, he died from wounds received in battle the same as though he had been killed on the field. He left a family of small children; the eldest, Miss Ada Sweet, the present Pension Agent, has had the care of the family. The boy who will inherit his father's honor and spotless name is about 10 years of age. This young family [is] dependent upon the exertions of their sister for a living. In view of these facts, is it possible that any soldier who ever faced an armed foe in the field or that ever battled for the flag could seek this girl's place? I've heard so, but "believe it not." To turn this brave soldier's daughter with her little sisters and brother dependent upon her, from the office of Pension Agent, a place she has filled such intelligence, fidelity, and honesty that no fault can be found, would indeed be a wrong.

(Signed) E. R. P. Shurly, late Captain and AAG, Camp Douglas.

APPENDIX C

E. R. P. Shurly's Thoughts Regarding
the Indian Question

BELOW IS AN ARTICLE WRITTEN BY EDMUND SHURLY, for the *Chicago Times* in 1869, in reply to a newspaper article submitted some days earlier by a minister in Chicago, praising the Western Indian and criticizing the U.S. government in its handling of the "Indian Question."

The Sympathetic Whipple;
A Gentleman Who Has Been Through The Indian Mill Reviews His Letter;
The Weaknesses of the Bishop's Position Pointed Out;
An Argument in Favor of Turning the Redskins Over to the Army.

There is no accounting for the eccentricities of men. An old writer says, "all men are insane on some point." For the last 13 years I have placed our worthy bishop in the ranks of these described by the "old writer." That the bishop is in the dark so far as the Indians are concerned will be attested by all those who have had occasion to come in contact with them. Bishop Whipple knows nothing of the wild Indian or he would not use the pen as he does. I would not ask him about the Indians who so ruthlessly murdered men, women and children within the bounds of his fair bishopric. Their wails of anguish still linger in the forests of Minnesota. These savages were some of the "half Christianized" that you find in the agencies. The bishop knows that it is impossible to tame the savage. Even in midst of prayer at the sanctuary, the war whoop summon their savage nature and nothing but "scalps" will bring back a Christian state of mind. I do not believe it possible to find one full-blooded Indian at any of the agencies that can be trusted. Moral suasion has been tried, and the "Quaker policy" has cost the lives of hundreds of those who have been struggling on the borders for a home.

There is not a savage tribe in existence but what holds the lands it roams over by conquest—having driven some other tribe of Indians from it. It is singular that the bishop and those of his kind have not a word for the hundred and fifty men, women and children who fell under the scalping knife of these fiends last summer—women dying by the most revolting means; children tied up and slowly tortured to death. There is no more treacherous kind in existence than the American Indian on the Plains, and how the bishop's sense of justice can allow him to say one word in favor of the Cheyenne is more than I can imagine. It was the duty of the troops at all hazards to recapture them. There is not one of them whose hands were not dyed with the blood of the settlers of Kansas.

I may be taking too much space, but such letters as the bishop's mislead the people, especially those of the East, who get their idea of the Indian from Cooper's novels, Indian agents or Bishop Whipple. They do not know that one Indian requires at least twenty square miles of territory to roam over and hunt; that one half of the continent would scarcely be space enough to support the game required for their sport and sustenance, and if they do not have it, a knife is unsheathed. Our Government has treated the Indians with fairness and liberality, perhaps more liberally than any nation ever treated her savage tribes. So far as Christianizing the wild Indian is concerned, it cannot be done. I will wager that one half of Sitting Bull's Indians have emblems and crosses to prove that they have been taken into the fold. I remember meeting a party of Cheyenne and Arapaho at Fort Laramie. One of the chiefs told me through the interpreter that he was a "good Indian." Father DeSmet made him so. He believed in "white man's god." He and his party tried to run off our stock the next morning. In nearly all the Indian wars the Indians are the aggressors. Powwows follow and all is done that can be done; but the more talk the more the Indian thinks the representatives of the general government are actuated by fear. Take the action of the government in abandoning the Powder River country in 1869. No sooner was it done and the order issued to abandon Forts C. F. Smith, Phil Kearny, Reno and some smaller camps and the troops had been withdrawn than the Sioux, Cheyenne and Arapaho followed down to the railroad. Men were killed by the savages half a mile from Cheyenne [the city]. Trains were attacked, settlers murdered, and the border made desolate, in violation of the treaty just made by them.

The Interior Department is to blame as the recent trial of Indian agents shows. I am not reflecting upon Bishop Whipple alone. The same mawkish sentimentality is shown toward condemned murderers in our prisons. Not a thought for the murdered one, for the bereaved friends, fatherless children. By taking the position the bishop does he unintentionally misleads. I say this from experience. If Congress wishes to stop this bloodshed upon the frontier let it:

1. Turn the government of the Indians over to the War Department. The Indian will know that he must behave or be punished. At the same time he will receive all that the government votes him.

2. Let Congress grant two hundred acres of land to each Indian family, without the power to sell. If the family becomes extinct then it shall be repossessed by the government.

3. All thefts, murders, etc., (for the first three years), to be punished by military court.

4. In the year 1890 do away with all tribal organizations; Indians twenty-five years of age to be citizens at that date and amenable to the civil law.

5. All annuities and supplies for Indians to be issued by the proper army departments.

6. Indians committing offenses are to have fair trial and be promptly punished if guilty.

7. The President to appoint a certain number of Chaplains who shall have charge of Indian schools with the necessary teachers, to be under the commanding officer of the post.

8. No Indian traders allowed. The commissary and quartermaster department to sell furs, etc. for Indians and furnish all they require at cost.

9. Six or more mechanical instructors to be appointed to each reservation to teach Indians.

One word in conclusion: All the mules and horses the Indians have are stolen from settlers and the United States. I cannot see the justice of the reverend bishop's that the Indians should be paid for lost ponies. There are thousands of poor families in the settled portion of the states who are suffering, many of them, the pangs of hunger who could go to those beautiful fertile valleys of Wyoming and Dakota and rear Christian homes in that wilderness. The sun does not shine upon a better or more beautiful land. There is an abundance of timber, coal and minerals. I cannot see the Christian virtue that secures to a few Indians thousands of acres of fertile land that God destined to reward those who till the soil.... That the Indian is not more responsible than the rattlesnake, or the mountain tiger, I will admit, but he must be treated the same. Nothing but fear will govern him. There were more valuable lives sacrificed by treacherous Indians last year than all the Indians are worth. I will point to the Pawnee Indians as a specimen of the civilizing effects of the Indian Bureau. The country has had enough of it, and, if Indian wars are to cease, put them in the hands of those who have solved the question for all nations, both ancient and modern, that is, her soldiers. The lowest in rank are fit for this service as well as the highest.

[Signed] E. R. P. Shurly. [254]

NOTES

1. Letter to James Brisbin from Edmund Shurly, n.d., James Brisbin Papers, MC 39, Box 1, Folder 3, Montana Historical Society [hereafter MHS] Archives, Helena, Montana.

2. From an unpublished manuscript titled "Chicago's Indian Fighter" dated April 8, 1889, James Brisbin Papers, MC 39, Box 2, Folder 16, MHS Archives, written in his hand and certainly intended for release to a newspaper or magazine serving the Chicago area. There is no doubt it is based on a letter Shurly wrote to Brisbin in about 1888 detailing his scrape with the Sioux in November 1867 as it elaborates on this letter and uses many of the terms and sentences Shurly used. Brisbin added additional detail not found in Shurly's letter, which could only have been revealed to him in a face-to-face interview that he had with Shurly. Whether the manuscript was ever published is unknown.

3. Shurly's official report to the Post Adjutant, Fort C. F. Smith. A copy is printed in *Bozeman Trail Scrapbook*, by Elsa Spear.

4. Undated, handwritten letter from Shurly to Brisbin, MHS.

5. Barry J. Hagan, *Exactly in the Right Place*.

6. Marian Winifred Shurly (b. 3-20-1827, d. 9-27-1892).

7. A. T. Andreas, *The History of Chicago*, p. 750.

8. Winston Churchill, *Churchill's History of the English-Speaking Peoples*, p. 339.

9. Ibid.

10. Jack Gieck, *A Photo Album of Ohio's Canal Era, 1825–1913*.

11.   Samuel Harden Stille, *Ohio Builds a Nation*.

12.   Henry C. Hagloch, *The History of Tuscarawas County, Ohio to 1956*.

13.   "Cosmus" is the name indicated in the 1860 Census for Buffalo. He apparently was not pleased with this name, for all other references to him in records refer to him as "C. J."

14.   Before 1860, many documents list the spelling of the name as "Shurley." After enlistment in the army Edmund petitioned to have his name changed on army documents to the current spelling, Shurly. Some early documents also show the name misspelled "Shirley" and "Shushley."

15.   A. T. Andreas, *History of Chicago: From the Fire of 1871 Until 1885*, p. 750.

16.   Armory D Company, 2nd District, 65th Regiment.

17.   Reference State Militia order dated Monday, August 19, 1850. Found in the Shurly collection, Box 2, scrapbook #1, Reuther Library, Wayne State University, Detroit, Michigan [hereafter the Shurly collection—Reuther].

18.   The Shurly collection—Reuther, Box 1, scrapbook. From an article in an unnamed Chicago newspaper titled "The Railway Mail Service; United States the First to Develop This System—Recollections of Mr. Shurly."

19.   Although seldom used by Mrs. Shurly, the name Charlotte does appear on at least one census record (1880 in Chicago).

20.   The Shurly collection—Reuther, Box 1, scrapbook. Utica newspaper article describing the first regimental reunion of the 26th NYV in 1885.

21.   The Shurly collection—Reuther, Box 2, scrapbook #2, p. 87. From an article written by Shurly in the *Chicago Daily Inter-Ocean* newspaper titled "Old Mason's Slaves ..." dated March 30, 1896.

22.   From an article in a Utica, New York, newspaper, probably the *Utica Daily Press*, dated October 18, 1903, describing the eighteenth reunion of the 26th Regiment in Utica; filed in the Shurly collection—Reuther, Box 1, scrapbook.

23.   Ibid.

24.   Cornelius Rightmire of Newberry, Pennsylvania, recorded, on June 4, 1912, his memoirs, which included memories of his participation in the Civil War

as a member of the 26th New York Volunteers Regiment. These memoirs are filed in the U.S. Army Heritage Center in Carlisle, Pennsylvania.

25.   Ibid.

26.   Ibid.

27.   Ibid.

28.   Ibid.

29.   Ibid.

30.   G. F. R. Henderson, *Stonewall Jackson and the American Civil War*, p. 103.

31.   Henderson, pp. 103–4.

32.   Henderson, p. 110 (italics added for emphasis).

33.   According to company muster rolls dated June and August 1861.

34.   Company C muster rolls.

35.   E. R. P. Shurly, "Reminiscence of the War of the Rebellion—1861." This is an unpublished account of several incidents during the early part of Shurly's Civil War service personally edited and signed by Shurly. The document was donated to the Bentley Library, Ann Arbor, Michigan, by the Michigan Commandery, Loyal Legion in 1936. The story elaborates on one he provided to *The Daily Inter-Ocean*, a Chicago newspaper, that appeared on March 30, 1896, a copy of which is filed in the Shurly collection—Reuther, Box 2, scrapbook #2, p. 87. The article's headlines were: "Old Mason's Slaves; They Figured in a Happy Incident of the Late War; How They Were 'Lost'; Federal Officer Succumbed to his Sympathies; Five Negroes That He Was Guarding Made Their Escape and Reached the North." Some of the wording in the newspaper article differs from that in the reminiscence.

36.   Ibid. The story elaborates on one he provided a Chicago newspaper, probably *The Daily Inter-Ocean*, appearing in an article dated July 21 around 1885 and now filed in the Shurly collection—Reuther, Box 2, scrapbook #2, p. 76. Headlines for the story were: "War Reminiscence; General Ord and the 26th Regiment Infantry NY Volunteers."

37.   U.S. War Department. *Records of the Rebellion*, Vol. 12, Series I, Part 1, p. 287.

38. See Bruce Catton, *The Army of the Potomac, Mr. Lincoln's Army*, p. 29 for good commentary regarding Banks and his army.

39. Henderson, p. 266.

40. John W. Shildt, *Stonewall Jackson, Day by Day*, pp. 54, 117. A marker titled "Belle Boyd & Jackson" marks the spot.

41. Henderson, p. 249.

42. Frederick H. Dyer, *A Compendium of the War of the Rebellion*. Also, National Archives, Official Records, Series I, Vol. 12, Part 1, Reports p. 555–58.

43. Henderson, p. 232.

44. Ibid., p. 240, and Dennis Kelly, *Second Manassas; The Battle & Campaign*, p. 3.

45. Henderson, p. 242.

46. For disposition of McDowell's forces May 29 to June 1, 1862, see Henderson, p. 271.

47. Shurly, *Reminiscence of the War of the Rebellion*. Shurly had been outraged by an article in the *National Tribune*, a Chicago paper, that gave credit for saving his regiment, the 26th NYV, to General Crawford. Shurly's original article was printed in the October 25, 1894, issue of the paper rebutting Crawford's claim.

48. Kelly, *Second Manassas,* p. 4. Pope was tied to Mary Todd Lincoln's family by marriage. His father was a federal judge and an uncle was a U.S. senator from Kentucky.

49. Charles S. McClenthen, *A Sketch of the Campaign in Virginia and Maryland from Cedar Mountain to Antietam*.

50. Ibid.

51. Reports of the amount of cash vary. One report says only $35,000 was taken, which seems light.

52. McClenthen, *A Sketch of the Campaign*.

53. Ibid.

54. Ibid.

55. Ibid.

56. Ibid.

57. Ibid.

58. Ibid.

59. The Shurly collection—Reuther, Box 1, scrapbook. Article in the *Washington Post* dated September 18, 1904, written by E. R. P. Shurly, responding to what Shurly knew to be false information.

60. McClenthen, *A Sketch of the Campaign*.

61. Ibid.

62. Ibid.

63. Ibid.

64. Ibid.

65. Frederick Phisterer, *New York in the War of the Rebellion, 1861–1865*, p. 2027.

66. Captain Charles Jennings died from his wounds on October 1, 1862, and is buried near his brother, Gilbert Jennings, and Edmund Shurly in the Rochester, New York, Mount Hope Cemetery.

67. Henderson, p. 479.

68. See Catton, *The Army of the Potomac; Mr. Lincoln's Army*, pp. 44–47, for an interesting description of the action around this homestead. It is located on State Route 28, three miles north of Centerville, near Dulles Airport.

69. McClenthen, *A Sketch of the Campaign*.

70. A fort, erected in 1866 to protect the Bozeman Trail in what is now Wyoming, was named after Major General Philip Kearny. As we see in Chapter 13, Edmund Shurly was stationed at this fort during the Sioux uprising along this trail in 1866–68 and nearly lost his life in a gun battle not far from the post.

71. Kearny, accompanied by a small party of soldiers in a blinding rainstorm, stumbled into a unit of Confederate soldiers and was gunned down trying to escape back to Union lines.

72. Dyer, Vol. I, p. 285. John Michael Priestly, author of *Before Antietam: The Battle for South Mountain*, was kind enough to point out where this information concerning Christian's appointment to Brigade commander could be found.

73. McClenthen, *A Sketch of the Campaign*.

74. Ibid.

75. Ibid.

76. Ibid.

77. Ibid.

78. Ibid.

79. Ibid.

80. Henderson, p. 527.

81. McClenthen, *A Sketch of the Campaign*.

82. Ibid.

83. Ibid.

84. Don Wisnoski, interview at the Utica, New York, Historical Society Museum, July 25, 2000.

85. McClenthen, *A Sketch of the Campaign*.

86. Henderson, p. 579.

87. Charles S. McClenthen, *Narrative of the Fall & Winter Campaign by a Private Soldier*.

88. Ibid.

89. Ibid.

90. Henderson, p. 579.

91. Henderson, p. 594.

92. Henry M. Field, *Bright Skies and Dark Shadows*, p. 294

93. The Shurly collection—Reuther, Box 2, scrapbook #1, p. 39, "What Became of an Illinois Legislator's Dog."

94. National Archives, Washington, D.C.

95. From George Levy, *To Die in Chicago, Confederate Prisoners at Camp Douglas, 1862–65*, used by permission of the publisher, Pelican Publishing Company, Inc.

96. The present location of the University of Chicago is some three miles south of its Civil War site. After the war the Camp Douglas area was transformed and by 1870 it was a fashionable residential area. Cottage Grove from 26th to 39th streets, was, by the mid-1890s, a major business district. Beginning in 1900 the area began a sharp decline and for the next fifty-two years, devolved into a notorious slum. Now cleared, the camp site has reappeared. White Oak Square, South Square, and part of Garrison Square are grassy fields and Prison Square is located on the east side of King Drive, between 31st and 33rd Streets.

97. Levy, p. 40.

98. Levy, p. 115. Thirty one hundred of the raiders were held at Camp Douglas.

99. The Shurly collection—Reuther, Box 2, scrapbook #1, p. 39.

100. Levy, p. 69.

101. Ibid., p. 225.

102. The article contains far too many details that could have been easily verified in 1882 for it to have been a fabrication, as believers in the "hoax" theory propose.

103. The Shurly collection—Reuther. From a January 29, 1882, article in the *Chicago Tribune*.

104. With luck that had not been seen since Stonewall Jackson marched in the Shenandoah, Early was able to pass north through the valley, unmolested, to Frederick, Maryland, where his soldiers attacked and looted. On July 11, his soldiers were passing Silver Spring, and on July 12 shelled the ramparts of the defensive ring around Washington, backing off only when they saw the Union 6th Corps arrive at the last minute and deploy in front of them. Had his skirmishers (snipers), positioned in farm houses opposite the Union defenses, seen and killed the tall slim figure dressed in black and wearing a stovepipe hat, watching from the barricades, Abraham Lincoln himself, and

had Thompson been able to hold to his schedule, the war would certainly have taken a turn in favor of the Confederates.

105. Shortly before the trial in which he was convicted in absentia, Dodd escaped from prison to Canada where he remained until returning after the war, in 1869, to live a respectable life in Wisconsin. His accomplices were not so lucky.

106. This man was probably not former President Millard Fillmore, also from Buffalo, though he may have been a relative. The article refers only to a "Judge Fillmore." I found that Millard Fillmore was a lawyer and active in local and national politics, but with no reference to a judgeship for the ex-president. During the Civil War, Fillmore became a staunch Unionist, helping to organize enlistment and war-financing drives.

107. The Shurly collection—Reuther. From an article by Colonel A. T. Burr dated January 28, 1882, appearing in the Philadelphia Press. Headlines of the article were: "In War Times; the Attempt to Inaugurate a Northwest Confederacy ..."

108. Ibid.

109. Ibid.

110. Ibid.

111. Ibid.

112. Ibid.

113. From an undated newspaper article in the Shurly collection—Reuther, Box 2, scrapbook #1, pp. 55–56.

114. E. R. P. Shurly, in a letter to the editor of the *Chicago Tribune* dated February 3, 1882. From the Shurly collection—Reuther.

115. Levy, p. 212, quoting from Curry, *Chicago: Its History and Its Builders* Vol. 2, p. 139; Andreas, *History of Chicago* Vol. 2, p. 308.

116. Levy, pp. 212–13.

117. Ibid., p. 224.

118. From an undated newspaper article. The Shurly collection—Reuther, Box 2, scrapbook #1, pp. 55–56.

119. Levy, p. 225.

120. Ibid.

121. From an undated newspaper article. The Shurly collection—Reuther, Box 2, scrapbook #1, pp. 55–56.

122. Ibid.

123. Ibid.

124. Colonel Sweet was promoted to brigadier general on December 20, 1882, as a result of his work in bringing down the conspiracy.

125. Edmund R. P. Shurly, in a letter published in the *Chicago Tribune* February 3, 1882, copy filed in the Shurly collection—Reuther.

126. The Shurly collection—Reuther, Box 2, scrapbook #1. Letter to the editor of the *Chicago Tribune* and published February 3, 1882.

127. William Powell and Edward Shippen, *Officers of the Army and Navy (Regular) Who Served in the Civil War*, p. 382.

128. From an article in the *Chicago Times*, August 25, 1889, filed in the Shurly collection—Reuther, Box 2, scrapbook #2, p. 66.

129. Levy, p. 289.

130. Ibid., p. 278.

131. From a letter to the editor of the *Chicago Tribune* on February 3, 1882 titled "The Conspiracy at Camp Douglas" by Edmund Shurly filed in the Shurly collection—Reuther. Unfortunately, Ada Sweet's father had engendered hatred in the city with his arrests of prominent people during the war. By 1882, Ada was facing efforts to have her fired from her job, which she needed to support her younger siblings. Edmund's reason for writing his letter was to show support for Ada Sweet. The Cleveland Administration eventually succeeded in having her removed.

132. The Shurly collection—Reuther, Box 2, scrapbook #1, p. 53.

133. The Shurly collection—Reuther, Box 1, scrapbook.

134. Ibid.

135. Reprinted by permission of the University of Nebraska Press from *The Bozeman Trail*, Vol. II by Grace Raymond Hebard and E. A. Brininstool, 1922, p. 146.

136. The Laramie Treaty of 1865 ceded land to the Crow inhabiting this territory at the time. A treaty with the Sioux was never consummated as Red Cloud walked out of the conference and would not sign a treaty not also signed by the president of the United States.

137. Dorothy M. Johnson, *The Bloody Bozeman; The Perilous Trail to Montana's Gold*, p. 49.

138. Ibid., p. 63.

139. Robert A. Murray, *The Bozeman Trail—Highway of History*, p. 5.

140. Due to the depression following the Civil War, veterans of both the North and South could not find work, so the army was able to recruit ex-soldiers from both North and South. The former Confederate soldiers were referred to as "galvanized Yankees."

141. Margaret Irvin Carrington, *Absaraka, Home of the Crows*, p. 279.

142. Johnson, pp. 188–89.

143. Lyle Edwin Mantor, *History of Fort Kearney*.

144. The reader is cautioned not to confuse Fort Phil Kearny, Wyoming Territory with Old Fort Kearney, Nebraska, where the 18th Regiment began its expedition to the Bozeman Trail. Note the minor difference in the spelling of the name.

145. Another legend, perhaps more suitable to modern-day sensibilities, has it that General Conners command found a lone teepee near this stream where a demented squaw lived. Because of her mental condition, her tribe had driven her away but provided her with sustenance.

146. Article in the *Chicago Daily Inter-Ocean*, January 25, 1897, filed in the Shurly collection—Reuther, Box 1, scrapbook.

147. Hagan, p. 32.

148. Johnson, p. 207.

149. Reprinted from *The Bozeman Trail,* Vol. II by Grace Raymond Hebard and E. A. Brininstool by permission of the University of Nebraska Press. Copyright 1922 by Grace Raymond Hebard and E. A. Brininstool, p. 179.

150. William S. E. Coleman, *Voices of Wounded Knee,* pp. xiii, xv, 8.

151. Charles M. Robinson, *A Good Year to Die,* p. xxiii.

152. Alexis De Tocqueville, *Democracy in America,* Vol. I, p. 26.

153. Cyrus Townsend Brady, *Indian Fights and Fighters,* pp. 62–64. These are the written words of Mr. R. J. Smyth, a teamster for Carrington, whom Shurly would have known.

154. *Chicago Daily Inter-Ocean,* January 25, 1897, the Shurly collection—Reuther, Box 1, scrapbook. The article states that Shurly was at Phil Kearny on December 21, 1866, when the Fetterman massacre took place.

155. Hebard and Brininstool, Vol. II.

156. Gen. Henry B. Carrington, Official Report of January 3, 1867 to the Assistant Adjutant-General, Department of the Platte, Omaha.

157. J. W. Vaughn, *Indian Fights: New Facts on Seven Encounters,* p. 92.

158. On December 26, Lieutenant Shurly found himself reassigned to Company H, 2nd Cavalry in the newly formed 27th when Brigadier General Philip St. George Cooke ordered the reorganization of the 18th Regiment. Colonel Henry Wessells replaced Colonel Carrington, who would assume command of the 18th, headquartered at Fort Caspar (now Casper, Wyoming). Though the timing of the reorganization was purely by chance, the public was led to believe it was because of the massacre, and Carrington was disgraced. His superior, General Cooke, out of spite, did nothing to clear his name as Carrington had been warning him of the need for more troops and ammunition since the summer, a warning unheeded by Cooke. It was years before Carrington could convince the public that the day Cooke ordered Carrington's reassignment, Cooke could not possibly have known of the disaster.

159. Fort Phil Kearny/Bozeman Trail Association, members of, *Portraits of Fort Phil Kearny.* The Fort Phil Kearny/Bozeman Trail Assoc. (Banner, Wyoming), 1993, pp. 160–66.

160. Handwritten order received by Shurly from General Bradley on a small scrap of paper; from the Shurly collection—Reuther, Box 2, scrapbook #2, p. 72.

161. Today, one can reach the site of Fort C. F. Smith by taking Interstate 90 to Montana exit 503 at Hardin and taking route 313 south 44 miles to the town of Fort Smith. The site is on private land. Local inquiry will lead one to the owner of the land who will likely permit entrance.

162. Handwritten comment by Shurly on a small scrap of paper; from the Shurly collection—Reuther, Box 2, scrapbook #2, p. 72.

163. Merrill J. Mattes, *Indians, Infants and Infantry*, p. 132.

164. Vaughn, p. 94.

165. James D. Lockwood, *Life and Adventures of a Drummer Boy*, pp. 177–81.

166. This report is found in both *The Bozeman Trail*, Vol. II, by Hebard and Brininstool, pp. 144–46, and *Indian Fights*, by Vaughn, pp. 94–95. Vaughn is very complimentary of Shurly, concluding his description of him with these words: "Apparently recovering from his disability [from Civil War wounds], Shurly entered the Regular Army as a 2nd lieutenant in the 18th Infantry on May 11, 1866.... He was brevetted lieutenant and captain in the Regular Army for gallant services at Fredericksburg and during other actions during the Civil War. *He was evidently a competent officer to have received commissions in the Regular Army despite the handicaps of his war injuries*" (italics added).

167. Reprinted by permission of the University of Nebraska Press from, *The Bozeman Trail*, Vol. II by Grace Raymond Hebard and E. A. Brininstool, copyright 1922, pp. 144–46. However, the authors do not reveal where they found this report or where it resides. References are made to the *History of Montana*, Vol. I, by authors M. A. Leeson and George Coutant both before and after the Shurly letter, suggesting this is where his letter may be found.

168. Hebard and Brininstool, Vol. II, p. 162.

169. Hagan, p. 115.

170. Vaughn, p. 98.

171. This had to have been Sergeant Norton, Company I, who was listed as having been wounded in the left shoulder in the fight.

172. Lockwood, pp. 183–85.

173. Ibid., p. 187.

174. Ibid., pp. 188–89.

175. For an excellent description of the Hayfield Fight see Roy E. Appleman's article in *Great Western Indian Fights,* written by members of the Potomac Corral of the Westerners, pp. 142–43. Also see Hagan.

176. Hebard and Brininstool, Vol. II, p. 167.

177. Hagan, p. 118.

178. *Portraits of Fort Phil Kearny*, p. 162.

179. Vaughn, pp. 106–10.

180. Lockwood, pp. 189–90.

181. Reprinted by permission of the University of Nebraska Press from, *The Bozeman Trail,* Vol. II by Grace Raymond Hebard and E. A. Brininstool, 1922, p. 165. The article was written by Finn Burnett.

182. Hebard and Brininstool, Vol. II. This estimate is by Finn Burnett.

183. Lockwood, p. 187.

184. The Shurly collection—Reuther, Box 1, scrapbook. From the *Chicago Daily Inter-Ocean*, January 25, 1897. Shurly was a lieutenant when the incident occurred. When the article appeared in the paper in 1897, Shurly had been brevetted a major "for bravery" three years before.

185. Letter to James Brisbin from Edmund Shurly, n.d., James Brisbin Papers, MC 39, Box 1, Folder 3, MHS Archives.

186. This is Shurly's estimate from his official report. There is some disagreement among local experts as to exactly where the fight took place. According to a footnote in *Portraits of Fort Phil Kearny*, p. 165, official records indicate the fight took place about twenty miles northeast of Fort Phil Kearny, near Goose Creek. A problem for historians is that in 1867–68 there were two roads, the old road and a new military shortcut, between Forts Phil Kearny and C. F. Smith. Shurly implies that he was on the old road, or Bozeman's original route, which followed Peno Creek (Prairie Dog Creek), and crossed a ravine. The late Mr. Glenn Sweem, a persistent local historian, accumulated

persuasive evidence pinpointing the battlefield's location on the old road where it passed near the intersection of routes 14 and 64.

187. William Powell and Edward Shippen, *Officers of the Army and Navy (Regular) Who Served in The Civil War,* p. 382.

188. Shurly letter to James S. Brisbin, MHS. I, as a dutiful great-grandson, have corrected spelling and grammar where appropriate and added factual corrections in parenthesis where, after twenty years, memory of insignificant detail failed Shurly.

189. Ibid.

190. James S. Brisbin, *Chicago's Indian Fighter*. James Brisbin Papers, MC 39, Box 2, Folder 16, MHS Archives.

191. A copy of Shurly's official report of the battle can be found in *Bozeman Trail Scrapbook*, edited and photos by Elsa Spear.

192. Ibid.

193. *The Daily Missoulian*, April 30, 1907, as reported in Mattes, p. 266.

194. Mattes, p. 271.

195. Special Order No. 71, June 16, 1868.

196. Elizabeth Burt, "An Army Wife's 40 Years in the Service, 1862–1902." Merrill J. Mattes wrote her diary into his book titled *Indians, Infants and Infantry*.

197. General William B. Hazen, acting inspector general, reporting after inspecting Fort Reno August 19, 1866, as reported by Johnson, p. 198.

198. The Shurly collection—Reuther, Box 1, scrapbook. From the *Chicago Daily Inter-Ocean*, January 25, 1897.

199. Hartz letter, 28 July 1868, Library of Congress. As reported in Hagan, p. 230.

200. The Shurly collection—Reuther, Box 1, scrapbook. From the *Chicago Daily Inter-Ocean*, January 25, 1897.

201. Shurly letter, 2 August 1868, file no. S-184-1868, RG 393, U.S. National Archives.

202. The Shurly collection—Reuther, Box 1, scrapbook. From the *Chicago Daily Inter-Ocean*, January 25, 1897.

203. Hagan, p. 230.

204. Shurly letter, 2 August 1868, file no. S-184-1868, RG 393, National Archives, as reported in Hagan, p. 231.

205. Joseph W. Cook, *Diary and Letters*, as reported in *The Post Near Cheyenne*, by Col. Gerald M. Adams, p. 27.

206. U.S. Army Continental Commands, Department of the Platte Records 1858–1895, Sherman's letter to Augur, Letters Received A-Y 1867–1869 (RG533, Roll 6) National Archives, as reported in *The Post Near Cheyenne*, by Colonel Gerald M. Adams, p. 7.

207. Adams, p. 7.

208. Adams, p. 13.

209. *Cheyenne Daily Leader*, July 4, 1868, as reported in *The Post Near Cheyenne* by Adams, p. 24. Reprinted by permission of Mrs. Gerald M. Adams.

210. Brisbin, last paragraph, MHS.

211. *Cheyenne Daily Leader*, July 18, 1868, as reported in *The Post Near Cheyenne* by Adams, p. 24. Reprinted by permission of Mrs. Gerald M. Adams.

212. Ibid., July 21, 1868.

213. Cook, p. 104. As reported in *The Post Near Cheyenne*, by Adams, p. 27.

214. Burt. Library of Congress, as reported in Mattes, pp. 168–70. The graves were moved to the Custer Battlefield Cemetery in 1888.

215. Burt, in Mattes, pp. 175–78.

216. Hagan, p. 224.

217. Burt, in Mattes, p. 175.

218. William Powell and Edward Shippen, *Officers of the Army & Navy (Regular)*, p. 382.

219. Linda W. Slaughter, *Fortress to Farm, or Twenty-three Years on the Frontier*, pp. 50, 29. Reprinted by permission of Virginia Dullum.

220. According to the *Chicago City Directory*, the Chicago street numbering system changed in 1909. Street numbers shown are "pre-1909" numbers.

221. The Shurly collection—Reuther, Box 2, scrapbook #1. Article in the *Chicago Times* in 1869.

222. Ibid.

223. Ibid.

224. Ibid.

225. There have been efforts recently to absolve the O'Leary's and their cow of setting the Chicago fire, suggesting that, because his testimony had holes in it, a neighbor, Daniel "Peg Leg" Sullivan may have dropped a spark while lighting his pipe. However, evidence that the fire started in the O'Leary cow barn is persuasive, and at least one wag has suggested that if one of O'Leary's five cows did not do it, then their horse or maybe the calf did; or perhaps Catherine O'Leary got up out of bed, went out in the barn, and kicked the lantern over herself.

226. Dates are taken from the family headstone in Mount Hope Cemetery, Rochester, New York. Both Edna and Arthur are buried there with their mother and father, along with the eldest daughter (Viola) of Edmund's son Burt.

227. The Shurly collection—Reuther, Box 2, scrapbook #1, p. 41. From an article in a Chicago newspaper dated 1882.

228. While Shurly lived in Chicago, this address was 55 Clark Street.

229. Andreas, p. 750.

230. This street number changed when Chicago renumbered its streets in 1909.

231. Andreas, p. 750.

232. The Shurly collection—Reuther, Box 2, scrapbook #1.

233. Named after the father of Adjutant William K. Bacon, killed at Fredericksburg.

234. The Shurly collection—Reuther, Box 1, scrapbook. Newspaper article, probably from the *Utica Daily Press*.

235. Ibid.

236. Ibid.

237. The Shurly collection—Reuther, Box 1, scrapbook. The article suggested that relics and souvenirs of the 26th may have been stored or displayed somewhere in Utica, possibly in the Munson Williams Memorial Building. However, in a visit to Utica on August 25, 2000, Don Wisnowski advised your author that the relics and souvenirs had been sold off or otherwise disposed of after 1956, and that only a record book, which was found to be of little value, remains.

238. The Shurly collection—Reuther, Box 2, scrapbook #1.

239. Author unknown.

240. The Shurly collection—Reuther, Box 2, scrapbook #1, p. 2.

241. These address changes are noted in the *Chicago City Directory* for the years indicated. The 1880 Census lists the address as 3224 Calumet; the *1880–88 Chicago City Directories* list the address as 3220 Calumet. Today this street is shown as South Calumet Street on city maps.

242. Augusta's sister married a Jennings whose son, Charles, would later practice medicine in Detroit with Edmund's brother, Ernest, and with Edmund's son Burt.

243. This name was unclear on the census record and the name does not appear anywhere else in the family records. It is possible this boy was not a nephew but instead was related to Edmund's friend from his Indian War days, General Andy Burt. Andy Burt is known to have visited Chicago a number of times after Shurly left the army and certainly would have kept in touch with him.

244. The 1900 Michigan Census also lists a Mr. Edwin Shurly, born June 1832, in England, and wife Sarah, born September 1836 in New York. I will leave it to others to research the curious possibility that they were related to "our" Shurly. Their address was nearly illegible and appeared to be: Casco Twp., … Allegan County (western Michigan, south of Muskegon).

245. Frederick Allen, "Technology at the End of the Century," *American Heritage of Invention & Technology Magazine* (Winter 2000): 12.

246. On November 15, 1965, the late Elsa Spear Byron, a noted historian in Sheridan, Wyoming, at the time, wrote Edmund Shurly's grandson, Burt Russell Shurly, Jr., asking what the initials "E. R. P." stood for.

247. Section C, south end of Lot 105.

248. On January 7, 1880.

249. On November 20, 1899.

250. From a brochure passed out at a memorial service for Shurly on March 28, 1909. Ending the eulogy is a verse by James Whitcomb Reilly.

251. Reprinted from the *Compendium of The War of The Rebellion*, by Frederick H. Dyer, p. 1414, and from *Registers and Sketches of Organizations*, p. 2027.

252. Official Record, Series I, Vol. 12, Part III.

253. Frederick Phisterer, *New York in the War of the Rebellion 1861–1865*, 3rd ed., Registers and Sketches of Organizations, p. 2027.

254. The Shurly collection—Reuther, Box 2, scrapbook #1. Article in the *Chicago Times*, in 1869.

BIBLIOGRAPHY

LIBRARIES AND COLLECTIONS

Burton Historical Library, Detroit Public Library, Detroit, Michigan. The Shurly collection.

Cheyenne Library, Cheyenne, Wyoming.

Colonel Bozeman Restaurant, Buffalo, Wyoming.

Fort Phil Kearny State Historical Site, Story, Wyoming.

History Museum, Carlisle Barracks, Carlisle, Pennsylvania.

Jim Gatchell Memorial Museum, Buffalo, Wyoming.

Kearney Public Library, Kearney, Nebraska.

Montana Historical Society, Helena, Montana. The James S. Brisbin Papers.

National Archives, Washington, D.C.

Sheridan County Fulmer Public Library, Sheridan, Wyoming.

Walter E. Reuther Library, Wayne State University, Detroit, Michigan. The Shurly collection.

CEMETERIES

Elmwood Cemetery, Detroit, Michigan

Mount Elliot Cemetery, Detroit, Michigan

Mount Hope Cemetery, Rochester, New York

NEWSPAPERS, PERIODICALS, AND DIRECTORIES

American Heritage of Invention & Technology Magazine, Forbes Magazine, Winter 2000.

Army and Navy Bulletin, December 1922.

Cheyenne Daily Leader.

Chicago City Directories, 1871–90.

Chicago Daily Inter-Ocean.

Chicago Times.

Chicago Tribune.

City of Detroit Historic Designation Advisory Board Final Report.

Detroit Census 1900, 1910, 1920.

The Detroit Collegian.

Detroit Directories, 1890–1900, 1902, 1907, 1915–17, 1919, 1920–21, 1923–24.

Detroit Evening Times.

Detroit Free Press.

Detroit News.

Detroit Times.

Michigan Census, 1900.

National Tribune, Chicago.

New York Census, 1840, 1850, 1860.

The Philadelphia Press.

Red Cross Detroit Chapter, Newsletter, 1917–19.

Utica Daily Press.

Washington Post.

BOOKS AND ARTICLES

Adams, Gerald M., Col. USAF (Ret.). *The Post Near Cheyenne, A History of Fort D. A. Russell, 1867–1930*. Cheyenne, WY: High Flyer Publications, 1996 (PO Box 20943, Cheyenne, WY 82003).

Andreas, A. T. *History of Chicago: From the Fire of 1871 Until 1885*. Chicago: A. T. Andreas Company, 1886.

Bacon, William Johnson. *Memorial of William Kirkland Bacon, Late Adjutant of the Twenty-sixth Regiment of New York State Volunteers, by his Father*. Utica, NY: Roberts, 1863.

Book, Herbert V. *Family Records*. Detroit: Author, 1963.

Brady, Cyrus Townsend. *Indian Fights and Fighters*. Lincoln & London: University of Nebraska Press, 1971. Original publisher: McClure, Philips & Co., 1904.

Brisbin, James S. "Chicago's Indian Fighter" (handwritten manuscript). James S. Brisbin Papers, Box 2, Folder 16, Montana Historical Society Archives.

Brown, Dee. *The Fetterman Massacre (formerly Fort Phil Kearny: An American Saga)*. Lincoln, NE: University of Nebraska Press, 1962.

Burt, Elizabeth. "An Army Wife's 40 Years in the Service, 1862–1902" (typescript). Burt Family Papers, Manuscript Division, Library of Congress, Washington, D.C.

Butterfield, Roger. *The American Past*. New York: Simon and Schuster, 1947.

Carlisle, Fred. *Chronography of Notable Events in the History of the Northwest Territory and Wayne County, 1531–1890*. Detroit: O. S. Gulley, Bornman & Co., 1890.

Carrington, General Henry B. Official Report of January 3, 1867 to the Assistant Adjutant-General, Department of the Platte, Omaha. (50th Cong., 1st sess., Senate Exec. Doc. 33, pp, 39–41.) First published 1887 upon request of the U.S. Senate for papers relating to the Fetterman massacre. A copy can be found in appendix C, J. W. Vaughn, *Indian Fights: New Facts on Seven Encounters*, pp. 223–230.

Carrington, Margaret Irvin. *Absaraka, Home of the Crows*. Philadelphia: J. B. Lippincott, 1868. Lincoln and London: University of Nebraska Press, 1983.

Catton, Bruce. *Picture History of the Civil War*. New York: American Heritage Publishing Co., 1960, 1988.

Catton, Bruce. *The Army of the Potomac; A Stillness at Appomattox*. Garden City, NY: Doubleday & Co., 1953.

Catton, Bruce. *The Army of the Potomac; Glory Road*. Garden City, NY: Doubleday & Co., 1952.

Catton, Bruce. *The Army of the Potomac; Mr. Lincoln's Army*. Garden City, NY: Doubleday & Co., 1951.

Churchill, Winston S. *Churchill's History of the English Speaking Peoples; Arranged for One Volume by Henry Steele Commager*. Avenel, NJ: Wings, 1994.

Clark, Champ. *Jackson's Valley Campaign, The Civil War—Decoying the Yanks*. Alexandria, VA: Time-Life Books, 1984.

Cockhill, Brian, ed. *Skirmish at Goose Creek: Edmond R. P. Shurly's Bozeman Trail Reminiscence. Magazine of Western History* 33 (Spring 1983).

Coleman, William S. E. *Voices of Wounded Knee*. Lincoln and London: University of Nebraska Press, 2000.

Cook, Joseph W. *Diary and Letters*. Laramie: The Laramie Republican Co., 1919, as reported in *The Post Near Cheyenne*, by Col. Gerald M. Adams.

Curry, Seymour J. Chicago: *Its History and Its Builders: A Century of Marvelous Growth*. Chicago: S. J. Clarke Publishing Co., 1912.

De Tocqueville, Alexis. *Democracy in America,* Vol. I. New York: Bantam Books, 2000, first published 1835.

Dyer, Frederick H. *A Compendium of the War of the Rebellion*. Dayton: The National Historical Society, in cooperation with The Press of Morningside Bookshop, 1979. This volume is found in the U.S. Army Military History Institute, The Army War College, Carlisle, PA. Compiled and arranged from official records of the Federal and Confederate Armies, it is a concise history of each and every regiment, battery, battalion, and other organizations mustered by several states for service in the Union Army during the Civil War. It contains a complete record of the battles, engagements, combats, actions, skirmishes and important operations, tabulated by States and showing the Union Troops engaged in each event. A summary of the service of the 26th New York is contained on pages 1414–15.

Field, Henry M. *Bright Skies and Dark Shadows*. Freeport, NY: Books for Libraries Press, 1890, 1970.

Fort Phil Kearny/Bozeman Trail Association. *Portraits of Fort Phil Kearny*. The Fort Phil Kearny/Bozeman Trail Assoc., 1993 (528 Wagon Box Road, Banner, WY 82832).

Gallagher, John. *A Survey of Detroit's History and Development*. Boston: Massachusetts Institute of Technology, as found at Internet www.mitalliance.org/gallagher. htm, 2003.

Gieck, Jack. *A Photo Album of Ohio's Canal Era, 1825–1913*. Kent, OH: Kent State University Press, 1988.

Grant, Ulysses S. *Personal Memoirs of U. S. Grant*. New York: C. L. Webster, 1885; New York: Penguin Books, 1999.

Hagan, Barry J. *Exactly in the Right Place: A History of Fort C. F. Smith, Montana Territory, 1866–1868*. El Segundo, CA: Upton and Sons, 1999.

Hagloch, Henry C. *The History of Tuscarawas County, Ohio to 1956*. OH: Dover Historical Society, 1956.

Hebard, Grace Raymond, and E. A. Brinistool. *The Bozeman Trail,* Vol. II. Lincoln and London: University of Nebraska Press, 1922, 1990.

Henderson, G. F. R. *Stonewall Jackson and the American Civil War*. New York: Da Capo Press, Inc., 1898, 1943, 1988. Originally published in two volumes and copyrighted by Longmans, Green & Co. New York, 1898, published in 1943 and again in 1988 in one volume. Written some twenty years after the Civil War by an English military analyst who had visited the battlefields and talked to veterans while memories were still fresh, this may be the best account of the battles and actions of Stonewall Jackson. This work is highly recommended to students of the Civil War.

History of Montana From the Earliest Known Discoveries. Laramie: Chaplin, Spafford & Mathieson, 1899.

Johnson, Dorothy M. *The Bloody Bozeman; The Perilous Trail to Montana's Gold*. New York: McGraw-Hill Book Co., 1971, and, Missoula: Mountain Press Publishing Co., 1983.

Kelly, Denis. *Second Manassas, The Battle & Campaign*. Eastern Acorn Press, 1983 (originally published by Civil War Times Illustrated, Box 8200, Harrisburg, PA 17105).

Krick, Robert K. *Stonewall Jackson at Cedar Mountain*. Chapel Hill & London: University of North Carolina Press, 1990.

Leeson, Michael A. and George Coutant. *History of Montana, 1739–1885*. Chicago: Warner Beers & Co., 1885.

Levy, George. *To Die in Chicago, Confederate Prisoners at Camp Douglas 1862–65*. Evanston: Evanston Publishing, Inc., 1994.

Lockwood, James D. *The Life and Adventures of a Drummer Boy*. Albany: John Skinner, 1893.

Lowe, David. *The Great Chicago Fire: In Eye Witness Accounts and 70 Contemporary Photographs and Illustrations*. New York: Compiled and edited by Dover Publications, Inc., 1979.

Mantor, Lyle Edwin. "History of Fort Kearney." Thesis for doctorate of philosophy, State University of Iowa, June 1934. Copy at Kearney Public Library, Kearney, NE.

Mattes, Merrill J. *Indians, Infants and Infantry: Andrew and Elizabeth Burt on the Frontier*. Denver: Old West Publishing Co., by Fred Rosenstock 1960, and Lincoln and London: University of Nebraska Press, 1988.

McClenthen, Charles S. *A Sketch of the Campaign in Virginia and Maryland from Cedar Mountain to Antietam*. Syracuse, NY: Master and Lee, 1862. Copy located at the U.S. Army Heritage Center, Carlisle, PA.

McClenthen, Charles S. *Narrative of the Fall & Winter Campaign by a Private Soldier*. Syracuse: Masters & Lee Book and Job Printers, 1863. Copy located at the University of South Florida, Tampa Campus Library.

Millis, Walter. *The Martial Spirit*. Cambridge, MA: Riverside Press, 1931.

Murray, Robert A. The *Bozeman Trail—Highway of History.* Boulder, CO: Pruett Publishing, 1988.

Phisterer, Frederick. *New York in the War of the Rebellion, 1861–1865*, Vol. 3. Albany, NY: Weed and Parsons, 1890; 3rd ed., D. B. Lyon Company, 1912. See pages 2027–39 for a brief history of the 26th New York Regiment and roster of officers.

Potomac Corral of the Westerners, Members of. *Great Western Indian Fights.* Lincoln and London: University of Nebraska Press, 1960.

Powell, Major William, and Edward Shippen. *Officers of the Army and Navy (Regular) Who Served in the Civil War.* Philadelphia: L. R. Hammersly & Co., 1892. Refer to page 382.

Priestly, John Michael. *Before Antietam: The Battle For South Mountain.* Shippensburg, PA: White Mane Publishing Co., Inc., 1992.

Rightmire, Cornelius. "Memoirs, June 4, 1912." Filed at U.S. Army Heritage Center, Carlisle, PA.

Robinson, Charles M. *A Good Year to Die: The Story of the Great Sioux War.* New York: Random House, 1995.

Sawislak, Karen. *Smoldering City: Chicagoans and the Great Fire 1871–1874.* Chicago & London: University of Chicago Press, 1995.

Shildt, John W. *Stonewall Jackson, Day by Day.* Chewsville, MD: Antietam Publications, 1980.

Shurly, Edmund R. P. "Reminiscence of the War of the Rebellion—1861," 1904. Personally edited and signed by Shurly, this document is stored in the Bentley Library, Ann Arbor, MI, and is a rewrite of an article he wrote for a Chicago newspaper in 1894.

Shurly, Edmund R. P. Letter, to James Brisbin from Edmund Shurly, n.d., James Brisbin Papers, MC 39, Box 1, Folder 3, Montana Historical Society Archives.

Slaughter, Linda W. *Fortress to Farm, or Twenty-three Years on the Frontier.* 1st ed. Jericho, NY: Exposition Press, Inc., 1972.

Spear, Elsa. *Bozeman Trail Scrapbook*. Sheridan WY: Author, The Mills Company, 1967. Copy #322 located at the Gene Eppley Library, University of Nebraska at Omaha.

Starr, Stephen Z. *Colonel Grenfell's Wars: The Life of a Soldier of Fortune*. Baton Rouge: Louisiana State University Press, 1971.

Stille, Samuel Harden. *Ohio Builds a Nation*. Lower Salem, Ohio: Arlendale Book House, 1939.

Tanner, Robert G. *Stonewall in the Valley*. Garden City, NY: Doubleday & Co., 1976.

Utley, Robert M. *The Indian Frontier of the American West 1846–1890*. Albuquerque, NM: University of New Mexico Press, 1984.

Vaughn, J. W. *Indian Fights: New Facts on Seven Encounters*. Norman: University of Oklahoma Press, 1966.

Ward, Geoffrey C. with Ric Burns and Ken Burns. *The Civil War; an Illustrated History*. New York: Alfred A. Knopf, 1991.

Wellman, Paul I. *Death on the Prairie: The Thirty Years Struggle for the Western Plains*. Lincoln and London: University of Nebraska Press, 1934, 1962, 1987.

Whittier, John Greenleaf. *The Complete Poetical Works of Whittier*, Cambridge Edition. Boston: Houghton Mifflin Company, 1894.

Williams, Thomas Harry. *Lincoln and his Generals*. New York: Gramercy Books, 2000.

Yenne, Bill. *Indian Wars: The Campaign for the American West*. Yardley, PA: Westholme Publishing, 2006.

INDEX